D0871837

FAILING OUR FATHERS

Failing Our Fathers

CONFRONTING THE CRISIS OF ECONOMICALLY VULNERABLE NONRESIDENT FATHERS

Ronald B. Mincy

Monique Jethwani

Serena Klempin

OXFORD
UNIVERSITY PRESS

OXFORD
UNIVERSITY PRESS

Oxford University Press is a department of the University of
Oxford. It furthers the University's objective of excellence in research,
scholarship, and education by publishing worldwide.

Oxford   New York
Auckland   Cape Town   Dar es Salaam   Hong Kong   Karachi
Kuala Lumpur   Madrid   Melbourne   Mexico City   Nairobi
New Delhi   Shanghai   Taipei   Toronto

With offices in
Argentina   Austria   Brazil   Chile   Czech Republic   France   Greece
Guatemala   Hungary   Italy   Japan   Poland   Portugal   Singapore
South Korea   Switzerland   Thailand   Turkey   Ukraine   Vietnam

Oxford is a registered trademark of Oxford University Press
in the UK and certain other countries.

Published in the United States of America by
Oxford University Press
198 Madison Avenue, New York, NY 10016

Library of Congress Cataloging-in-Publication Data
Mincy, Ronald B.
Failing our fathers : confronting the crisis of economically vulnerable, nonresident fathers / Ronald
B. Mincy, Monique Jethwani, Serena Klempin.
pages cm
ISBN 978-0-19-937114-3
1. Absentee fathers—United States.   2. Fatherhood—United States.   3. Father and child—United
States.   4. Single mothers—United States.   5. Fatherless families—United States.   I. Jethwani,
Monique.   II. Klempin, Serena.   III. Title.
HQ756.M558 2015
306.874'2—dc23
2014022088

9 8 7 6 5 4 3 2 1
Printed in the United States of America
on acid-free paper

Contents

Acknowledgments

NO BOOK INVOLVING so many methods could have been written without saying thank you to so many who have helped or supported our work in one way or another. We owe the biggest debt to our spouses, partners, parents, and children, who have patiently endured less than our complete attention during "family times" to allow us to complete this work. At the other end of the spectrum, we are grateful for the financial support that we received from the Ford Foundation and the Open Society Foundation's Campaign for Black Male Achievement. Special thanks are due to our program officers, Kilolo Kijakazi and Shawn Dove, who believed in our work and endured the many twists and turns until this project was completed. Next we would like to thank Gretchen Dovholuk, the project manager for the Center for Research on Fathers, Children, and Family Well-Being during the formative years of our project. She completed so many grant, effort, financial, and narrative reporting requirements of the University and our donors, so that we could focus on the research. We also owe a great debt of gratitude to our colleagues, Irwin Garfinkel at Columbia University and Sarah McLanahan at Princeton University, who have created such a sprawling and effective research community around the Fragile Families and Child Well-Being Survey, which is the source of much of what we and so many others have learned about vulnerable nonresident fathers over the last 20 years.

Fortunately, however, our research went far beyond what we could learn from the analyses of survey data. Instead, 43 fathers being served by H&R Block and fatherhood/employment programs located throughout New York City and Chautauqua, New York, shared their stories with us and with our readers. We are very grateful for the privilege. We thank the staff of these programs at Strive and Seedco, and the staff at H&R Block who helped us recruit these fathers and provided space for our interviews. We are also grateful for the army of smart and dedicated graduate students at the Columbia University School of Social Work who conducted the interviews, gathering over 500 pages of transcripts that we analyzed for this book.

Special thanks go to James Singletary, Emily Wong, William Buford, Vera Dumont, Zee Cee Randall, James Singletary, Atavia Whitfield, Cameron Rasmussen, and Valerie Edwards, our research assistants who help us code the qualitative data and conduct literature reviews for various chapters, and to Elia De La Cruz and Hyunjoon Um, who undertook analyses for the manuscript. In addition, our colleagues Daniel Miller and David Seith have been generous in allowing us to expand upon analysis of a conference paper, presented at the Annual Meeting of the Association for Policy Analysis and Management. This list of thanks would be incomplete without special mention of Jo Turpin, who provided stellar research assistance and spent countless hours editing the entire manuscript. Her work helped us find that plain voice we had so long forgotten after writing so many pages in scholarly journals for our research colleagues.

We also thank the five anonymous reviewers of an earlier draft of the manuscript, senior staff especially, Jennifer Burnszynski, our long-time colleague, Elaine Sorensen, and Debra Pontisso at the Federal Office of Child Support Enforcement, and David L. Levy, founder and former president of the Children's Rights Council, for many conversations that helped us understand the current state of play of policies affecting vulnerable nonresident fathers and their families. Finally, we thank the editorial and production staff at Oxford University Press, especially Dana Bliss and Brianna Marron, for believing in this project, helping us see its broader relevance, and guiding us through the publication process.

Despite these many thanks, the views represented here are our own and do not represent the views of our the Ford Foundation, the Open Society Foundation, the Columbia University School of Social Work, or the Federal Office of Child Support Enforcement.

About the Authors

Ronald B. Mincy, PhD, is the Maurice V. Russell Professor of Social Policy and Social Work Practice at the Columbia University School of Social Work (CUSSW) and Director of the Center for Research on Fathers, Children and Family Well-Being (CRFCFW). He is also a co-principal investigator of the Fragile Families and Child Well-Being Study.

Monique Jethwani, PhD, is a lecturer at the Columbia University School of Social Work (CUSSW), where she is teaching Human Behavior and the Social Environment, Adolescent Development, and Clinical Practice Evaluation.

Serena Klempin, MSW, is a Research Associate at the Community College Research Center, Teachers College, Columbia University. She was most recently a Research Associate at the Columbia University School of Social Work's Center for Research on Fathers, Children and Family Well-Being (CRFCFW).

Preface

My child arrived just the other day
He came to the world in the usual way
But there were planes to catch, and bills to pay
He learned to walk while I was away
And he was talking 'fore I knew it, and as he grew
He'd say, "I'm gonna be like you, dad
You know I'm gonna be like you"

[Chorus:]
And the cat's in the cradle and the silver spoon
Little boy blue and the man in the moon
"When you coming home, dad?" "I don't know when
But we'll get together then
You know we'll have a good time then"

CAT'S IN THE CRADLE
Words and Music by HARRY CHAPIN and SANDY CHAPIN
© 1974 (Renewed) STORY SONGS, LTD.
All Rights Administered by WB MUSIC CORP.
All Rights Reserved
Used by Permission of ALFRED MUSIC

Though his wife penned the words to *The Cat's in the Cradle* several years earlier, it was the birth of their son that caused Harry Chapin to reflect on the cost that success in the breadwinner role imposed on American fathers and their families. The song told the story of a middle-class father who ignored his son's constant pleas for attention, while focusing instead on his job and his responsibilities as a provider. Nevertheless, the son, who regarded his father as a hero and role model, followed in his father's footsteps. In pursuit of his own career and success as a breadwinner, the son was too busy to heed his father's golden-year pleas for a relationship. This became a theme song in the counterculture that was emerging in the mid-1970s around family issues, topping the charts in December 1974. Over the following decade and a half, such sentiments matured into a demand for greater work-life balance and gender equity, both in the family and the workplace.

Chapin's generation would achieve those aspirations, at least among college-educated men and women. But about half of the sons of this generation did not complete college, and as a result they would have a very different legacy. Despite working as hard as their fathers, many were unable to form or sustain their families, in part because of a general decline in earnings for men without post-secondary schooling. Others, particularly Black and Latino fathers without college degrees, never had the opportunity to work as hard work or as consistently as their fathers. Instead, many remained chronically unemployed for most of their adult lives. Some of these fathers missed substantial portions of their children's tender years behind bars as a result of the incarceration boom that began during that same period.

As a result, about half of the children born between 1970 and 1984, spent some portion of their lives in a single-parent family. In response, the United States built up a public-benefits infrastructure designed to support single mothers and children. This infrastructure included a multibillion-dollar earning subsidy program that would ensure that working mothers could support their children through work, and the federal child support enforcement program designed to make financial support from fathers a certainty. Ironically, these important policies also began in 1974, anticipating the demographic trends that Chapin and his fans did not foresee. Yet this infrastructure treated economically vulnerable fathers as perpetrators, rather than victims-in-common with single mothers and the children they could not support. It set up increasingly elaborate schemes to ensure that they supported their children financially and made collection of such support swift and certain, even if there was no blood in the turnip. When fathers failed to pay, it made no distinction between volition and ability, but instead heaped on financial and then criminal penalties, assuming that eventually the deadbeats would get the message. Yet a commitment effort to build an infrastructure to increase employment and earnings among men lacking post-secondary schooling was intermittent at best.

Of course research, conducted at the nations' universities and think tanks informed the construction of this infrastructure, but until recently, fathers have been in the background of studies and demonstration projects on which policy-makers rely. Many studies have focused on inner-city minority fathers. However, the breadth of the on-coming crises among men lacking post-secondary school-ing who would become fathers and thus subject to the punitive aspects of this infrastructure went largely unnoticed. New studies on fathers have picked up dramatically over the past two decades and stereotypes about nonresident fathers as irresponsible, sexual predators are beginning to shatter under the weight of new evidence. The research reveals that some nonresident fathers who fail to provide support are not unwilling, but are simply unable, to support their children. They are broke. Further, the number of fathers who are caught in this position far exceeds the number of Black and Latino men residing in the nation's largest cities. As a result, policymakers are beginning to understand that if they want to increase the resources available for children, some assistance to these fathers may be required. Unfortunately, wars, recessions, health care reform, changes in the economies of Asia, Europe, and Latin America, and turmoil in the Greater Middle East have so preoccupied the nation's attention that many Americans who were once close observers of our nation's efforts to reform wel-fare and reduce child poverty have gotten sidetracked.

The resolution of several urgent matters may allow policy debates related to welfare, child poverty, and working poverty to return to center stage. We are no longer involved in a war with Iraq. We anticipate troop withdrawals from Afghanistan. The unemployment rate is slowly, but consistently, declining from historically high levels reached in 2010. Nevertheless, efforts to reduce high levels of inequality left in the wake of the recession are emerging. In the weeks follow-ing his January 2014 State of the Union address, President Obama announced a series of policy initiatives designed to underscore his ongoing leadership, despite the intransigence of Congress. Among these new initiatives were provisions to expand the minimum wage and the Earned Income Tax Credit, the latter of which is our nation's largest anti-poverty program. Absent was a special Earned Income Tax Credit for noncustodial fathers, made all the more conspicuous because in 2008, then Senator Obama proposed such an expansion for noncustodial fathers earning up to $34,000, similar to the cutoff used to designate vulnerable non-resident fathers in this book. Mr. Obama, now a two-term president with major accomplishments in healthcare reform and the urgent matters discussed above, has a public mandate to address the issue of inequality. He certainly has more leverage as president than he ever did as a freshman senator. New initiatives such as "My Brother's Keeper" indicate that his commitment to helping fathers and children has surely not waned. Why then did his proposal not include the issue he had advocated for in the Senate, an expansion of the Earned Income Tax Credit for noncustodial fathers? Did these fathers fare better or worse than other men during the Great Recession? Is it important to help nonresident fathers return to full employment? Or did their employment losses make work-based initiatives targeting nonresident fathers infeasible? These are among the issues that readers will better understand after reading this book.

But the book is not primarily about policy. Instead, it draws upon the most recent quantitative and qualitative research, including our own, to describe economically vulnerable nonresident fathers, who they are, and their numbers in the United States. Additionally, we explore the nature of their relationships with their children and their children's mothers, and what barriers they face in making a living in this new post-industrial/post-recession economy. We also examine the unintended consequences of policies designed to secure financial support for their children, the effectiveness of the few policies that have been designed to offer relief, and how we can improve upon policies that do both.

The approach of this book differs from most studies about fathers in a few important ways. First, most recent studies take the view that nonresident fathers who are divorced, and those who never married, come from completely different worlds. A similar strand runs through the literature on differences among nonresident fathers by race and ethnicity. While there are important differences, there are also significant similarities among divorced and never-married fathers, with the similarities far more important than their differences. In particular, if we are concerned about the policies that can help these fathers become better providers and nurturers for their children, then the differences between their marital status at birth and their race and ethnic origins may be nearly irrelevant.

Second, without neglecting the views of mothers, we approach roles as providers and nurturers through the fathers' lens. Our reason for doing so is simple. The literature on poverty, inequality, and families is already dominated by surveys and interviews of mothers and, to a lesser extent, children. To complete the picture, we need to hear from the fathers themselves. We accomplish this by asking the fathers important questions about their work, their family background, and their relationships with children and mothers, in addition to the impact that policy and programs have on their lives. Because what they tell us is very important, we end each chapter with a profile of one of the fathers, whose experiences best illustrate the themes of the chapter that follows. We include six additional profiles in the Appendix because the circumstances of these fathers differ so dramatically and it was hard to choose which father best illustrates a particular theme. These stories helped us understand how fathers made meaning of the social, economic, demographic, and policy changes we explore in this book. Therefore, we urge our readers to consult these fathers' stories as well. However, we also want our readers' understanding to be informed by more representative samples than was feasible to collect or analyze in the form of in-depth interviews. Therefore, we explore the same topics using studies, including our own, based on large, more nationally representative sample surveys. Because most of these surveys relied upon mothers' reports, even when asking questions about nonresident fathers, the results should adequately represent mothers' views on these topics.

Our multimethod approach has another advantage. Like other qualitative studies, our in-depth interviews can pull at readers' heartstrings, but the information they provide may not represent the views of all the fathers who have similar characteristics and circumstances. While quantitative studies can identify which topics (e.g., work and visitation) are related, they often leave unanswered questions about how and why these relationships exist. This is where in-depth interviews can help. The fathers' voices and the stories they tell about themselves and their children help us and our readers interpret the findings from quantitative studies and form a connection to the fathers beyond the statistics they represent. By listening to nonresident fathers, our research reveals the complexities of their lives and forces us to move beyond stereotypes, labels and misconceptions. We hope the in-depth interviews help our readers feel empathy and keep an open mind toward vulnerable nonresident fathers, while the quantitative studies help them to place fathers' voices in context. The result, we hope, is a balanced view of these fathers, their children, and their families, and the taxpayers who are called upon to help support them.

Today, more than 5 million men are unable to provide financial support for their children who live elsewhere. This is a population far larger and more diverse than the inner city, unmarried, Black and Latino men who have so long been the focus of the debate on disadvantaged fathers. Some of these fathers were without regular jobs even when the economy was growing. Over the last 20 years, some states have responded to the plight of these chronically unemployed fathers, making it easier for these fathers to meet their child support obligations, if nothing else. In other states, fathers in similar circumstances are still treated as if they are willfully avoiding their financial obligations to children. They are subject to sanctions resulting in rapidly accumulating debts and, until quite recently, incarceration as well.

Before the Great Recession, many other fathers were working, but they could not make ends meet if they paid all the child support they owed. The Great Recession was an enormous setback for these working-poor fathers, one that will take years from which to recover. The Great Recession taught some states that they had to be more responsive to the changing financial circumstances of working-poor fathers, but in other states the same fathers continued to accumulate debts while unemployed, making it more difficult for them to recover.

However, whether they were working at regular jobs or not before the Great Recession, most of these fathers were significantly involved in the lives of their children, but their child-support obligations and long-term debts created significant strain. Though they wanted their children to avoid the same problems they experienced due to a lack of education, the barriers they faced to involvement left them too little time to help close the gap between their own children and those who grow up with both parents. Fortunately, over the past 20 years, some states and localities have learned how to help these fathers meet their child support obligations, and become more engaged in the lives of their children. Unfortunately, these innovations are not available throughout the country. To help vulnerable nonresident fathers increase their earnings and disposable income, other ideas that seemed radical only 20 years ago must be further developed and tested. Making changes will involve a vigorous public debate because no consensus has been reached around many of these emotionally charged issues. We hope that after reading this book, you will be more interested in this debate and better prepared to participate.

Juan's Story

Juan is a 31-year-old Puerto Rican father, living with his girlfriend and her 9-year-old daughter in a rental apartment, close to where he was raised. Currently, he has been looking for a job. Previously, he worked as an armed guard for a security company, but had to leave for just over six months to attend to some personal problems. At the time, Juan was earning between $25,000 to $30,000 per year, and the company told him they would rehire him when he returned from his absence. However, upon his return, there was no longer an opening, and now Juan will have to wait. He has been waiting 11 months. In the meantime, he has applied to other jobs but cannot find work. This is only the second time that Juan has been unemployed, and it's definitely the longest. It has forced him to live off his savings, money that he had planned to use for his college tuition, or for the down payment on a home.

Juan did not complete high school, instead earning his GED. He attended college but had to drop out during the first semester, as he just didn't have the money to continue. It was also at this time that he first learned he was going to be a father. At 20, he didn't initially feel ready for parenthood, but he wanted to be responsible and felt he needed to take care of his daughter first. Juan takes his parental responsibilities very seriously. "You know, every man should be responsible for supporting their children financially. That's no, you know, no questions asked; you have to do that." But he strongly values education, and believes it will help him to achieve his goal of a high-paying position, and he wants to find a way back to school. That is one of the reasons he hopes to return to his former job. His salary allowed him to save money. "But the reality is that college costs money and it's not cheap. So that the only problem I have, personally, was the money. I didn't have the money." But Juan knows he has the motivation and the desire. "Cause I'm driven, I want—you know, I want a bachelor's degree. You know, I want that and it's not only, you know, to get a better job. You know, to get more money, yeah, that's cool of course but you want it for yourself. You know, know that you did something, achieve something in life. Which is an education, which is the most important thing, you know? An education will get you real far no matter what; that's what I believe."

Juan grew up in New York City with his mother and eight siblings. Although they were poor and struggled to make ends meet, his mother was strong and always provided food and shelter for the family. Juan never knew his father. He had abandoned the family when Juan was just a small child, and was never there for any of his children, financially, emotionally or otherwise. "You know I never had a father figure. Which is one of the reasons is why I think I'm a good father, because I do not, uh, want my children growing up the, the same way I grew up. You know, without a father figure."

Juan has two children, an 11-year-old girl and a 3-year-old boy, both of whom live with their mothers. He has supported his daughter informally her entire life, an arrangement that has suited both parents. After the birth of his daughter, her mother applied for TANF benefits. When this occurred, Juan was assessed for child support but he mistakenly made the payments directly to the mother of his daughter instead of child support enforcement. Because he had moved, he never received any notifications of the error, and debt continued to accrue, until it reached $11,000. Juan found out about it quite by accident, but worked with a judge and paid the amount in full. The mother of his daughter no longer receives welfare, and the case has since been closed. However, he continues to support his daughter informally, and both parents work together to make life better for their child "You know she moved on with her life, moved on with mine, but we both together for our daughter." Juan also supported his son informally, but that changed when his mother, too, applied for public benefits. Now, he has a standing child support order for his son set at $25. per month, but it was recently increased to $50.

Despite the fact that he does not live with either child, Juan identifies first and foremost as a responsible father. He believes that being a father means being there emotionally and financially, or really anytime he can be involved in the lives of his children, and he has worked hard to build a close relationship, maintaining an active presence in their lives. Juan sees his son twice weekly and saw his daughter daily since they both lived in the same neighborhood. However, she and her mother have moved to Staten Island and he sees her less frequently, although they speak often over the phone. Juan wants to make sure he is emotionally available to both children and that they understand they can come to their father if they are upset or uncomfortable. He feels it is important to set a good example to both children and wants them to be proud of their father.

Though Juan is fortunate that he has savings in the bank, he worries that he will exhaust his money before he finds a job. The last time he was unemployed, he was forced to work off the books, something he'd like very much to avoid. During that time, he was forced to sell some of his personal possessions, which was very difficult, but he felt strongly that his children came first. Despite everything, Juan still feels hopeful about the future, and sees the next five years as better than the present. He firmly believes education holds the key to his future success. "You know, there's no other way."

1 Introduction

LURKING NOT TOO far from the front line of the cultural war over the state of the American family is the specter of the nonresident father, who leaves the critical work of raising his children to single mothers and taxpayers. According to defenders of the traditional, heterosexual, nuclear family, such as Kay Hymowitz,[1] David Blankenhorn,[2] David Popenoe,[3] and Charles Murray,[4] nonresident fathers have abandoned a critical script in American life, which had assured the health and well-being of American families for decades. According to this script, young adults graduate from secondary school, find stable employment, commit to a lifelong heterosexual partner through monogamous marriage, and bear and rear children who can contribute to a well-functioning society. By abandoning this script, these fathers create new cohorts of poor, dependent children who are prone to violence, delinquency, and teenage pregnancy and are at risk of child sexual abuse. What's more, they leave mothers overburdened with the responsibility of raising children alone, potentially increasing their exposure to domestic violence. In doing so, nonresident fathers also undermine an American institution, namely the nuclear family, and contribute to growing social inequality.

Defenders of family diversity, like Stephanie Coontz[5] and Judith Stacey,[6] have little to say about nonresident fathers, directly. Instead, they argue that the resident father is largely a mythical or undesirable figure. According to Coontz, during

America's industrial age, economic insecurity drove many non-White, immigrant, or working-class men to spend long hours, weeks, and months away from their wives and fathers trying to earn a living during lives cut short by harsh and risky working conditions. The achievement ideology requiring native-born, upper class White men to make their place in the world by business or professional accomplishments left them little time to spend with their wives or children. In other words, unless their children were farmers or artisans, the children of industrial America were as fatherless as children are today.

According to Stacy, the nostalgia for the nuclear family disguises that for some, marriage was not necessarily an ideal. Some homemakers found that work inside the home was not fulfilling and desired options in addition to marriage. Others recognized that the relationship itself was the problem, creating new family patterns of divorce and remarriage. Still others did not want or desire marriage. Because these options largely ignored same-sex couples, none spoke to the aspirations of gays and lesbians. The traditional nuclear family structure, as Stacey observed, has given rise to a new postmodern family, a byproduct of which is the nonresident father.

Liberal politicians, entertainers, and members of the media, without rigid public positions in the debate about the marriage script, have been more direct in their critique of nonresident fathers. They have focused especially on the predatory sexual and irresponsible behavior of unmarried Black nonresident fathers. Though his tone has become much more supportive in recent years, in his 2008 Father's Day speech at a Southside Chicago church, President Barack Obama criticized these fathers for being absent from the lives of the children, saying:

> Yes, we need more money for our schools, and more outstanding teachers in the classroom, and more afterschool programs for our children. Yes, we need more jobs and more job training and more opportunity in our communities. But we also need families to raise our children. We need fathers to realize that responsibility does not end at conception. We need them to realize that what makes you a man is not the ability to have a child—it's the courage to raise one.[7]

This echoed a 2006 speech by Bill Cosby at a Northwest Baltimore church event designed to urge Black fathers to become more involved in the lives of their children. Cosby derided those who had children by more than one mother, saying, "This is a great evening because we're calling on men to come claim their children, that's part of being a man. You cannot be a man at all if you haven't claimed your child. Some of you have three, four, five of them. You have more children than you have jobs."[8]

Both comments appear to have been inspired by Timothy McSeed, the infamous "player" portrayed in a late 1980s documentary, narrated by Bill Moyers on the Vanishing Black Family. In the documentary, McSeed, a 27-year-old, unemployed Black father of six children by four women, celebrates his virility by dancing around the delivery room with his newborn child, exclaiming "...I am the king." In other scenes he explains his failure to use birth control methods, by saying "...girls don't like them things," and says that, through welfare, government was providing the support he failed to provide. Although he was only one of four Black men portrayed in the documentary—some who were victims and others heroes—he remains the most enduring image of unmarried nonresident fathers in the record of the documentary.

Nonresident Fathers: The Residue of Marital Decline

Though the marital script represents a cure for some, a trouble for others, and a placebo for those not involved in the great American family debate, there is plenty of social science research in support of its demise. Noted sociologists such as Stephen Nock[9] have described the central role of the marital script in men's lives and the individual and social consequences when Americans abandon this script by separating childbirth from marriage. Marriage institutionalizes the relationship between men and women as spouses and as parents, ensuring involvement and dictating how men should behave not only as husbands, but also as fathers.

According to Andrew Cherlin[10] however, the rules for non-marital relationships have not been institutionalized in the United States, and the social norms about everyday behavior for nonresident fathers and their children are relatively unknown. More recently, Harvard sociologists Kathryn Edin and Tim Nelson have described the abandonment of the marital script. In their view, the traditional quest for a monogamous relationship among young men has been exchanged for a euphoric commitment to non-marital children, made unworkable by an equivocal and distrustful relationship with the children's mothers.[11] The result is what they describe as "serial paternity" of fathers who have children by multiple mothers. Such fathers, they argue, are highly involved with their younger children and much less involved with children they conceived at an earlier age. This behavior is indicative of a paternal instinct, a determination on the part of some men to raise their own children even after having lost contact with their older children because of failed relationships with the children's mothers.

Increasing tolerance of a variety of family arrangements has contributed to the growth of nonresident fatherhood.[12] According to Arland Thornton, who has been tracking American family attitudes for decades, researchers began to observe the changing landscape of the American family in the late 1950s with declines in attitudes rejecting single lifestyles, declines in preferences for marriage, and increasing concerns about the confines of marriage. Into the mid-1980s and beyond, the acceptance of single lifestyles, including divorce, became more widespread while unfavorable attitudes toward marriage declined. Despite this decline, more recent cohorts of young Americans want to delay marriage. More generally, marriage became one of many family-related options available to Americans who, as Andrew Cherlin argues, became less concerned about the significance of marriage to the community and larger society and more concerned about whether marriage, divorce, parenthood, or any other family choice suited their individual needs and desires.

The 1960s and 1970s brought further changes to the landscape. Though the birth control pill was viewed as the icon of changing sexual attitudes in the 1960s, its initial beneficiaries were married women, primarily White and middle class.[13] Use of this new birth control method changed the marital relationship, allowing women to decide when to have children and the number of children, shifting a woman's role as wife and mother. It was not until the 1970s that the pill had greater acceptance among single women, with just under 6 out of 10 college women reporting that they had sex. These changes were driven by, among other things, increased educational opportunities and delaying marriage. The tumultuous times created change and uncertainty, but what was certain was that the sexual revolution was here to stay.

Americans began to accept sex between unmarried consenting adults, with little change in this attitude over the next two and half decades. In addition, the mid-1970s witnessed dramatic changes in attitudes regarding cohabitation and non-marital childbearing. While cohabitation was rare and taboo in the 1960s, by the mid-1970s adults still disapproved of cohabitation, but it was widely accepted by adolescents. By the late 1990s, attitudes of young people about cohabitation shifted from mere tolerance to a belief, shared by the majority, that cohabitation was an effective strategy for testing the quality of relationships prior to marriage. Changes in attitudes about non-marital births were not as sweeping, but still important. Americans became much more tolerant of this outcome compared to most of its alternatives.[14] In particular, Americans believed that marriage was a better outcome for adult women than unmarried motherhood and that children were better off if raised by a married couple. However, few were morally offended by a non-marital birth, and the majority of male adolescents believed that if a woman became pregnant, raising the child as an unmarried mother would be better than abortion, adoption, or a shotgun wedding.

Economic Trends and Vulnerable Fathers

Other important reasons for the decline in marriage and marital births are the disappointing trends in male employment and earnings since the mid-1970s. Elliot Liebow conducted an ethnographic study of Black "street corner" men in the early 1960s. He found that the men's employment prospects were grim, and that even when they were able to find jobs, the work seldom paid enough to adequately support a family. These economic struggles were profoundly damaging to men's self-confidence and identity, particularly as husbands and fathers. More recently, William Julius Wilson, the Harvard sociologist,[15] has done more than any scholar to draw attention to the role of mid-1970s declines in manufacturing and the decentralization of urban population and employment in eroding job opportunities for inner-city Black men.

Other sociologists have kept their attention focused on the plight of young Black men in the inner city. Even at the end of the long economic expansion of the 1980s, Yale sociologist Elijah Anderson[16] found them to be demoralized by the scarcity of employment opportunities and the negative stereotyping of their gender and race. Out of a sense of desperation and hopelessness they turned to involvement in the underground economy and criminal activity. At a University of Pennsylvania conference, held just before the onset of the recent recession, Anderson[17] identified three distinct types of work in the informal economy that took the place of regular jobs for this population: (1) legal activities conducted outside the marketplace (i.e., bartering labor and goods among friends and relatives); (2) semi-legal activities (i.e., small businesses operated out of the home under the radar of regulation); and (3) illegal activities (i.e., drug dealing, prostitution, street crime).

In a qualitative study of low-income nonresident fathers living in poverty-stricken areas of Philadelphia, Pennsylvania, and Camden, New Jersey, Katheryn Edin and Tim Nelson,[18] as part of a new generation of sociologists, identified similar distinctions within the underground economy, defining them as (1) off-the-books work: unregulated, employer-based work; (2) informal businesses: unregulated entrepreneurial work; and (3) hustles/drugs—unregulated entrepreneurial work that is also illegal. Most fathers were working at least part-time doing regular work, but most also felt compelled to engage in some level of underground work to make ends meet, although they would have preferred to solely engage in regular work. Drug dealing was viewed as incompatible with fatherhood, and thus most chose unregulated work, either off the books or entrepreneurial informal businesses, to supplement their income. Edin and Nelson conclude that lack of opportunity in the regular labor market was the main motivation pushing men to do unregulated work.

While these urban socialists have pointed to the deteriorating labor market conditions, another member of the new cohort of urban sociologists, Alford Young, looked at the views of young Black men for an explanation of their condition.[19] He found that the worldviews and understanding of the current employment environment were also barriers to regular work. In particular, the men he interviewed in Ypsilanti, Michigan, a southern Michigan suburb devastated by the closing of automobile-part assembly plants between the mid-1960s and the early 1990s, were generally unaware of recent employment trends, such as the increasing demand for service sector jobs, and they expressed determination to avoid jobs they considered menial.

Although the deteriorating jobs and earning prospects of inner-city Black men are compelling, they may only represent the worst of far more general trends that impact the employment opportunities and earnings of all men. Government employment data show that virtually *all* men who reached working age by the mid-1970s, not just those residing in inner cities, have experienced stagnating or declining earnings for more than a quarter century, making the cost of supporting children especially burdensome.[20] This secular trend was also unexpected because prior to 1974, men's earnings rose when the economy expanded. Since then, average male wages, after adjusting for inflation, remain at $43,000 annually, whether we are experiencing an economic boom or bust. Earnings actually fell for men who did not attend graduate school. For example, according to Northeastern University economist Andrew Sum and colleagues, between 1979 and 2007, the hourly earnings of 20- to 29-year-old men, including those without earnings, fell by 26 percent for high school dropouts, 27 percent for high school graduates, 10 percent among men with some college, and 3 percent for college graduates. According to Sum and his colleagues, these reductions in earnings contributed to the declines in marriage, marital stability, and marital births in America about which so much has been written over the last four decades.

Today two out of five births in America are to unmarried women, and the majority of births to American women over 30 years old are non-marital births. Further, while the majority of these births are to cohabiting couples, few of these cohabiting couples marry.[21] What's more, the divorce rate has stabilized at 50 percent, so that more than half of American children will spend a significant portion of their childhood in a household without their biological father. As a result, nonresident fatherhood has become a growing phenomenon, especially among young men who lack post-secondary schooling and high earnings.

Oddly, thought leaders on the fringe of the American mainstream appear to be the only ones talking about the growth of nonresident fatherhood outside the inner city. Focusing solely on White Americans, libertarian scholar Charles Murray notes growing economic, social, and behavioral distance between economic classes, arguing that this trend differs from our traditional understanding of class structure.[22] To place his discussion in context, Murray uses residents of two towns, Belmont and Fishtown, simplifying the characteristics of each for an easier interpretation of results. He restricts his discussion in several ways, first, by limiting his population to adults who are between the ages of 30 and 49. The types of jobs are also limited, with residents of Fishtown possessing a high school diploma or less, and holding jobs in the blue-collar sector. In Belmont, citizens complete at least a four-year college education and are high-level professionals. The Fishtown residents correspond roughly to families with income in the bottom 30 percent of the US income distribution, and Belmont residents represent the top 20 percent of the US income distribution. Murray uses the two groups to demonstrate divergent trends among the working- and upper-middle classes.

To explain the gaps between the two groups, Murray identifies four virtues—marriage, honesty, religiosity, and industriousness—that he asserts founded and sustained our democracy. He argues that the loss of personal virtues is greatest among the segment he terms the "new lower class," a subset of the working class. However, outside factors beyond personal control may have contributed to gulfs in behavioral norms. Thus, Murray blames declining industriousness for declines in employment rates, hours of work per week, and labor force participation. Declines in employer demand for less-educated workers caused by immigration, global competition, core inflation, business deregulation, labor-saving technology, the rising female labor force participation, suburbanization of employment, and other factors, noted by MIT labor economist Frank Levy[23] and others, play no role in Murray's assessment. Similarly, Murray believes that high levels of non-marital birth change the culture of a community, casting doubt as to whether White working-class communities are capable of "socializing the next generation."

Though he excluded women under 30 who bore half their children outside marriage, Murray was correct to note the increase in non-marital births in working-class White communities. Unmarried parents in the United States rarely married or stayed together over the long term, even if they were cohabiting. Therefore, nonresident fatherhood was growing in working-class White communities as well as in inner-city, mostly minority communities. While the latter growth has been well documented, the former has been virtually ignored. If the number of non-marital fathers in working-class White communities was growing during a period in which their earnings, employment, and labor force participation were falling, then we should expect an increasing number of White nonresident fathers who are unable to support their children.

Economically Vulnerable Nonresident Fathers

That nonresident fatherhood among economically vulnerable men has become so widespread became apparent during a recent conference of some of America's leading family economists and sociologists at the long-standing Institute for Research on Poverty (IRP) at the University of Wisconsin. Tim Smeeding, the IRP director and conference co-convener, showed that men who were least likely to support a family were most likely to be fathers. By age 30, nearly three out of five male high school dropouts were fathers; nearly two out of three men with only a high school degree were fathers; while just two out of five men with a bachelor's degree or more were fathers.[24] Writing in the same volume, Northeastern University labor economist Andrew Sum and his colleagues showed that just over a quarter of high school dropouts and 3 out of 10 high school graduates were married, compared with almost half of young men with a college degree or more.[25] Together, these data mean that the great majority of young less-educated men, not just those in the inner city, are (or will eventually become) nonresident fathers.

According to the most recent data available from the National Survey of Family Growth, there are 7.5 million nonresident fathers in America; about 5.3 million earned no more than $40,000. We think of these fathers as vulnerable nonresident fathers because most are poorly educated, fully employed, but they do not pay their child support obligations in full. More than 75 percent of nonresident fathers earning at most $40,000 per year have no post-secondary schooling, and more than 75 percent of these fathers are employed mostly full-time. Child support payments are automatically deducted from the wages of full-time workers who have child support orders. As a result, the nonresident father with a full-time job and a child support order cannot duck his child support obligations. Nonresident fathers who are self-employed or working at irregular jobs must pay their child support directly. If they do not pay their child support, they may be unable to do so, or are working irregular jobs and thus are concealing their income.

One of the difficulties with studying nonresident fathers is that those who do not provide adequate financial support for their children are reluctant to admit that they have nonresident children. For this reason, few surveys collect data on nonresident fathers directly, and those that do usually undercount nonresident fathers. Instead, the Current Population Survey, a large monthly survey used by the Labor Department to estimate basic employment and earning trends in the United States, asks mothers if their children have nonresident fathers. If they do, surveys then ask if a child support order has been established on behalf of the child, and if so, whether those child support orders are paid in full, partially, or not at all. Since many nonresident fathers have children by more than one mother, the number of nonresident children exceeds the number of nonresident fathers. Researchers at the Urban Institute use special computations to align reports of the number of men who say they are nonresident fathers with the number of children that mothers report as having nonresident fathers.[26] The result is a data set with a complicated name, the Transfer Income Microsimulation Model (TRIM 3). TRIM 3 is also an important source of information about nonresident fathers.

A third source of information from which we will draw quite extensively in this book is the Fragile Families and Child Well-Being Survey. This is a survey of parents of children born between 1998 and 2000, who have been followed over the past 15 years. The survey is the first to include a large subsample of children born to unmarried mothers and fathers and to collect a wealth of new information about nonresident fathers, from the fathers directly and from the mothers of their children.

Recently, with colleagues, we used TRIM 3 and the Fragile Families and Child Well-being Survey to study the link between a nonresident father's income and his child support payments.[27] We used these two data sources because TRIM 3 provided details about all nonresident fathers, while Fragile Families provided data on the fathers of younger children only. Nevertheless, the two data sources provided remarkably similar estimates of the relationship between income and child support payments.

Using TRIM 3, we found that there were approximately 9.5 million nonresident fathers, but only about 4 of 10 had child support orders. According to both TRIM 3 and Fragile Families, only two of five nonresident fathers paid all the child support they owed; while only one of three nonresident fathers making no more than $40,000 paid all the child support they owed. Why did so few nonresident fathers, making what appeared to be a comfortable living, fail to pay all the child support they owed?[28]

Because, like the fathers earning the minimum wage we studied with our colleagues, doing so would cause fathers who earned four times as much to be defined as poor or nearly so.[29] Taking into account normal household expenses (e.g., rent, food, clothing, healthcare, and transportation) as well as federal, state, and other taxes, a father making $20,000 a year with a child support obligation (for one child) of $3,400, would have little money left by the end of the year. In fact, his income would be $6,354 below the federal poverty line for a single person. A father making $30,000 with a child support order of $5,100 would be $1,304 below the poverty line. The man who earns $40,000 with a child support order of $6,800 would be $3,011 above the poverty line after paying all household expenses. Although he is not living below the poverty line, he has little left for any additional expenses that he may incur. This can include a vacation or gifts, but it may more likely include unforeseen medical expenses, car repair, or routine household maintenance, thus pushing him back into poverty.

Two children to support make the situation even worse. Men earning $20,000 per year with a child support order of $4,000 are $7,000 below the federal poverty line, very close to being insolvent. Those earning $30,000 with a child support obligation of $6,000 are $2,204 below the poverty line. Finally, a nonresident father with two children earning $40,000 per year with a child support order for $8,000 has little to show for his efforts, living only $1,811 above the poverty line. Nonresident fathers earning $40,000 or less, supporting either one or two children, must budget carefully in order to afford their child support obligations. Almost any unforeseen expenditure will impoverish them, risking arrears and penalties.

In summary, changes in family-related attitudes and behavior, along with long-term declines in male earnings, have led to a large population of nonresident fathers, perhaps nine percent of all adult men between 15 and 44 years old, who are unable to provide adequate support for their children. Prior to the 2007–2009 recession, these fathers were among the working poor or near poor. Child support payments are automatically deducted from the earnings of most regularly employed workers. So if they failed to pay the full amount of child support due, it was most likely because they did not earn enough money. Willful noncompliance is an option only for fathers who escape child support payments while they are between regular jobs, or fathers working off the books. Although men of color are overrepresented among vulnerable nonresident fathers, more than half of the men in this population are White, and more than two-thirds of them worked full-time. Put differently, most Americans have a brother, cousin, nephew, or ex-husband who is a vulnerable nonresident father, and yet we know little about this population as a whole, how much they contribute to their children's needs, what efforts they make to stay in contact with their children, what barriers they face in making these efforts, and how their financial and other contributions might be increased.

Overview: How and What We Present

This book answers these and related questions by undertaking new analyses and examining studies based on recent large sample surveys and small-scale interviews. However, because these sources leave important gaps, we also answer these questions through the voices of vulnerable nonresident fathers themselves who were interviewed in New York State between February and August 2009, following an effort to help them meet their child support obligations.

In 2006, New York State became the first state in the country to offer a tax credit for nonresident parents (mostly fathers) who worked and supported their children by paying formal child support.[30] Expansion of the federal Earned Income Tax Credit (EITC) in 1996 provided strong incentives for single mothers to leave welfare for work. Building on this experience, legislators in New York State hoped that a similar tax credit would spur employment and child support compliance among low- and moderate-income nonresident fathers, the only group left poor after paying payroll taxes. State and federal policymakers throughout the country wanted to know more about how the credit in New York State was working. To help them, we wanted to speak with fathers who were eligible for the credit program. These fathers had to be nonresident parents of at least one child under the age of 18 years, for whom child support was awarded by the State of New York, and residents of the State of New York who were themselves over the age of 18. Their earnings could not exceed $33,995 in the 2008 tax year, and the child support they owed for the tax year had to be paid in full.[31]

As a result of our attempts to find fathers like those whom New York legislators sought to help, we became very skeptical of the way the problem of nonresident fatherhood has been framed. In addition to the unwed, inner-city fathers who have caught the attention of most researchers, policymakers, and members of the media, there are hundreds of thousands of economically vulnerable nonresident fathers who are having difficulty supporting themselves and their children, despite being stably employed for most of their adult lives. This book amplifies their stories by drawing upon recent research and new analyses about nonresident fathers, based on large sample surveys. But first, a little more about how we found the fathers we interviewed, because this experience provides lessons as well.

To find fathers who met the criteria for receiving the New York State credit for nonresident parents, we first visited agencies that provided voluntary income tax assistance (VITA) at no cost to low- and moderate-income people. VITA is a program funded by the IRS and is usually operated by nonprofit organizations. Unfortunately, in 2009 when we went into the field for our interviews, most

VITA sites in New York City were placing childless workers, including nonresident fathers, on a waiting list. They would be served only after the VITA sites served families with children. So we sent interview teams to H&R Block offices throughout New York City. H&R Block offices have been very popular locations for low- and moderate-income women who file for the federal EITC, and H&R Block had been very helpful to Kathryn Edin and her colleagues who studied how low-income and working-poor families access and spend the federal EITC.[32] Nevertheless, in the 100 hours we spent at H&R Block, we did not encounter a single father who had received or applied for the New York credit for nonresidential parents, even though the credit had been in existence for 3 years. In fact, the earnings of most men we encountered at H&R Block exceeded $34,000, which would make them ineligible for the credit.

The rewards and eligibility requirements of the New York State credit may explain why we were unable to find more low-income nonresident fathers at the H&R Block sites. Essentially, the credits were set so much lower than the federal EITC that fathers with qualifying incomes were unlikely to be able to pay their child support in full. For example, the typical father earning $21,000 a year would receive a $290 credit. If he earned $15,000 a year, he would receive $458 from the credit. However, the credit program requires that applicants for the credit pay their child support—about $2,550 for one child—in full for the tax year. What are the chances that someone earning just $15,000 could afford to pay one of every $6 he earned in child support, after meeting other living expenses? The maximum credit ($970, after deducting the cost of tax preparation) would go to nonresident fathers earning between $6,000 and $9,000 annually. Such fathers would earn too little to be full-time/full-year workers.[33] They might have worked part-time or full-time, but for only part of the year. If so, they probably could not afford to pay all the child support they owed.

After recruiting only four nonresident fathers at H&R Block, who we thought would have been eligible for the credit if they had applied, we turned to programs that were providing employment services to fathers who could not meet their child support obligations. Although these programs typically served chronically unemployed fathers, by February 2009 when we began our interviews, the nation was already 14 months into the worst recession since the Depression of the 1930s. As a result, many nonresident fathers who were stably employed in regular jobs paying up to $40,000 prior to the recession had begun to seek help from local programs or had been ordered to do so to avoid harsher sanctions for failing to meet their child support payments. Unfortunately, none of the programs in New York City served White fathers. So we turned to similar programs in Chautauqua County, New York, to recruit White fathers who might be interested in the study.[34]

Chautauqua County is a community in the western portion of the state. The city of Jamestown in Chautauqua County had been a center for the manufacturing of wood products such as furniture, as well as a major producer of mattresses. The town was once called the "Furniture Capital of the World," but many of these industries had moved away from the area in recent years.

In Chautauqua, we interviewed nine (White) nonresident fathers who met the study criteria.[35] The fathers were as economically vulnerable as their counterparts from New York City, including several who were ex-offenders. Most lacked a four-year college degree, and could not make a decent living in an economy that had adapted even less effectively to the decline in manufacturing employment than New York City. They suffered from the same structural changes that, according to Wilson, Anderson, and others, have hurt the employment prospects of inner-city minorities, with adverse consequences for employment, earnings, savings, and family life of prime age men. Unable to support their families financially, many have become nonresident fathers who are unable to meet their child support obligations. Finally, mounting child support debt, amplified by the recession, made it impossible for them to pursue the kinds of training or higher education needed to put them on a higher path of earnings.

In total, we interviewed 39 nonresidential fathers (9 White, 16 Black, 13 Latino, and 1 Other). Besides awareness of and eligibility for the credit program, interview topics included family background, current family composition and living situation, relationship with children, child support, organizational involvement and support, employment history, educational attainment and goals, and personal finances and expenses (current income, taxes, savings, and debt). To analyze these interviews, we used an interpretive approach, which we describe more fully in a journal article.[36] Through these interviews, as well as our own and others' studies based on large sample surveys, we hope to reframe the way that Americans understand vulnerable nonresident fathers. Chapter 2 describes what we mean by vulnerable nonresident fathers and why we think this population needs help in order to meet the obligations that Americans expect them to meet. Chapter 3 describes efforts by vulnerable nonresident fathers to sustain their roles as breadwinner, despite limited means. Chapter 4 describes their thoughts about the link between their own education and their economic vulnerability, as well as their thoughts about the educational aspirations for their children, and the effects of these attitudes on their engagement with their children around education. Chapter 5 describes the challenges that vulnerable nonresident fathers face when attempting to remain involved in the lives of their children. Chapter 6 describes programs and policies that can help these fathers fulfill financial and nonfinancial roles in the lives of their children. Finally, Chapter 7 provides a list of other sources where readers can get useful information about vulnerable nonresident fathers and efforts to require and/or enable them to meet society's expectations.

Many fathers expressed their appreciation for an opportunity to participate in the interviews and have their voices heard, as Jeffrey, a father we profile in the Appendix, said. "I would just like to thank you for this opportunity to get my voice heard. Because you know, we're not heard often. So this is a great, platform. Thank you very much." The response of another father we profiled in the Appendix, Michael, was similar. "I'm happy I got the opportunity to sit with you. Yeah, you know. If this is going to help the cause, I'm all for it, you know, and that's pretty much it."[37] Fathers enthusiastically agreed that they enjoyed talking with the interviewers and that they wanted to contribute to "the cause," with the cause being the difficulties facing nonresident fathers, especially in the formal child support system. Fathers hoped their stories might facilitate an understanding of this population and guide other fathers in similar situations. We hope this book accomplishes that charge.

Franco's Story

Franco is a 45-year-old man who describes himself as Hispanic and Puerto Rican. He is fluent in both English and Spanish. Franco is also a newlywed, having married just a year ago. This is his second marriage, as the first ended in divorce in 1990. Franco and his wife live with her daughter and her daughter's husband, and their four-year-old daughter, in a rental apartment. He has been unemployed for four months, a situation that has not been easy for him. However, his wife and her daughter and son-in-law all work and help with household expenses, which makes things a little less scary, at least for the moment.

The middle child of three children, Franco and his brothers lived with their mother and father, but it felt a bit like growing up without parents since neither spent much time at home. Franco remembers his father as always working. He would get up early in the morning and did not return home until late at night. Because he owned two businesses, a grocery store and a fish market, he was always at work. As Franco reflected, "not really spending time with my father was a big influence on me and my brothers."

His mother worked in a school, teaching, and also attended school herself, as a student. Her schedule did not allow much time at home, either. Franco and his brothers did not have a great deal of supervision from either parent and as a result, the boys often felt left on their own. "Yeah, we always seemed like the family was always split. My father would work and he would be over here, my mother would work and be over here, and we would be right in the middle." Franco remembered some good times that he and his brothers spent with their mother on special outings to the beach or the Botanical Gardens, but there were also less pleasant memories. Franco got in trouble at school for hitting other children, for getting into fights or talking back to his teacher. As he noted, he would get confrontational and very physical. Looking back, he felt that he overreacted to things but just couldn't help himself. He acknowledged that maybe he just wanted attention and that the easiest way to get it was with bad behavior. But for whatever reasons, when he did get into trouble there were always consequences at home. Sometimes, Franco was physically punished. Other times, he lost privileges like watching television or being able to go outside. Franco's brother also got into trouble, but it was more serious. He had problems with the law.

Franco is a father and had four children with his first wife, now all in their early to mid-twenties. None lives with him. Since 1990, when Franco and his wife initiated divorce proceedings, he has had a child support order for all four children, set at $32 per week in total. The money was taken out of his paycheck automatically. During short spells of unemployment or injury, Franco would petition the court to have the amount reduced so he did not fall into arrears. At only one point did he run into trouble, but it was resolved successfully. Now, he no longer is obligated to pay support, as his youngest child just turned 22 and has aged out. However, Franco still wants to help his children when he can. When his youngest son needed a pair of sneakers, he was happy to be able to purchase them for him.

Franco's youngest son is a pre-law major at Columbia University—a fact that makes Franco very proud, since he has only a high school diploma. None of Franco's brothers has more than a high school degree, nor do his parents. His son will be the first. His daughter is also going back to college, as is his other son. Franco wants to follow in his children's footsteps and return to college, too, to get a degree in business. He wants to one day own a limousine company. But for now, it is only a wish because he would need financial aid, and when he locates full-time work, he will need to find the time to attend school. His priority right now is to find a job.

Franco has been looking for work for the past four months, looking for job openings and sending out resumes. He would like a job as a chauffeur or a driver. His last job was driving an access-a-van, a service for people who are disabled or sick, to take them to appointments. He had worked there for two years, prior to the company going out of business, earning close to $34,000 a year with overtime. He enjoyed the work because he enjoyed being around people, talking to them, and finding out about their children and their families, though he didn't always like the New York traffic. As Franco recalled, "interacting with the people was one of the best parts of the job."

Franco has been looking for job openings, but the stress of being unemployed weighs heavily on him. He tries to focus on a search rather than what he is going through. "I just keep encouraging myself. The economy is real, real, I mean real tight." He looks forward to working again and wants to work but cannot find an opening. Franco does not want to take a job off the books because he is afraid that an employer might take advantage of him, and then he has no recourse. Though Franco had worked off the books several years ago, he felt the risks of the informal job market far outweighed any benefits. "Off the books if the guys says, look, I'm out of business today, you're out of a job, that's it, you have no compensation." There are also tax risks and Franco did not relish the prospect of the IRS chasing him down. The security of formal employment is an important issue for Franco.

Presently, he receives unemployment benefits that have allowed him to continue to contribute to the household and help to maintain economic stability, an impossible outcome had the job been off the books. Franco is also aware that accidents can and do happen, and that drivers run this risk, making off-the-books jobs uncertain. "Well, if you worked off the books, you'll get the money right there, but how is that going to help you if God forbid you get into an accident and you can't work for six months." His daughter, who works for Workforce One, helps him when she sees potential openings, notifying him immediately. Franco appreciates that she gives him an "inside scoop" and also helps him with updating his resume.

Though Franco does get unemployment benefits, it still is just barely enough to pay all the bills, and Franco works hard to make sure he does not fall behind. To make ends meet, the family has a very tight budget, and tries to live within their means. Even with budgeting, Franco worries about paying his bills. So the family prioritizes the bills, paying the most important ones first. But Franco still worries.

And then, you know, my wife and I have been budgeting more, so that definitely helped. And we just live on what we have—our means. We have enough this, we have enough of that, and then we just try to space it where we can pay this at this time, pay a little bit more here. That's what we do— budgeting more, which helps a lot. Some weeks are a little less, some weeks are a little more. It just gets me to the next week.

When he had a job, he felt he had enough to live on. Now, he lives with daily uncertainty. To relieve the stress, the family tries to enjoy simple things, like riding bikes or having dinner out occasionally. Franco and his wife also have a membership in a local gym. It is inexpensive, and he is able to work out and forget about his problems, at least for a little while.

Even though the family's finances are tight, Franco still tries to save a little money each month. A full-time job will allow him to save more money, with the goal of saving for a vacation, putting money aside for his college education, and saving for a car that he can use for a chauffeur business. But for now, he buys small things for his children when they need them. Because they are now adults, he sees them less often than he'd like. It's hard, because his children have busy lives with work and school. Sometimes, he feels like it's a distant relationship and that's difficult for him. But he still reflects that having children and watching them come into the world was a privilege. Franco takes pride in the fact that he watched them grow up and enjoyed sharing activities with them and helping them. "That was like the best."

2 Employment

ON TOP OF the long-term erosion of male earnings, which we discussed in Chapter 1, the recession of 2007–2009 was like a full blast of wind in the face of a biker already peddling furiously to climb up a long and steep hill. Male joblessness rose more than female joblessness during every recession since the early 1980s. However, the Great Recession—called this because of its depth and severity—had the twin distinction of creating the largest postwar male jobless rate and the largest male-female jobless rate gap. Because of the disproportionate harm the recession caused men, Mark Perry, in his testimony before the members of Congress, coined the term "the mancession" to describe the 2007–2009 recession.[1] One reason for this disproportionate harm is that manufacturing and construction, traditionally fields that have been male dominated, were particularly hard hit by the 2007–2009 recession. Unfortunately, these industries have also been particularly slow to respond to recovery and may never achieve their pre-recession employment levels.

Not only was the increase in male joblessness larger than in previous recessions, but its effects are far from over. According to labor economists at the Federal Reserve, the government agency responsible for promoting economic growth while keeping prices stable and unemployment low, the male unemployment rate rose from just over 4 percent to 11 percent between December 2007 and August

2009.[2] As of July 2011, 4 out of 10 adults and young adults working or looking for work reported that they had been unemployed for more than six months. Three out of every four of those unemployed had been looking for more than a year, and unemployed workers have been without work for an average of 30 weeks, the highest rate of long-term joblessness since the federal government began collecting such data.[3]

Long-term joblessness has been particularly high among 20–45-year-old men, who are likely to be the fathers of young children. Jobless men in this age group have been looking for work for an average of 28 weeks to 41 weeks.[4] These long jobless spells eat into their savings, destroy credit worthiness, and, in some cases, result in the loss of their homes. Thus, the low-wage path on which young men have traveled for four decades has been compounded by long-term unemployment.

Victims of "the Slowdown"

According to a recent survey by the Pew Research Center, conducted 30 months after the recession, the Great Recession caused layoffs, pay cuts, reduced hours, or involuntary part time employment for more than half of the American workforce.[5] About a third of the adult workforce was laid off at least once during the 2007–2009 recession. Carl Van Horn and his colleagues at Rutgers University's Heldrich Center have been surveying the job-related attitudes of American workers over the last 15 years. Three-fourths of Americans who responded to the Heldrich Center Survey in September 2010 had lost a job, or had a friend or family member who lost a job since the recession began. It should not be surprising, therefore, that vulnerable nonresident fathers were also hurt by the recession. Although no nationally representative sample exists, many vulnerable nonresident fathers we interviewed were laid off because of what they described as a "slowdown" in the business of their former employer.

Finding a new job was difficult for most Americans who were laid off during the recession. National data show that in 2010, it took the average laid-off worker 33 weeks to find a job.[6] The Heldrich Center's record of the consequences of the recession began in March 2009, just three months before the recession officially ended. Nevertheless, two years later, they found that a third of workers who had lost their jobs by March 2009 were still looking for work, and more than one in six had become discouraged and had stopped looking for work altogether.[7] Later snapshots show that just over one in five workers who had been displaced by August 2009 had found new jobs almost 18 months later, and just over one in eight found full-time jobs.[8] Just as the unemployment rate of men rose to higher levels than the unemployment rate of women, men who were laid off also found it more difficult to find new jobs than women.

Similarly, some laid-off working-poor fathers found another job not long after being laid off, only to be laid off again within a few months. Princeton University economist Henry Farber, who has been studying displaced workers during every recession since the early 1980s, found that about one in five displaced workers experienced such repeated layoffs during the 2007–2009 recession.[9] Similarly, more than one-in-three workers interviewed by the Pew Research Center Survey had at least two layoffs during the recent recession, and two in eight had been laid off three or more times. There is no reason to believe that laid-off working-poor fathers were more successful at finding new jobs.

Among the working-poor fathers who were still employed, many also suffered a slowdown or cut in pay because of the recession. This was a common experience among American workers. For example, almost a quarter of currently employed workers who responded to the Pew Research Center Survey took a pay cut, with full time workers only slightly less likely to do so than part-time workers, men more likely than women, and workers in families with income less than $30,000 more likely to take pay cuts than those in families with higher incomes. Though happy to have a job, any job, half of the part-time workers interviewed by the Pew Research Center wanted a full-time job, the majority blaming the recession for their inability to find full-time work.

A few of the fathers whom we call laid-off working-poor fathers were not actually laid off during the recession. Instead, they withdrew from the labor force because of a personal or health-related situation, which they or a family member experienced. Still, the recession prolonged the unemployment spell they experienced when they were able to return to the labor force. For example, Juan, one of the fathers we interviewed, was a 31-year-old Puerto Rican father of two children with different mothers. Over the past 10 years he has worked as a security guard. He resigned, for personal reasons, from a $25,000-a-year security-guard job at which he had worked for the past seven months in downtown New York. But since he returned, he has been unable to find work. He explained:

> I went back to my old employer to, to go work with them again but, uh, I don't know what it is they give me a little run around they said since I been out for more than six months. I'm ready to go back to work and, um, you know, I'm just waiting for them to give me the okay. In the meantime, I'm still looking for other jobs, in the meantime, even though I want to go back to my original job.

Now his biggest concern is that the recession will be so severe that he will exhaust his savings before he finds another job. National surveys describing the impacts of the recession on American workers more generally do not tell us how the recession affected labor force re-entrants.

Did Nonresident Fathers Fare Better or Worse Than Other Men During the Recession?

As we have just seen, experts are just coming to grips with the consequences of the recession for American workers and their families, including the characteristics of workers (and families) who were hurt most. We know, for example, that the recession was harder on men than women. In particular, the increase in the unemployment rate was higher for men than it was for women, and this has been true in every recession since the early 1980s.[10] After being laid off, more men left the labor force than women, and it took longer for unemployed men to find new jobs than it took unemployed women. We also know that employment and earnings of younger workers and minorities fell more sharply than employment and earnings among older and White workers.[11] Studies also show that lower income and less-educated workers suffered more severe consequences than higher income and more-educated workers.

But we do not know if nonresident fathers and their families suffered more or less than other fathers or other men. One way to answer this question is to focus on the characteristics of nonresident fathers in relation to those of other fathers or other men. Even this is difficult because collecting data on nonresident fathers is so difficult.

Society expects (and the law requires) nonresident fathers to support their children financially. Therefore, men who fail to support their children tend to deny that they are nonresident fathers. This results in three kinds of distortions in the picture of nonresident fathers that emerges from large surveys, which are usually more reliable than small selective surveys or qualitative studies. First, large surveys miss many nonresident fathers. Second, the nonresident fathers we know about from these sources tend to be better off financially; they also have better relationships with their children's mothers and, partly as a result, tend to interact with their children more frequently than the fathers we miss. In sum, nonresident fathers who remain hidden from large surveys are more economically vulnerable, have more strained relationships with the mothers of their children, and see their children less frequently.

Third, rather than miss survey respondents who deny their nonresident-father status, most surveys rely on mothers to get information about nonresident fathers, but the picture that emerges may be "tainted" by the mothers' feelings about these fathers. Mothers who are on pretty good terms with their former partners say pretty good things about them. On the other hand, if the fathers' name still leaves a bad taste in her mouth, a mother may exaggerate how bad the father really is. For all these reasons, interviews conducted by researchers who persuade nonresident fathers that they will not be criticized or penalized for their failure to support their children financially are important ways to fill out what we learn about nonresident fathers from large national surveys and census data.

Researchers at the University of Bowling Green tried to assess the most accurate source of large survey information about nonresident fathers.[12] They looked at three large national surveys, two of which asked men two questions: (1) if they were nonresident fathers, and (2) if they provided financial support for their nonresident children. In both surveys the second question immediately follows the first question. The third survey, called the National Survey of Family Growth (NSFG), asked men the same two questions, but at very different points in the survey interview. Estimates of the number of nonresident fathers from NSFG were substantially larger than estimates from the two other surveys, leading these researchers to conclude that the NSFG missed fewer nonresident fathers. According to the survey, which was undertaken between 2006 and 2010, there were almost 9 million nonresident fathers in the United States in the years bracketing the recent recession. After reproducing this estimate, we analyzed NSFG data on men to understand how nonresident fathers differed from resident fathers and other men in terms of the characteristics likely to influence how vulnerable they were to the recession.

Almost one of three men was a resident father; just over one in nine was a nonresident father. The average nonresident father was about 35 years old, about six years older than the average man, but about the same age as the average resident father. In other respects, however, nonresident fathers were more economically vulnerable than resident fathers and other men. More than five of every eight nonresident fathers were high school graduates or dropouts, while fewer than four of every nine resident fathers, and the total population of all men, completed this little schooling. Finally, more than half of nonresident fathers were Black or Latino, while less than one in three resident fathers were men of color.

Because they were more likely to be men of color and less likely to have postsecondary schooling, the recession probably took a bigger toll on nonresident fathers than it did on resident fathers. For example, more than 8 out of 10 nonresident fathers were employed, compared with 9 of 10 resident fathers. More than half of nonresident fathers earned less than $40,000 annually, while only a third of resident fathers had such low earnings.

Focusing our attention on this lower-earnings group underscores how vulnerable they were to the recession and the trends in play over the prior four decades resulting in declining earnings and labor force participation, especially among less-educated men and men of color. While fewer than 4 of every 10 nonresident fathers earning less than $40,000 were White, White men made up more than a third of nonresident fathers earning $40,000 or more. Employment rates among nonresident fathers earning less than $40,000 were high (7 of 9), but employment rates among nonresident fathers earning $40,000 or more were even higher (9 of every 10). Longer hours were partly responsible for the higher earnings of the latter group since almost all worked full-time, while only 7 of every 9 nonresident fathers earning less than $40,000 worked full-time.

Family ties compounded the difficulties faced by more economically vulnerable nonresident fathers. Five of every nine nonresident fathers earning below $40,000 were married or living with a female partner, compared with five of eight nonresident fathers earning $40,000 or more. Therefore fewer of the more vulnerable group could share expenses with a spouse or female partner. Despite having less money coming in, the more vulnerable group also had as many resident children and more nonresident children to care for. That's right, more than two out of five nonresident fathers who supported their kids through the courts were the family men working in low- and moderate-wage jobs with pictures of their wives (or partners) and children on their walls. Unless the mother of the child in the picture worked, his job paying less than $40,000 a year was barely enough to sustain the family at twice the poverty level. However, counting the child support owed for his nonresident child or children, the family's financial picture looked a lot less rosy. What's more, nonresident fathers with lower earnings (2 of every 11) were more likely to be responsible for three or more nonresident children than nonresident fathers with higher earnings (2 of every 15).

These 5 million vulnerable nonresident fathers (about nine percent of adult males between 15 and 44 years old in the United States) are a far larger group than the inner-city fathers who have been the focus of much research over the past few decades. The overwhelming majority worked full-time before, during, and after the recession, though many had higher paying jobs before the recession. Further, though men of color and less-educated men were overrepresented in this group, 4 of 11 vulnerable nonresident fathers, by our designation, were White, and more than 6 of 11 had some post-secondary education. Given their characteristics, particularly those that are known to affect employment and earnings (e.g., race and education) we suspect that nonresident fathers experienced more hardship than most men and most fathers, but perhaps not drastically so.

Another way to gauge the relative impact of the recession on nonresident fathers is to estimate whether their employment is lower than the employment of resident fathers, when two otherwise identical fathers live in the same city (and therefore are subject to the same labor market conditions). We made such estimates using data on resident and nonresident fathers from a relatively new Fragile Families and Child Well-Being Survey. Our estimates accounted for many of the characteristics that make it more likely that men will become nonresident fathers. These same characteristics account for how much employment rates fall when unemployment is high and include the fathers' age, race, education, and prior incarceration, as well as other characteristics. After taking into account a wide array of other factors, our estimates show that nonresident fathers who live in cities with high unemployment rates are four percent less likely to be employed than resident fathers living in the same city.

Making Ends Meet

Many of the fathers we interviewed described a gradual downward spiral of their employment status and earnings after first being laid off. Such cascading was also evident among many workers who responded to national surveys about the Great Recession. Princeton University economist Henry Farber notes that among the 50 percent of job losers who found new jobs after being laid off during the 2007–2009 recession, there was a substantial increase, as compared with previous recessions, in the proportion of full-time job losers who were working part-time in their new job at least six months after the 2007–2009 recession. The Pew Research Center Survey shows that just over one in four workers who lost and found a job during the first 30 months of the recent recession replaced a full-time job with a part-time job. Of course, moving from a full-time job to a part-time job usually meant lower pay and losing benefits, such as pensions and health insurance. The Heldrich Center Survey shows that over half of the workers who were able to find new jobs after being laid off took a pay cut; others found jobs paying the same, but offering fewer hours than the jobs they had prior to the Great Recession.[13]

Beside reduced earnings, job satisfaction was generally lower when workers lost and found a job during the recession. While almost three of five workers interviewed by the Heldrich Center who lost and found jobs since the recession thought their new job was just a steppingstone to something better, almost 8 of

10 similar workers interviewed by the Pew Research Center were satisfied their new jobs (compared with almost 9 of 10 workers who did not lose their job) and just short of 6 in 15 of these workers said their sense of identity was affirmed by their new jobs (compared with 8 of 15 who remained working through the recession).

Because many had been unemployed for so long, more than three-quarters of job seekers surveyed by the Heldrich Center said they would be willing to change careers in order to find a job.[14] Among re-employed workers interviewed by the Pew Research Center, three out of five had already changed careers or had thought out about doing so, and more than one in three enrolled in a job training programs or went back to school.

Although unemployed workers cut back on expenses, bills still mounted. According to the Pew Research Center Survey at the beginning of the recession (2008), only one out of 15 American workers said they could not meet their basic expenses. By May 2010, one of nine Americans admitted having such trouble. So they depleted their savings and unemployment insurance, if any, and doubled up or borrowed from friends and family. Some even applied for food stamps to help them get by. Almost a quarter of Americans earning under $30,000 had little money to meet daily expenses. Many unemployed workers doubled up in more affordable housing arrangements with friends and relatives, and borrowed money from friends and family.[15]

The working-poor fathers we interviewed who found no comparable work after losing their regular jobs during the recession experienced the same hardships and tried to recover in the same ways. For example, Franco, the working-poor father we profiled before the beginning of this chapter, would like to follow in the footsteps of his children and go to college to get a business degree. Then, he would start a business of his own, a limousine service. But his more immediate concern is to find a regular job after being unemployed for four months. His family is on a very tight budget. To make ends meet, he and his wife are doubling up with her daughter and son-in-law, and Franco is using his unemployment benefits to contribute to household expenses.

However, Franco's experience looking for work differs from the typical experiences reported by the Pew and Heldrich Center studies in several important ways. When Franco had been unemployed in the past, his child support debts would mount and become one of his chief concerns. So he worked off the books to pay his child support debt. However, his employer took advantage of him, and he does not want that experience again. He learned from that experience to reduce his child support debt whenever he was unemployed. He was also afraid that he might be injured or laid off, but off the books work did not provide workman's compensation or unemployment insurance. Now that his children were no longer minors, he no longer had to pay child support, so he avoided off the books work. As we shall see, these are typical experiences for working-poor fathers during the Great Recession.

Chronically Unemployed Workers: Experiencing the Consequences of Incarceration

While the bulk of the fathers we interviewed were laid-off working-poor fathers like Franco, the next largest group was chronically unemployed fathers. According to University of Chicago professor Waldo Johnson, who has spent most of his career studying these fathers, chronically unemployed fathers face multiple employment barriers, including diminishing blue collar jobs, lack of education and skills training, a shift to service economy, and criminal records.

Most of the chronically unemployed fathers we interviewed had felony convictions. As a result, they had longer and more frequent periods without work at regular jobs than laid-off and current working-poor fathers.

These fathers suffer from what Edin and Nelson call chronic joblessness.[16] The decline of prospects for finding regular work negatively impacts a father's ability to provide for himself, his family, and his child or children, and forces the parents to remain unmarried; as a result, the family is destined to collapse (p. 376). Harvard University professor William Julius Wilson sums it up nicely, "The disappearance of work has adversely affected not only individuals, families, and neighborhoods, but the social life of the city at large. A neighborhood in which people are poor but employed is different from a neighborhood in which people are poor and jobless. Many of today's problems in the inner-city ghetto neighborhoods—crime, family dissolution, welfare, low levels of social organization, and so on—are fundamentally a consequence of the disappearance of work."[17]

Nonetheless, Edin and Nelson found that chronically unemployed fathers preferred regular jobs over irregular work. Similarly, most of the chronically unemployed fathers we interviewed preferred regular jobs because of the Social Security, worker's compensation, health benefits, and life insurance that many such jobs provided. Additionally, the chronically unemployed fathers we interviewed thought that regular jobs made them more desirable to both their child(ren) and their children's mother(s), and that such jobs would give them more access to their child(ren). This echoed Edin and Nelson's findings. The chronically unemployed fathers in their study felt that regular jobs would give them a level of respectability among their families and their communities, and could potentially afford them the opportunity to reconnect with their children and their mothers, or allow them to enter into new relationships with other women (p. 386–387).

Felony Convictions Damage Future Employment Prospects

According to Harvard University sociologist Bruce Western, the "war on drugs" has given the United States a dubious distinction. We now imprison more people than any nation on earth.[18] His report to the Pew Charitable Trusts (with his colleague Becky Pettit) shows that one out of every 100 adults is in prison or jail.[19] Since men are much more likely to commit drug-related crimes than women, men are also more likely than women to be swept up in the net of mass incarceration. This means that our prisons are bursting with nonresident fathers. According to a report from the Bureau of Justice Statistics, just over half of the men in state prisons are fathers, and five of every eight men in federal prisons are fathers. Besides the growth of incarceration, a wide array of "get tough on crime" laws passed in the 1990s have reduced badly needed assistance to prisoners once released. Michelle Alexander, a legal expert, argues that policymakers used the War on Drugs to reproduce a Jim Crow–like experience that is imposed on Black men. In addition to incarcerating them in record numbers, mass incarceration policies in many states made ex-offenders ineligible for cash, food, housing, and educational assistance.[20]

Inmates and vulnerable nonresident fathers share many of the same characteristics that make it difficult for them to find regular jobs. In particular, they are likely to be men of color and to have little schooling. With his colleagues Stephen Raphael and Michael Stoll, from the University of California (a state which has one of the largest prison populations in the country), Georgetown University professor Harry Holzer shows that most inmates are Black and Latino men, and 7 of 10 have less than a high school diploma.[21] Without social supports and facing limited employment and earning prospects, many ex-offenders violate parole or commit new crimes, which lands them back behind bars. According to the Bureau of Justice statistics, 3 of 10 ex-offenders are arrested within six months of release. Six months later, this figure rises to seven of nine. Since unemployed workers took almost 33 weeks to find another job, this means that the average prisoner would be rearrested before he found a regular job. In three years, more than two of every three ex-offenders faced arrest.

Since one spell of incarceration often turns into another, once incarcerated, inmates lose contact with their children, but they also lose contact with friends and relatives who can help them find regular jobs. This further reduces their employment and earnings prospects after they are ultimately released. As a result, researchers typically find that incarceration reduces the employment and earnings of men who have been incarcerated. For example, Holzer and his colleagues reviewed the available evidence on the cost of incarceration, focusing on studies that took into account other factors, such as race, ethnicity, and education, that affected employment and earnings. They found that men who had been incarcerated earned 10 to 30 percent less than other men and were 20 to 30 percent less likely to be employed than other men.[22] Western and Pettit's report to the Pew Charitable Trusts found that a spell of incarceration costs the average ex-offender nine weeks of employment each year, 40 percent of lifetime earnings, and 11 percent of their annual wages.[23]

Most chronically unemployed fathers we interviewed faced one or more work-related obstacles as a result of having been incarcerated. Harry Holzer and his colleagues found that employers rarely used background checks, especially if they were small- to medium-sized firms. Nonetheless, employers routinely asked job applicants about criminal records, and they were very reluctant to hire ex-offenders or applicants with large gaps in their employment histories. As a result, the chronically unemployed fathers we interviewed went for long periods without a regular job and, when they did find regular work, it was part-time or low-wage work. Because of their low and unstable earnings, these fathers faced financial problems, including difficulty meeting their child support payments.

Clearly, their economic circumstances were bleak. The frustrations that these fathers felt because they were unable to find regular work had a crippling effect on them and their families. They were unable to be self-sufficient adults and were unable to support the children with whom they lived, or to meet their child support obligations to other children who lived with their ex-wives or former partners. Without good regular jobs, these men were pushed into jobs that were legal in and of themselves, but off the books. One of the chronically unemployed fathers we interviewed and profiled in Chapter 5 sums up the experience this way, "If McDonalds ain't calling, you know things changed."

Work and the Chronically Unemployed

Work in the underground economy was an important part of the complex arrangements that laid-off working-poor fathers used to make ends meet during the recession. It was the main strategy for the chronically unemployed before and during the recession. This should not be surprising because several large- and small-scale studies underscore the importance of the underground economy for vulnerable men or fathers. In his studies of low-income neighborhoods in Philadelphia, Yale University professor Elijah Anderson writes at length about the importance of the underground economy for an older generation of men, whom he calls "old heads," who used to be employed in manufacturing in the 1970s and 1980s.[24] The disappearance of these jobs from large urban areas by the 1990s left these men with limited prospects to earn family-sustaining wages. So, many worked in lower paying jobs, particularly municipal services such as transportation and sanitation, but supplemented their regular earnings with irregular, and sometimes illegal, earnings. The jobs available to younger cohorts of men were mainly in low-paying service industries and occupations, so irregular and often illegal earnings, especially drug trafficking, became a primary strategy for making a living.

More recently, Columbia University sociologist Sudir Alladi Venkatesh, who has written much about irregular work in the inner city, was careful to distinguish between illegal and underground work, describing the latter as untaxed but legal activities.[25] This is part of a growing list of studies about less-skilled men and the informal economy. Other researchers, like Venkatesh, go into inner-city communities to observe or interview small groups of mostly Black and Latino fathers, without a college degree, who regularly work in the underground or illegal economy, because of the difficulty these men have securing regular work at family-sustaining wages.[26]

People who work off the books are, at minimum, committing a crime by evading taxes, and many such people are unwilling to admit such illegal activity. Therefore, very few large, more representative, surveys collect any information, certainly not reliable information, about irregular work. As a result, we know little about irregular work outside inner-city areas, where most qualitative researchers conduct their interviews. This means that we know little about irregular work among White men, who rarely live in the nation's largest cities, where Blacks and Latinos are concentrated, or about men of any race or ethnic group who also work at regular and irregular jobs. One important exception is the work of Lauren Rich, formerly with the University of Pennsylvania. Using data from the first wave of the Fragile Families and Child Well-Being Survey, conducted in 1998, Rich finds that such work was quite common.

Rich found that, in the week prior to the birth of their children, almost 11 of 13 unmarried fathers worked in the regular economy, compared with 12 of 13 married fathers. However, two of every seven unmarried fathers combined work in the regular economy with work in the irregular economy. This tendency to combine regular and irregular work was not much lower among married fathers, nor were there differences in the extent to which fathers combined regular and irregular work, between unmarried fathers who lived with the mothers of their children (resident) and those who did not (nonresident). The average unmarried father who combined regular and irregular work earned just over $19,416,[27] and earnings were about the same for resident and nonresident unmarried fathers. Even accounting for inflation, this means that when their children were born, the average unmarried father (resident or nonresident) in the Fragile Families and Child Well-Being Survey was economically vulnerable, by the definition we adopt here.

Married fathers, who combined regular and irregular work, earned more than twice this amount ($41,114). Fathers who combined regular and irregular work earned slightly more than fathers who earned all their income from regular jobs—about five of seven fathers. Fewer than 2 of 10 fathers worked at irregular jobs, exclusively.

Among the fathers we interviewed, those with felony convictions seemed confined to the underground economy for a very long time, while those without such convictions appeared to work at irregular jobs primarily to make ends meet after losing their regular jobs. Unfortunately, Rich's study tells us nothing about the relationship between prior incarceration and underground work because the first wave of the Fragile Families and Child Well-Being Study does not include information about incarceration. The Rich study does suggest that fathers who combined regular and irregular work probably did so because it was hard for them to hold down a full-time, full-year, regular job. Compared to fathers with only regular earnings, those with both regular and irregular earnings were more likely to be unmarried high school dropouts, to have four or more children, and to be drug users and heavy, rather than light, drinkers. Men with these characteristics are also likely to wind up in prison or jail. Interestingly, after taking account of these characteristics, White fathers were no less likely than Blacks or Latino fathers to combine regular and irregular work.

We should also keep in mind that our interviews occurred in 2009, at the height of our nation's most severe postwar recession, while Rich's study used data from 1998, the end of the longest postwar economic expansion. As a result, the chronically unemployed fathers we interviewed, almost all of whom were ex-offenders, probably had much more difficulty finding a regular job than working-poor fathers, almost of whom had been employed at such jobs prior to the 2007–2009 recession.

The impression that underground work is the exclusive domain of less-educated, minority fathers arises from the tendency of researchers who undertake small-sample studies to focus on minority communities in their fieldwork. This is understandable, given the cost of conducting such research and the need for

researchers to speak with as many disadvantaged fathers as they can in whatever communities they choose to conduct their fieldwork. Nonetheless, this focus
tends to "ghettoize" the issue of vulnerable nonresident fathers, leaving policymakers and the public with the impression that less-educated White fathers rarely
encounter the challenges encountered by similarly ill-prepared men of color. As
Ronald, whom we profile in the Appendix, shows, the chronically unemployed
White fathers experienced plenty of challenges of their own.

Because he dropped out of school, had a substance abuse problem, and had a
felony conviction for drug trafficking, Ronald was unable to find a regular job in
the two years since he had been released from prison. Though at one point his
off-the-books job paid well, market conditions had changed, so he now relies
upon doing small jobs for friends to earn money. His family income was so low
that at one point they were temporarily homeless. Though he was subsequently
married, his children were born out of wedlock, so the birthing costs for his
two children, which were paid for by Medicaid, were now part of his child support order.

Adjusting Employment Arrangements to Meet the Child Support Expense

Besides supporting their children informally, which was the third highest priority among the usual expenditures of the fathers we interviewed, formal child
support payments were one of the expenses that fathers had to meet even while
looking for regular jobs or working in irregular jobs. Formal child support payments were their second highest priority for usual expenditures, but making
these payments called for substantial changes in their employment arrangements. Some fathers were able to make these arrangements, others were not.
Working-poor fathers usually had more flexibility than chronically unemployed
fathers in adjusting their employment arrangements to meet the demands of
child support. For example, many working-poor fathers used unemployment
insurance like an asset, saving it for a rainy day. After being laid off, they tried
to avoid collecting unemployment insurance until it became clear that their savings, belt-tightening, and earnings from irregular jobs were not enough to make
ends meet. However, the pressure of sanctions by the courts (including possible
jail time for contempt) forced several fathers we interviewed to meet their child
support obligations immediately by applying for unemployment insurance, taking on additional irregular work, or forgoing unemployment insurance in favor
of taking a regular job at lower pay than the jobs they lost. David, a 24-year-old,

White, working-poor father, whom we profile in the Appendix, employed several of these strategies. Dwight, a chronically unemployed father, whom we profile in Chapter 4, employed fewer strategies, because he had few options other than off-the-books work. In fact, the money he earned working off the books helps him to avoid being sent back to prison if he defaults on his child support order.

In other small-scale studies, fathers also claimed that meeting their child support obligations required substantial work-related changes. For example, policy analysts Maureen Waller and Robert Plotnick reviewed several qualitative studies about the child support experiences of low-income fathers.[28] They found a lot of support for the idea that some fathers quit their regular, low-paying jobs after learning how much of their earnings would be deducted to pay child support, while others worked at irregular jobs to make up for regular earnings lost to child support payments. However, these studies focused primarily on adjustments made by chronically unemployed fathers and fathers of children on welfare.

The findings based on large and more representative surveys provide contradictory support for the idea that formal child support payments require big employment-related adjustments for vulnerable nonresident fathers. For example, University of Wisconsin professors Cancian, Heinrich, and Chung found that debts associated with birthing costs, like the debts accumulated by David and Ronald above, were related to lower earnings from regular jobs and lower child support payments.[29] Harvard University researchers Richard Freeman and Jane Waldfogel found no evidence that men living in states with more aggressive child support enforcement policies were less likely to seek regular jobs.[30] However, some weak evidence supporting this relationship was found by Harry Holzer and his Urban Institute colleague Elaine Sorensen, from whom we have learned much about the ability of nonresident fathers to pay child support, and Paul Offner, a former Wisconsin state senator and aide to former Senator Patrick Moynihan, author of the controversial Moynihan report in the 1960s.[31] Unfortunately, their study was limited to Black men between 25 and 34 years old.

Two studies using the Fragile Families and Child Well-Being Survey have addressed the effects of child support orders (and debt) on job-seeking in the underground economy. Again, the work of Lauren Rich has been helpful. Along with her colleagues Irwin Garfinkel (Columbia University) and Quin Gao (Fordham University), Rich found that fathers in cities with stricter child support enforcement policies worked *fewer* hours at irregular jobs.[32] However, along with a colleague, Daniel Miller, and his colleague, we examined more recent data from the Fragile Families and Child Well-Being Survey.[33] We found no relationship between arrears and irregular work by nonresident fathers. However, we found that fathers with arrears that were as high (or higher than) their earnings worked fewer hours per week at regular jobs, while fathers with arrears that were much lower than their earnings worked more hours per week at regular jobs.

Regular Work Preferred

Some laid-off working-poor fathers made ends meet by working off the books; almost all chronically unemployed fathers did so. Nevertheless, both groups preferred regular to off-the-books work, though they evaluated these employment options differently. Working-poor fathers had held regular jobs more recently and more frequently than chronically unemployed fathers, and those who were laid off expected to find a regular job in the near future. They point to a long list of reasons that they preferred regular to irregular jobs. Like Franco, they feared being caught and penalized by the IRS for failing to report irregular earnings. They also appreciated the way regular jobs provided the documentation they needed for filing taxes, filling out housing or future employment applications, and setting or modifying their child support orders. Further, like Franco and David, working-poor fathers also appreciated the perks associated with regular jobs, such as paid vacations, health insurance, workmen's compensation, and unemployment insurance. Most of all, they appreciated the regularity of hours and protections against being shortchanged by their employers for the hours they actually worked on regular jobs or for which they were promised work by employers in the regular economy. In his study of fathers served by Detroit-area employment programs, University of Michigan sociologist Alford Young points out that for these men, regular work is preferred because it offers a sense of economic stability and fringe benefits.[34]

This stability of employment arrangements was also the feature of regular jobs that chronically unemployed fathers relished most. The earnings of chronically unemployed fathers, like Ronald and Dewight, were whipsawed by changes in commodity prices, weather conditions, and a host of other factors—like an enclosed space in which to work—over which they had absolutely no control. In their study of nonresident fathers served by responsible fatherhood programs in the 1990s, Young and his Urban Institute colleague Pamela Holcomb observe that low-income fathers are not satisfied with the menial jobs available to them, which pay so little that they cannot afford to support their nonresident children financially, without impoverishing themselves or their families (p. 1).[35] Further, according to Jennifer Hamer, employers often underpay these men for their work, particularly if they have a criminal record (p. 177).[36] Young says it best, "these jobs are not particularly fulfilling economically, emotionally or materially (p. 152).[37]

However, because their earnings were also lower and more volatile than the earnings of working-poor fathers, chronically unemployed fathers also relished, rather than feared, their ability to reduce their tax and child support liabilities by hiding their irregular earnings from the IRS and child support enforcement. Several qualitative studies support the ambivalence with which chronically unemployed fathers view irregular jobs (i.e., they dislike the limited and unpredictable hours that characterize irregular jobs, but relish being able to keep more of their irregular earnings by evading taxes and child support payments.[38] However, to our knowledge, only Elijah Anderson's study also observes differential evaluations of the advantages and disadvantages of regular and irregular work by fathers with more or less secure attachments to regular jobs.[39]

Professor Anderson's contrast between "decent" and "street" daddies bears some resemblance to our contrast between working-poor and chronically unemployed fathers. Cohort differences among non-college-educated Black men in inner-city Philadelphia are the primary reason for the contrast in Anderson's study. His "decent daddies" are mostly older men who have lost touch with good paying jobs because of the decline in manufacturing employment in large central cities, especially in the North and Northeast, since the 1970s. For the same reason, relatively few less-educated younger Black men in these neighborhoods had ever worked high-paying manufacturing jobs. Given the low-paying service jobs available to them, these younger men fueled the growth of "street" daddies mainly through irregular and often illegal work.

Whether they were chronically unemployed or working poor, the difficulties these fathers faced finding regular jobs at all, or regular jobs that paid as much as they earned before the recession, meant that they were unable to meet their child support obligations. However, the welfare reform law passed in 1996, which was intended to "end welfare as we know it," not only imposed strict work requirements on mothers, but also provided aggressive new tools to enforce payment of child support. How did economically vulnerable fathers fare in this new environment?

Kelly's Story

Kelly is a 29-year-old white father. He has a daughter who is now nine years old and lives with her mother. She currently has a formal child support order, but that was not always the case. Earlier, both parents worked together to make sure their daughter had what she needed, but that changed after her second birthday. Kelly feels that boyfriends influenced his daughter's mother, changing the relationship from one where the parents worked together, to one where they barely got along. His visitation has also been sharply cut, something he finds deeply troubling, and the courts haven't seemed to help. To try to cover his expenses, including his child support obligation, Kelly has been forced to work off the books for the past year, a decision that comes with very mixed feelings.

When Kelly was younger, he changed jobs frequently. It was never a problem because he was able to find a new job very quickly, and he was still trying to determine what he wanted to do. What he really wanted to do was go to college and move to a new city. However, when he found out he was going to be a father, he put his college dreams on hold and began to work. "Well, I became a father kind of unexpectedly and had to start working. And at that point, you know, I had dreams of going to college, moving away, things like that, and then kind of life got serious and I started working, and just, yeah, couldn't really decide what I saw myself doing for the rest of my life." His frequent job changes, job separations, and now, off-the-books work do not give him a clean work history and make it more difficult to find a job, especially now that he really needs one.

Kelly had paid child support for close to seven years at a level that he felt was unreasonable, but he nevertheless paid it successfully. Things changed drastically when he decided to return to college. In order to fully commit himself to his studies, Kelly quit his job; however, without a job he began to fall behind on his child support payments. Because he had left his employment voluntarily, regardless of the circumstances, he was unable to modify his order. In an attempt to try to rectify the situation, Kelly took a part-time job, working close to 30 hours a week as a delivery driver, in addition to taking a full course load at college. It was a grueling schedule and Kelly was left with little to show for his efforts, since child support enforcement garnished 65 percent of his wages. He was forced to leave college after three semesters.

> Um, the reason why at first that I had fallen behind was I gave my two weeks' notice to my—to my job and started going to college full-time, um, and that was when I was told that it doesn't matter since I voluntarily left my job I'm capable of making that money and so the whole time when I was in college, I worked part-time just to try and keep up with, you know, the child support, and that was hard taking 18 credits of course work, and then working 25, 30 hours a week, you know, to come home with $40.00, because all the rest went to child support. That was fun times.

Regardless of his initiative, Kelly's arrears continued to grow. Child support enforcement suspended his driver's license, twice, which was essential for his job, though he was still making weekly payments. Despite numerous phone calls to try to resolve the situation, he was unsuccessful. A lawyer might have been able to help, but Kelly didn't have the money. He did, however, have a note from his employer, stating that he needed his license for his job and that he had lost his position because of the loss of his license. Despite everything, the decision was not appealed, and Kelly found himself at the mercy of child support enforcement and "whatever they see fit. And I guess they saw fit to take my license, which was kind of a prerequisite to my job."

Kelly was still determined to modify his order and tried again for a second time. Because his license was still suspended, he had to rely on a friend for a ride to court. However, his friend forgot his commitment and Kelly missed his court date. He lost the decision by default since he failed to appear. It's hard for Kelly not to feel bitter about his situation. He knows other fathers—fathers who have reasonable child support orders. Because Kelly had once been capable of earning a comfortable salary, he felt that he was being penalized, regardless of the fact that he has been unable to find employment for the past six months. Every week without a job is just one more week of additional debt.

More recently, Kelly was charged with willful nonpayment of child support. The judge demanded that Kelly make a lump sum payment of $1,000 toward his child support debt by his next court date in three weeks. Kelly fell far short, raising only $90, and was incarcerated. "And the judge came up with this arbitrary $1,000.00 that he thought that I should bring in to prove that I'm trying to pay my child support. Well, there's no way I was going to be able to bring $1,000 in a three-week period or whatever it was by the next court date. And so I brought in like whatever I could scrape up. It was like $90 or something along with paycheck stubs and things like that that showed that I had worked, and I had been paying and trying. And he wouldn't—he didn't look at my paycheck stubs at all, didn't care, and put me in jail. So that was an experience. I've—I've never been in jail before in my life, and I wouldn't have thought that child support would be the thing to put me there."

In addition to prison and the suspension of his license, Kelly had his tax refunds seized and applied to his child support arrears. He did not mind that his state and federal tax refunds were taken; however, child support also took his tax rebate that was to be applied to his property taxes, putting his home in jeopardy. Now he risks the very real possibility of being homeless. "But child support even took my—I get a rebate from the STAR program to help me with my property taxes and school taxes, and child support even took those checks, so now I have to pay the full amount of my taxes, which basically is going to end up causing me to lose my home...it's not even a check that's addressed to me. I don't get to spend it. It just helps me pay my taxes and, uh, they took that, which is just—that's asinine." Additionally, he is in danger of having his license revoked for a third time. The last time that happened, Kelly had to establish three separate arrears accounts, each with 13 percent interest. He really doesn't know if he could afford to reinstate his license again, with every day one day closer to having his license taken from him.

While waiting for his job prospects to improve, Kelly makes ends meet by working at odd jobs and doing without. He has learned to live on very little, sustaining himself by purchasing only the most necessary items. "Um, I'm—I've found that I'm pretty good doing without. Um, I don't go out, I don't really spend money that I don't have to spend. Just, you know, the—the job here, there, is enough to, you know, buy some milk, or some stupid stuff, and that's—it. Hanging out with friends is free."

3 Child Support

PROVIDING FINANCIAL SUPPORT for their children is a major concern for most vulnerable nonresident fathers. If they provide such support, they meet their children's needs, fulfilling the most fundamental expectation that society has for them. They also improve their chances of keeping the gate to their children open and building lifelong relationships with them. If they do not provide adequately, they not only lose these things, but place themselves at risk of sanctions, including driver's license suspensions, financial penalties, and possible jail time for contempt of court.

Administering the child support enforcement program is no easy task. Whether the parents are divorced or unmarried, they usually arrive at the doorstep of child support enforcement after a disappointing relationship that ultimately failed. If divorced, child support enforcement officials usually have all the information they need to determine an appropriate child support order. If unmarried or separated without a legal decree, much of the information needed to determine the child support order may be unavailable. This makes setting a reasonable support order a difficult task. Responding to changes in the father or mother's circumstances that might warrant a change in the child support order adds further complications. Finally, if the father fails to pay, after the order is set, child support enforcement agencies are often responsible for collecting the amounts due. The 1996 welfare reform legislation gave child support agencies a full arsenal of weapons, which are designed to function like a heat-seeking missile. This arsenal has been built up over the years to get child support from fathers who simply refused to pay, because society gave them no good reason to prioritize their child support obligations over their other financial needs. Today, society has sent a clear message: when parents no longer live together, children's needs come first, and the formal child support process is the primary arena through which those needs are met. Paul Legler, a key Clinton administration official who helped design this new system, stated: "The vision for child support enforcement that guided much of the development of the legislation is that the payment of child support should be automatic and inescapable—like death or taxes" (p. 538).[1] Against this backdrop, it can be difficult to distinguish between fathers who simply will not pay, and those who cannot pay. Because the proportion of nonresident fathers who cannot pay has grown so dramatically, it is now more important than ever to make such distinctions. When we don't, things can go terribly wrong for vulnerable fathers like Kelly, whom we profiled at the end of Chapter 2.

Informal Child Support

Vulnerable nonresident fathers provide financial support for their children formally and informally. Rutgers University professor Chien Chung Huang and his colleague, Hillard Pouncy, used mothers' reports from a nationally representative survey to study mothers who were eligible to receive formal child support.[2] Divorced and legally separated fathers usually provided financial support through a formal child support order.[3] These fathers provided more financial support to their children than fathers who separated without a legal proceeding and nonresident unmarried fathers. Informally separated and unmarried fathers were also more likely to provide financial support for their children informally. Whether divorced, separated, or never married, many mothers did not want formal child support orders, either. Their independence was more important to them than the fathers' financial support; they knew the fathers of the children were unable to pay the amounts that Family Court would order; or they felt that formal child support orders would derail the positive relationships these fathers had with their children.

Although we know little about informal child support provided by separated fathers, many studies have shown that both unmarried mothers and fathers prefer informal arrangements to the formal child support system. With Lenna Nepomnyaschy, Irwin Garfinkel has shown that these informal arrangements last for the first three years of their children's lives.[4] Thereafter, informal financial support falls to very low levels, prompting mothers to seek help from child support enforcement agencies to collect child support due, or to seek cash assistance and other benefits to support their children. Under federal law, mothers receiving such benefits must sign over their rights to child support to the state in exchange for public benefits. After this transfer of rights, states use their considerable resources to collect child support from these fathers through the formal child support enforcement system. Despite this substitution of formal for informal child support, the total amount of child support the father pays continues to fall.

More than three out of four of the fathers we interviewed lumped formal child support payments with bills, debts, transportation, and household expenditures as their top three expenses. However, only one-quarter of these fathers ranked informal child support among their top three expenses. Nevertheless, those who supported their children informally had much to say about their reasons for doing so. By their account, these fathers placed their own needs or formal child support payments on the back burner in order to provide informal child support for their children. For example, Charles, whom we profile in the Appendix, was unable to buy the new clothes and other items he needed, because he placed the needs of his child first. His top three expenses were diapers, clothes for the baby, and carfare, but he couldn't recall the last time he bought clothes or anything else for himself. "It's a struggle. . . . I can't afford it. I've got a child. Every time I want to buy clothes, something comes up. 'Oh, your daughter needs this, your daughter needs that.' I don't get mad. I've got to do what I've got to do. . . . You lay down, you had the baby, you've got to take care of your responsibility."

When fathers had young children, like Charles, sacrificing their own needs in favor of their children's needs was relatively easy. However, fathers with older children sometimes felt that they were being asked to sacrifice their own needs in favor of their children's wants, which sometimes seemed frivolous. For example, Michael, whom we profile in the Appendix, has a 14-year-old daughter who needed money to buy clothes, sneakers, a hairdo, and a manicure. He was uncertain how to respond to the request for this last expenditure. "The nails done that's money I call that money waste. Blowing it, to get your nails, but I'll do it just [because], you want it done. I hate to be, no, you don't need your nails done, okay, here you want money to get nails, here whatever."

He gave her the money because doing so facilitated the kinds of experiences he never had with his father growing up. The same logic drove the way he thought about expenditures he made on his son's behalf. He tried to do the things with his children that he wished his father would have done with him, especially things that involved spending time together. For example, Michael bought a bike and a sled, so that he and his son could play together.

> We used to race each other down this hill, you know, and I would always beat him and then you know, um, one day I let him win, I let him win one time. Just once I let him win, you know, just to make him feel he can do it, he just got to work hard, you know. Cause, um, normally I wouldn't let him win, you know, but I said well let me, he's getting a little bit too frustrated that he can't beat me or so. . . . I would take him out and I bought him a frisbee, big giant frisbee sleds and him and I would get on it and shoot down the hill and stuff like that and I would take him out and play with him in the snow, that sort of thing. I always try to just give my kids a father, cause I never had one, you know, so like I know how I felt with not having one, you know, what I mean?

As this quote illustrates, fathers also used informal support so that the time they spent with their children would help them sustain their relationships and make the time spent more enjoyable and memorable. For example, Jeffrey, whom we profile in the Appendix, often bought his son the toys and equipment needed to make their time together fun. When his child was dropped off, his mother always made sure he had clean clothes for the visit. But Jeffrey's son, who like Jeffrey is very athletic, wanted to play basketball with his dad. So Jeffrey bought him basketball outfits and some sneakers so that they could play together. He also bought him some toys, especially wrestling figures, like the ones Jeffrey played with as a child. Jeffrey also monitored the food they ate because eating well would, he believed, help his son grow taller.

> But he likes wrestling, and so I had a bunch of wrestling figures coming up, so my father bought them for me, so I'm giving [them to] my son and let him do that. So, you know, I try—and food, you know, fast food, you know, he loves that. Um, I'm trying to wean him off that, maybe nuggets. I spend about $20 on chocolate milk a day, you know, so when he comes over, everything is chocolate milk with food, chocolate milk just to drink, so you know. Hopefully it works, you know, like they say it makes your bones strong, helps you grow, because I'm 5'11". His mother's not tall, so you know, we'll see.

Thus through informal financial support, fathers were meeting their children's needs or making the time they spent with their children more enjoyable, thereby building their relationships with their children. For some, providing informal support meant not meeting their formal child support obligations in full. Others paid informal support over and above formal support, because the formal child support they paid was not enough to meet all of their children's needs. However, most paid their child support through the formal system, and their experiences doing so varied widely.

Formal Child Support

In 1979, University of Michigan professor D. L. Chambers published the financial corollary of the package deal, entitled *Making Fathers Pay*.[5] This highly influential book showed that following divorce or separation, many fathers simply ignored legal child support orders, but through aggressive enforcement practices employed by some counties in Michigan, the courts were able to collect the child support due. One county in particular, Genesee County, relied heavily upon incarceration as the ultimate sanction for these "deadbeat dads." In addition, a few other counties found success in collecting child support by garnishing child support payments from fathers' wages, even before they defaulted on their support payments. This innovation paved the way for "automatic wage withholding," which is now the generally accepted practice for collecting child support payments. But the book also established the view that getting tough on delinquent obligors was the best way to ensure that their children received the support they needed.

Since that time, several studies have countered the image of the "deadbeat dad" with the image of the "dead-broke dad," by showing that many low-income nonresident fathers were unable rather than unwilling to pay child support. The work of Elaine Sorensen, formerly with the Urban Institute, a Washington-based think tank, has been extremely important in this regard. With one of the authors of this book, she created mirror images of mothers and fathers in the child support enforcement system. We showed that the proportion of mothers who received the child support they were owed was about the same as the proportion of fathers who owed and paid the child support due. We also showed that the proportion of mothers who were not poor, despite not receiving the child support they were owed, was about the same as the proportion of fathers who owed child support and did not pay, despite being non-poor. Finally, and most important, we showed that the proportion of mothers who were poor after they did not receive the child support they were owed was about the same as the proportion of fathers who were poor and did not pay. In other words, though we were unable to match mothers and fathers of the same children, it looked to us as if the child support enforcement system included both deadbeat and dead-broke dads. What's more, for each deadbeat dad, we could find a single-mother family that was not thrust into poverty as a result. But for each dead-broke dad, we could also find a single-mother family that was. Not surprisingly, dead-broke dads (and the mothers of their children) were younger and less educated than the deadbeat dads (and the mothers of their children) and the former were more likely to be never married, Black, or Latino.

In another study, with her colleague Chava Zibman, Sorensen showed that nearly 6 of 10 nonresident fathers who did not pay child support had limited ability to do so, and that tougher child support enforcement was unlikely to change this outcome.[6] Furthermore, among those who were paying, low-income fathers paid a higher fraction of their income than did those with higher incomes. University of Wisconsin professors Maria Cancian and Dan Meyer, who have done much work on the unmet needs of mothers in the child support enforcement system, have shown that the number of poor female-headed families who did not get the child support they needed was far greater than the number of dead-broke dads.[7] This was probably because, as we showed earlier, many dead-broke dads had children in more than one household. Nevertheless, Cancian and Meyer agreed that besides making child support enforcement tougher on the deadbeats, something had to be done to enable the dead-broke dads in the system to support their children.

In other studies, using data from his home state of Wisconsin, Meyer and his colleagues showed that the regressive feature of child support guidelines lead lower income fathers to default on their child support orders more frequently than higher income fathers.[8] With colleagues from Columbia University, one of the authors of this book reached the same conclusion for the nation as a whole.[9] Both Formoso and Peters produced similar findings in their studies of child support arrears in the state of Washington, noting that as income decreased, the extremely regressive child support guidelines used in the State of Washington increased the likelihood of defaulting and accumulating arrears.[10]

These extremes are misleading. Besides the dead-broke dads who have very low incomes and are unable to meet their child support obligations, and the deadbeat dads who are capable of paying but refuse to do so, there is a continuum of vulnerable fathers who experience varying degrees of difficulty paying child support. For example, with Urban Institute colleague Laura Wheaton, Sorensen showed that at most one-quarter of nonresident fathers earning less than $34,000 (in 2009 dollars) paid the full amount of child support due.[11] As earnings fell, this proportion fell as well. So at most, 3 of 19 nonresident fathers earning about $14,500 paid the full amount of child support due. At earnings near the poverty guideline for a single-person household ($10,380), no more than five percent of nonresident fathers paid the full amount of child support due.[12] However, not all nonresident fathers have child support orders, so these estimates may have overestimated the number of fathers who comply with their child support orders.

The government's own studies agree with these findings. A 2002 report by the Office of Inspector General divided nonresident fathers with child support orders into three income tiers—high, middle, and low.[13] The report found that the low-income tier contained the highest percentage of non-payers. For example, fathers with no reported income complied with only 17 percent of the amount of child support they owed, while those with earnings over twice the poverty line complied with 62 percent of the amount owed. When Sorensen and her colleagues looked at arrears in nine states with high levels of arrears, they found that 7 of 10 fathers with child support arrears had either no reported income or earned no more than $10,000 a year.[14] Like many of the fathers we interviewed, many of these fathers with arrears and no reported earnings were working at irregular jobs. But this, too, presents a distorted picture of a pattern of child support debt. The Office of Child Support Enforcement studied earning and child support debt in the country as a whole. They found that 39 percent of arrears owed to the government was from fathers with no reported earnings, 26 percent was from fathers with up to $10,000 in earnings, and 30 percent from fathers who earned between $20,000 and $40,000.[15]

Though child support orders varied among the fathers we interviewed, the variation in arrears was even greater.[16] The amount of monthly child support payments ranged from $0, for fathers with temporarily suspended orders, to nearly $1,500. These extremes were outliers, however. Only two fathers had suspended orders and only two had orders over $1,000. The bulk of the orders were fairly evenly distributed among low ($25–$75), medium ($100–$300), and high ($400–$700) orders. The amount of arrears owed ranged from $0 to an estimated $40,000–$50,000. The largest group had low arrears, defined as between $25 to $3,000, and the next largest group had no arrears. Half of the remaining fathers had medium arrears, defined as between $3,001 to $10,000, and the remaining group had either high or very high arrears. This is remarkable, given that almost none of these fathers earned more than $40,000 before the Great Recession.

Two main factors were associated with the amount of arrears owed: the amount of monthly child support owed, and the length of the case. The fathers we interviewed with low monthly orders had lower arrears, while those with higher monthly orders had higher arrears.[17] Every father with a high order had arrears, but the amount of arrears was evenly divided between low to medium, and high to very high arrears. Both of the fathers with very high monthly orders, those paying between $1,000 and $1,500 a month, had high arrears, one of them very high. This pattern is just what we would expect based upon the government's studies and the work of Sorensen and her colleagues.

Stereotypes such as "deadbeat dad" suggest that fathers resent and avoid child support on principle simply because they do not want to pay. The fathers we interviewed had far more complex relationships with the child support enforcement system. When they did grow frustrated with the child support system, it was not because they did not care to support their children financially. Instead, they were frustrated because they felt that the methods used to establish, monitor, and enforce their payments were unjust. In short, fathers' relationship to the child support system depended upon their perception of the reasonableness of their orders. The amount of the order and the amount of arrears mattered far less than how reasonable the order was in comparison to the fathers' income and the individual's perceived ability to pay. Lin reached the same conclusion when she spoke with divorced fathers in Wisconsin about the relationship between paying child support and fathers' perceptions of the fairness of the child support orders.[18] When fathers believed that the amount of their child support orders did not correspond with their ability to pay, they were more likely to fall behind on their child support and accumulate arrears. The same was true for many of the fathers we interviewed.

Willie, a chronically unemployed father whom we profile at the end of Chapter 5, saw his order increase dramatically by default. He has been struggling ever since. Willie initially owed $25 a month for child support because he was unemployed when the case was initiated in 2001. Two years later, in 2003, he missed a court date and his child support order was raised to $508 a month in his absence. He tried to have the order modified, but due to various complications, including the fact that his daughters' mother missed two court dates, he was never able to do so. Although he sent whatever money he could to child support, typically about $25 a month, his arrears grew to $38,000. The idea that child support would ever expect him to be able to pay $508 a month seemed ludicrous to him as he barely earned that much, even when he was working. "I have never issued—I have never sent a payment of $508. I don't think I'll [be] sending no payments of $508....Cause I never made—McDonald's only paid you $140 a week. I never made $508 to be paying $508 a month."

Charles, a 32-year-old Black father whom we profile in the Appendix, lives at home with his mother because he is currently unemployed. Though he has a security license and has worked as a bouncer/bodyguard at nightclubs, he has never worked a legitimate on-the-books job. His child support order for his 15-month old daughter has only been in place for about six months, but he already owes $1,000 in arrears. These arrears accumulated even though the order was originally set using a lower guideline for near-poor fathers, which reduced his order to $50 a month. Because he missed a court date that he did not know he needed to attend, the order was raised in his absence to $60 a week, or about $240 a month. Charles believes strongly in the importance of supporting his daughter financially, and buys diapers and other necessities whenever he can. However, he feels the child support order is simply too much for someone who is not working. "I'm not paying $60 a week. I don't have a job. How am I going to pay you $60 a week? That's a lot. That's for somebody who has a job. I'm not able to pay . . . $60 a week for a person who's not—currently not working, it's a lot."

Chronically unemployed fathers were not the only ones who struggled with child support orders that did not reflect their income. Jeffrey, a working-poor father, has been paying child support for his six-year-old son for the past two years. After being laid off the first time, Jeffrey took a job at a lower wage and was able to get his child support order modified from $1,600 a month to $532 a month. But the second time he was laid off, he was unable to get a second modification. So his order is far out of reach. Despite the high order, he only owed $400 in arrears. His income has been highly inconsistent, while his child support order, other than the one modification, has remained consistent. Jeffrey did not mind paying child support, but he knew the laws, and knew he should only be required to pay 17 percent of his income for one child. The fact that he was paying more than 17 percent, not the fact that he has to pay, frustrated him. If the order had been kept in line with his income, he probably never would have begun to accumulate arrears. "I went to the child support website, you know, because I know, like I said, they say 17 percent. Now I said I need some kind of understanding of why I'm paying well over 17 percent for one child, which I don't mind paying child support. I just need to know why I'm paying over 17 percent."

In contrast, when fathers felt that their child support orders were matched with their income and ability to pay, they were often, as Ernest states, "okay with the support." Ernest is a 42-year-old African American father who lives in a shelter-like home. He previously worked various jobs and "job hopped." He did seasonal work with FedEx, worked in a warehouse, did light construction and landscaping, but he is currently unemployed. He has had a child support order for his 11-year-old daughter, and one for his 7-year-old son, for the past eight years. He owes $7,000 in arrears, but his order is temporarily suspended to allow him time to find a job after attending a substance abuse program and an employment training program. His order was originally set at $50 a week, but had gone up to $100 a week to account for his arrears before it was suspended. Even though he owes a substantial amount of arrears, he feels that the child support system has been willing to work with his circumstances, so he says, "I really don't have a problem."

Brandon is a 24-year-old White father who lives at home with his parents. He worked in a carnival for about three years, starting from the beginning of 2006 through the middle of 2008, when he was laid off. After that, Brandon worked off the books, making between $700 and $1000 a week, tearing down apartment buildings, though he reported that his income for 2008 was zero. But even this work slowed down after November 2008, and now he earns money by helping out neighbors with odd jobs. He has been paying child support since the birth of his six-year-old son, but during that time, has only accumulated a little over $500 in arrears. Presently, his order has been reduced to $25 a month because he is unemployed. He feels the reduction is fair given his situation, and also trusts that once he does find work again, the child support order will increase in proportion to his income.

In addition to the relationship between the amount of the order and the likelihood of arrears, we noticed another, though similar, arrears pattern among the fathers we interviewed. Fathers with low arrears generally had child support cases for shorter lengths of time, while those who had cases for longer lengths of time owed high (or very high) arrears.[19] All seven fathers we interviewed who had a child support case for less than a year owed no or low arrears, while only those who had a child support case for more than five years owed high or very high arrears.

One reason that fathers felt their child support orders were unreasonable was that their orders failed to adequately account for their financial obligations for children in multiple households. This was reflected in two ways among the fathers we interviewed. Besides their nonresident children for whom they were paying child support, almost two of five fathers had other resident children for whom they were financially responsible, but for whom they did not pay child support. Half of those with additional children had resident biological children with their current wife or girlfriend. A quarter lived with their girlfriend or wife's children. Two fathers had nonresident biological children for whom they did not pay child support, and two fathers had both additional resident and nonresident children. Second, several fathers had complex child support cases involving nonresident children with more than one mother. More specifically, the majority of fathers had a single child support case for one child. However, seven also had a single child support case, but for multiple children. Another seven fathers had two separate child support orders. Finally, one father had more than two child support cases. He had four separate cases, one for each of his four children with four separate mothers.

Michael, a chronically unemployed father, had two child support cases: one in New York for his 14-year-old daughter and one in Georgia for his 12-year-old son. Between the two cases, he owed over $500 a month in child support. When he was working in Georgia, he was earning $800 every two weeks, but after child support was withheld, his checks only amounted to $295. After child support, his monthly take-home pay of around $600 was not even enough to cover his rent, which was $700. "Child support was taking all my money.... Could you imagine? You work for two weeks and get 295. Them people don't care man, they didn't care. If, if, I would have became homeless as long as they took they child support money."

Michael recently filed a petition to modify his order, but it was denied. The judge instructed him to attend a fatherhood program, to continue sending whatever money he could to child support, and to return to court in two months. Despite his high order, Michael owes only $1,300 in arrears. Ironically, it is possible that the low arrears may have contributed to the judge's refusal to modify the order, as he could have perceived the low arrears as an indication of Michael's ability to pay. But at what cost? Michael was paying his child support, but could not afford his rent. He eventually moved to New York to live with his mother, where he has been for the past year, until he becomes more financially stable.

Child support experts have begun to worry that even they have not understood how many vulnerable nonresident fathers there are with complex cases, like Michael, and additional financial obligations. Since it was founded in 1966, the Institute for Research on Poverty (IRP) at the University of Wisconsin has been a gathering place of experts undertaking basic research and providing counsel to policymakers working to reduce poverty in the United States. In 2009, IRP organized a conference for scholars and policymakers that focused on young disadvantaged men. Editors of a volume summarizing the findings of the conference noted that the more disadvantaged men are, the more they are likely to be fathers (p.147).[20] With his former graduate student Marilyn Sinkewicz, Columbia University professor Irwin Garfinkel, a pioneer among child support researchers, expressed a related concern. By ignoring such complexity in the child support cases of many, especially vulnerable, nonresident fathers, he feared that earlier studies, including his own, vastly overestimated fathers' ability to pay child support.[21] Professors Cancian and Meyer, who organized the conference, expressed another concern, namely that child support orders for fathers with simple cases may be inappropriate for fathers (and mothers) with complex ones. In particular, child support orders generally try to make certain that children do not receive less financial support from their fathers when their fathers become nonresident. For most families, this means that child support orders should not exceed the fathers' ability to pay and should decline as the number of children increase, because simple families enjoy economies of scale in providing for their children. When states use standard child support guidelines to set child support orders for complex families, conflicts arise among these goals, which cannot be easily resolved.[22]

The Economy and Child Support Compliance

The government's own data suggest that since the Great Recession, fathers have been even more prone to default on their child support orders and accumulate arrears.[23] In 2009, the federal Office of child support enforcement saw a decrease in annual total child support collections from the previous year for the first time in its history. Included in this overall decrease was a three percent decline in the average amount of child support collected per case. The year 2009 marked the first such decline in average amount collected per case since 1994.[24] Child support officials directly attributed this decrease to the downturn in the economy and high unemployment rates.

The sources of child support payments and the recipients of child support payments in 2009 provide telling signs of the effects of unemployment crisis on child support payments. First, when fathers are working at regular jobs, their employers automatically deduct child support payments and send them directly to state or local child support enforcement agencies. When fathers are unemployed and collecting unemployment insurance, their child support payments are deducted from their unemployment insurance and sent directly to the same agencies. In 2009, the amount of child support collected from automatic wage withholding decreased for the first time, while the amount collected from unemployment insurance benefits of fathers like David, whom we profile in the Appendix, tripled.[25]

Second, there are two types of child support cases: those in the private system, and those enforced by state child support enforcement programs, which we shall call the public system. In turn, there are two kinds of cases in the public system, cases for mothers receiving public assistance and cases for mothers who have asked for help. In 2009 the number of cases in the public system for mothers receiving public assistance increased, contributing to an increase in "hard-to-collect" cases. In 2009, 63 percent of child support cases not attached to public assistance received payment, while only a third of those involving public assistance did.[26]

The trouble with these assertions is that there may have been other factors, unrelated to the recession, that were changing at the same time, and these, rather than the recession, may have played some role in the reduction in compliance and increase in arrears. For this reason, we need to look at changes in compliance over long spans of time, and take account of other factors that might have affected child support payments. This is not an easy task, because the relationship between unemployment and child support compliance involves several pathways.

When the unemployment rate rises, some fathers remain employed, but their earnings fall, so they stop paying child support or pay less than the full amount due. In this case, there is an indirect pathway between unemployment and compliance, through earnings. Many researchers have found evidence supporting this indirect pathway. Several of these studies use data on individual earnings and child support payments in Wisconsin, where this information is uniquely available.[27] Other studies use variations in average earnings (or proxies for earnings) and child support receipt in different states and years.[28]

Fathers also partially or fully default on their child support orders when they lose their jobs, but their child support payments become due before they find new jobs. This pathway between unemployment and compliance is direct. In these cases, changes in unemployment rates reduce compliance rather quickly. Some of the fathers in these first two situations may have their child support orders reduced—called a downward modification—and pay child support, though at a lower amount. In these cases, child support violations are temporary. There are two problems here. First, the pathway between unemployment and compliance becomes indirect, through changes in child support orders. Second, to properly assess the pathway requires making allowances for the delay involved in getting the child support modification. Attorneys who advocate on behalf of vulnerable nonresident fathers, like Ron Henry and Hatchet and Lieberman, claim that getting a downward modification is a costly, uncertain, and time-consuming process. Therefore, many fathers give up before completing the process, or never attempt to modify their orders.[29] This claim receives support from at least two studies by Meyer and his colleagues at the University of Wisconsin, who have made good use of their ability to match earnings and child support orders in their home state.[30] These studies show that child support orders rarely change in response to changing economic conditions.

After taking account of these indirect effects and delays, several studies have found that the remaining effects of unemployment on compliance are negligible.[31] Unfortunately, few of these studies focus on years in which the economic downturn was as severe as the recent recession.

To fill this research gap, one of the authors of this book revisited the relationship between unemployment and child support compliance, with colleagues at Columbia and Boston Universities. The first study used data on child support payments by vulnerable fathers from the Fragile Families and Child Well-Being

Survey.[32] Our study began one year after the children were born (1999), and ended in 2010, months after the Great Recession was officially over. We took account of many factors—such as the fathers' age, race, and marital status at the child's birth—besides local unemployment rates that might have affected child support compliance. However, we focused on the overall relationship between unemployment and child support compliance, without trying to distinguish between the various pathways, through earnings and child support orders. We also used mothers' reports of fathers' child support payments, but our strongest results used the unemployment rates in metropolitan areas in which the fathers reported living. We found that when unemployment rates increased, mothers were less likely to receive all or some of the child support due.

A second study used national data from the same large-scale survey the US Department of Labor uses to track employment and earnings trends. Again, we took into account many factors, besides local unemployment rates, that might have affected child support compliance and focused on the overall relationship between unemployment and child support compliance, without trying to distinguish among the various pathways. This time, however, we focused on a somewhat earlier period, 1993–2009, that included most of the 1990s economic boom, the brief recession of 2001, the jobless recovery of 2003–2006, and all of 2009, six months after the end of Great Recession.[33]

Again, we found that mothers living in metropolitan areas with higher unemployment rates were less likely to receive the full amount of child support due. These results were much smaller than the results of the first study, probably because the time horizon was longer and included less of the Great Recession and none of its aftermath. The study used a nationally representative sample of single mothers owed child support, rather than a sub-sample of mothers owed child support by economically vulnerable fathers. Nevertheless, these overall results appear to have been driven by reductions in child support receipts by mothers who had children with more economically vulnerable fathers. These mothers were never married and poorly educated, were required to give up their rights to child support to the government in exchange for public benefits, and were getting help from child support enforcement agencies to collect child support, probably because they could not afford help from private attorneys.

"IT'S BETTER THAT WAY": WHEN AUTOMATIC WAGE WITHHOLDING HELPS
MAINTAIN COMPLIANCE

Interestingly, we also found that downturns did not affect whether or not mothers received any child support, nor the amount of child support they received. This was probably because of the practice of automatically with-holding. Since 1988, federal law requires most employers to pay child support on behalf of their employees automatically, even if fathers have never defaulted on their child support orders. In most cases, the employer pays the full amount the father owes. Meyer and Cancian note that this requirement reduces the variability in income for single mother families and their children, which is almost as important as the amount of money such families receive.[34] As Bartfield and Meyer have shown, automatic withholding means that such fathers cannot adjust the amount of child support they actually pay, nor can they adjust whether or not they pay any child support.[35] When they get laid off, workers who had been stably employed in regular jobs can also get unemployment insurance, which provides the documentation they need to modify their support orders. Once the child support modification and unemployment insurance are in place, their new lower payments are also automatically deducted from their unemployment insurance benefits. This is exactly what happened to David, a working-poor father whom we met in Chapter 2, who is greatly relieved by the way this all worked out. As he puts it, "I don't have to worry about it [child support]."

"I WOULD HAVE BECOME HOMELESS": WHEN AUTOMATIC WAGE WITHHOLDING BECOMES A BURDEN

For fathers with reasonable orders, like Franco and David, this automated process helps fathers, mothers, and children because it ensures that routine payments will be made without placing the burden of initiating and monitoring payments on them. But for fathers with unreasonable orders, the opposite is true. Once automatic wage withholding goes into effect, the fathers have little recourse other than to file a petition for a modification. However, as we show below, such modifications often do not work. So fathers with unreasonably high orders who are subject to automatic withholding may be actively driven into poverty, or they may chose to work, at least part-time, at irregular jobs to shield some of their earnings from child support.

After working a 48-hour week, Samuel, a chronically unemployed father from Chautauqua, received $58 from what would have been a paycheck for at least $560. For the past 10 years, Samuel's child support order had been set at $360 a week, or about $1,440 a month.

> I worked like 48 hours, and I was making pretty good money. And the boss comes up to me and hands me my check. It was like—I think it was like

$58. I was like, uh. And I worked hard. I was working next to a guy that was making like $15—I was doing the same thing. He was making $15-something an hour, you know what I mean. . . . I got a check for $58. I mean that's ridiculous, you know. It's hard to work for a dollar an hour . . . and they were saying, well, you could go apply for food stamps and get your $58 a week, go apply for food stamps. Yay, lucky me, you know?

As a result, Samuel quit his job three years ago, because he felt there was no way he could live on $58 a week. Meanwhile, he currently owes between $15,000 and $18,000 in arrears. Although he tried to have his order modified, he was unsuccessful. When he sought advice about how to manage his child support, he was merely told that he could apply for food stamps.

"THEY WILL WORK WITH YOU": SUCCESSFUL CHILD SUPPORT
MODIFICATIONS

Because their payments are not automatically withheld by their employers, fathers without stable jobs pay child support directly, so they have the ability to default on their child support payments or pay less than the full amount due. This includes fathers who are self-employed, working at irregular jobs, and those who are still unemployed, but without unemployment insurance. These ideas of Bartfield and Meyer led us to believe that when we interviewed fathers toward the end of the 2007–2009 recession, the chronically unemployed fathers would be plagued by arrears, while working-poor fathers—whether still looking for regular jobs or regularly working at new (or old) jobs paying less than their pre-recession earnings—would be relatively debt free.[36] However, we were wrong. Instead, arrears were more strongly associated with the factors identified previously—the amount and length of the order. That arrears would be lower for those with recent child support cases is fairly intuitive. The role of the amount of the order in the accumulation of arrears was less obvious. As it turned out, it was not the amount of the order, but this amount in comparison to the father's income that explained which fathers had high (or very high) arrears and which fathers did not.[37]

Regardless of employment status, some fathers were more successful than others in modifying their child support orders, making success with the modification process a critical determinant of arrears. Put differently, working-poor fathers and chronically unemployed fathers, like Willie, were nearly equally likely to have child support orders that they were unable to pay. What made the difference was whether they, like Brandon and Franco, were able to obtain and sustain the types of child support modifications that kept orders in line with income.

All 10 of the fathers with low child support orders, including five who were chronically unemployed and five who were working-poor, got the biggest child support modification possible: a self-support reserve. Under New York State law, fathers whose adjusted gross income was at or below the single-person poverty level could have their child support orders set to $25 per month. Those with adjusted gross income at or below 135 percent of the poverty level could have their child support orders set to $50 per month. All 10 fathers with child support orders reflecting this self-support reserve provision had no or low arrears. Fathers who had obtained more modest downward modifications of their child support orders also tended to have lower child support orders and low arrears. In contrast, out of the seven fathers with high to very high orders and high to very high arrears, only two had ever received a modification and, like Willie, both modifications occurred before the 2007 recession.

Franco learned to work with the child support enforcement system the hard way. At one point he had fallen into arrears while unemployed and received notice that his driver's license was going to be suspended. He went to court to explain that he was trying to look for work in his profession as a commercial driver, and that a license was a requirement. Although he was afforded some leniency, his license was ultimately suspended. "I said if you take my license, I can't work, so I went to the judge and I spoke to her, and I said, look, Your Honor, I mean, I'm looking for work. Right now there's no work. . . . She said okay, we'll give you some time, but then they turned around and took my license and I said how I'm going to work?"

Nevertheless, he learned from this experience and came to believe:

So as long as you show the court that you're looking for work, they will work with you. But if you don't go back, and now they expect you to pay every week, say $50 a week, now you haven't been working in three months, that's $600. Now you're back, now they're going to hit you with the interest—now they're going to come after your license, so you always have to let the court know what's going on. Because I was always in court regular, like if I was working or if I wasn't, they would have my information, so if I wasn't working, I would just go back, you know, and let them know I'm not working. Like one time I hurt my back, so I wasn't able to work, so I just went back, told the judge, look, you know, I had an injury to my back. So the judge, you know, she was fair. She would say look, I'm going to give you like two months, three months, you come back, you let us know the information, so every time I was working, they would say where are you working at, and I would say here, and they would say could you pay this, and I would say, no problem, and they would keep it according to the order.

After paying child support for nearly 18 years, and receiving modifications when he needed them, the child support case for Franco's youngest son, now 21 years old, had no arrears and the case was successfully closed.

"I'M PRETTY SURE IT'S A LONG PROCESS": OBSTACLES TO CHILD SUPPORT MODIFICATIONS

As we showed above, studies using large-scale administrative databases, especially in Wisconsin, support the views of attorneys who advocate on behalf of vulnerable nonresident fathers. These fathers face many difficulties in getting their child support orders modified.[38] According to the fathers we interviewed, the most important barriers were missed court dates, either by mothers or by the fathers themselves, the fathers' ignorance and intimidation about the modification process, and delays in processing petitions for modifications.

Recall that one of the reasons Willie was unsuccessful in getting his child support order modified was that his case was postponed twice because the mother of one of his daughters failed to show up for the modification hearing. His arrears continued to grow during the period the case was adjourned. An even bigger problem was that fathers were generally ignorant of the conditions that would make them eligible for a child support modification. In particular, many of the fathers, like Kelly, whom we profiled in Chapter 2, believed that attempts to get more schooling so that they could better support their children were reasonable grounds for child support modification. Unfortunately, this was untrue.

In the State of New York, as in many states, a father's attempt to get additional education in order to improve his ability to support his children is not adequate grounds for a modification. Instead, as law professor Baron explains, most states permit child support modifications when one or the other parties to a child support agreement shows that "the circumstances of the parties have changed so that the current order is unconscionable." When incorporating this language from federal law (the Uniform Marriage and Divorce Act), most states use words such as "substantial and continuing change," while other states incorporate language such as "substantial and unanticipated change," which would preclude taking a low-wage job or a part-time job while attending college.[39]

In addition to the possibility of court postponement, the delay between filing a petition for a modification and obtaining the initial court date also proved burdensome, particularly for fathers with fluctuating incomes, like those who worked in construction. For example, Thomas, a working-poor construction worker, did not attempt to modify his order when he was not working. Construction work was so volatile that by the time he would actually be able to obtain a modification he would be working again. Furthermore, once he did have a job, he felt he could not afford to take a day off from work to attend court.

> Well, one of the things is, you see, the system is a system and I'm not going against it, but I truly think one of the things they should try to do is look into it, because, for example, construction work—it has its ups and downs. And when—today I'm working. I've been at work for two or three months, and tomorrow I'm not working. So by the time I go down there and file the petition—I have to file the petition to wait a period of time to see a judge. So you're now waiting a period of time to see a judge, I'm back in the field, and I never really take off a day once I'm working to go down and see the judge in that court. They just come and go, and those monies that I should have went to just—you know, they just keep going. And because I never go to a court date, it never gets, you know [modified].

Consequently, Thomas owed a total of $19,000 in arrears between his two child support cases, one for his 12-year-old daughter, and one for his 3-year-old daughter and 2-year-old son. Although the case for his two younger children was fairly reasonable (about $150 a month), the case for his older daughter was high (about $500 a month). The combined $650 a month was far more than his unemployment insurance could comfortably cover. Without a modification, his arrears will continue to grow.

Given the experiences of fathers like Thomas, it is not surprising that many fathers felt intimidated by the child support system. Diego, a working-poor father, had been paying child support for his 15-year-old daughter for about a decade. Despite being unemployed for two years, having a high child support order of about $480 a month, and owing $7,000 in arrears, he never attempted to modify his order because he feared it would be a long and difficult process. "I usually let it be like that, just...go with the flow with that. I never try to go back to court and let them know that I'm unemployed and, cause the process, I'm pretty sure it's a long process, you know what I mean....As far as modification I don't, I don't go through."

Modifications and automatic wage withholding can be effective tools in managing child support. Timely reviews of child support orders and modifications, when appropriate, can increase compliance with orders both by improving fathers' view of the system and by ensuring that orders match income. Nevertheless, government auditors have found many problems with the methods that many states use to review and approve petitions seeking downward modifications of child support orders.[40] As the experiences of the fathers we interviewed show, the challenges associated with obtaining modifications and with ensuring that automatic wage withholding is accurate can draw fathers deep into debt. What's more, states rarely reduce the amount of the arrears owed to them.[41]

Help from Fatherhood Programs

Increasingly, courts are referring vulnerable fathers to programs that provide a variety of services to help fathers manage their child support obligations. At one end of the spectrum are employment-related services for chronically unemployed fathers who need training in job readiness, resume writing, soft and basic skills, and classroom instruction leading to the GED. Since the recession, however, many of these programs have expanded their services to working-poor fathers who already have these qualifications and plenty of prior work experience. They need help finding regular jobs comparable to the jobs they had before the recession, even if this means learning new skills.

For example, Antonio, whom we profile in Chapter 6, lost his job because of his drinking and drug use. After undergoing successful treatment, Antonio found work as a substance abuse counselor, working in this capacity for two years, at a job he loved. Unfortunately, the nonprofit agency where he worked suffered cutbacks and Antonio, one of the newest hires, was one of the first to lose his job. Although his unemployment benefits were not enough to pay the child support orders for his two children, Antonio feels this was only a small setback. As a result of being ordered into Strive, a fatherhood program, Antonio attends sessions about child support and other issues that impact fathers. But the greatest help has been working with their employment specialists.

> They have wonderful, wonderful services.... They've helped me tweak my resume to the point that it is damn near perfect. They helped me put together a wonderful cover letter. And really I feel like I have that edge now, and I will say that, because since January I've had quality interviews, quality callbacks since utilizing their services, because I wasn't using a cover letter before coming here.... I've had some quality interviews, and as I've said just recently, right now, I have two offers on the table, two potential offers.

Antonio has found the fatherhood program to be a helpful and supportive environment. "Yeah, this has been a great place for me." If one of these results in a firm job offer, he will be able to get back on his feet, make his child support payments, and get back on track with his life.

In addition to the job placement services he received at Strive, Michael has found friendship and camaraderie. Based upon the poor experiences he had with similar programs in the past, he expected neither. He had two child support orders, one for his son in Georgia, and one for his daughter in New York. Unable to find work, Michael could not pay these orders. However, when he went to court to seek a modification of the orders, the judge ordered him to enroll in the Strive program. Michael has been pleasantly surprised. "I thought it probably be another one of them, you know, hole in the wall places, you know, but you, as you could see they're not, you know. They, they, so I was just glad that, you know, I'm, I'm here and I'm involved with them cause they really, they really, try to help you out, you know."

Michael has been frustrated with the child support system. He feels as if fathers' concerns are not always heard and sometimes get lost. But Michael feels that he is getting the help that he needs at Strive, his fatherhood program.

> At least here child support court sent me to Strive to get help and to get involved in programs so at least I can say they trying to work with us fathers because the short time I've been at Strive; Strive is a beautiful place and it's a short time that I, that I've been with Strive and, um, um, I'm actually glad that the court sent me here."

Michael has found the environment so nurturing that he wants to stay and plans to ask the judge to let him remain as long as possible.

> But um, even after my court date in June I'm gonna continue with Strive. I'm gonna stay with, stay with Strive and I'm gonna tell the judge that I'm gonna stay with, stay with Strive. I want to stay with them as long as, as long as possible cause I have something that's materializing with Strive and Strive is helping me do it so. It's, it's it's gonna get better. It is, it's gonna get better.

At the other end of the spectrum are services designed to help fathers interface with the child support enforcement system, especially help modifying their child support orders. Some programs do this by providing legal support through court advocates or attorney consultations. After all of the difficulties that he has encountered with child support, Kelly found assistance through a case manager at the fatherhood program he is attending, a program he was referred to by the courts. "The first person—the first time that I've ever had anybody say that they would even help me, uh, to fill out the modification papers, because they kind of read like stereo instructions, was here through this [fatherhood program], so yeah."

Earlier, Kelly had not been so fortunate. Though he had sought a modification twice, both requests had been denied. Kelly wanted to attend college, a lifelong dream. He also hoped to learn new skills that might increase his earning potential. However, as he discovered too late, voluntary unemployment, even to attend college or acquire new skills, is not reason to modify a support order. Though he had tried to work a part-time job and attend school full-time, Kelly found he could not do both, leading him to withdraw from school after three semesters. During this time, he was unable to pay his support order in full and fell behind, resulting in arrears and penalties. Had Kelly had access to programs and information earlier, he may have avoided this situation entirely, one from which he is still trying to extricate himself, years later.

In contrast, David felt punished by the child support system for behavior that he regrets; he fooled around prior to his marriage. But he does not regret becoming a father and wants to be a good one to all of his children. The fatherhood program helped him to temporarily modify his order and to reinstate his driver's license. For the time being, it has made the payments more manageable and in line with his current employment situation. David has been unemployed for close to six months, and the family has managed to live off his unemployment checks and the money his wife earns from her home day-care center. But even with careful budgeting, it has been hard for the family, made even more difficult when child support threatened to put a lien on his guitar, drums, and car, the very things he needs to earn money. David was able to modify his child support order through a local fatherhood program before too much time passed.

> I'm unemployed. So but even then, I was coming here (fatherhood program) and she's (social worker)—she said, you know, that's too high. They shouldn't be charging you all of—all of that. They're not supposed to be, so then we went—she helped me get—fill out papers to get my driver's license back, and when I had did that, the support had told me that it was going to be back down for the original while I was on unemployment...

Unfortunately, there are not enough of these programs to serve the more than 5 million vulnerable fathers who need them. Without these services, the system is working for some fathers, yet not for others. This variability is a cause for concern because, as the next section makes clear, the child support debt can have far-reaching implications for fathers' overall financial stability.

Legal advocates who work with economically vulnerable nonresident fathers point out that they face a number of sanctions for child support noncompliance that place them, their families, and their children *in a vicious cycle where the goal of providing for families and children is thwarted by policies and practices that boomerang when applied to low-income people (p. 37).*[42] Once a father starts to fall behind on child support payments, several enforcement measures can be taken, often to the detriment of the father's economic security. For example, low-income fathers who spoke with researchers, legal advocates, and policymakers at a colloquium in Washington in the late 1990s complained of the effects of sanctions for child support non-compliance on their ability to make a living. The most worrisome sanctions were driver's license suspensions, financial penalties, and jail time.[43] More than a decade later, the chronically unemployed and working-poor fathers we interviewed had the same complaints.

"A NO WIN SITUATION": SUSPENSION OF DRIVER'S LICENSE

The suspension of driver's licenses can really hurt fathers' economic security, as many depend on their licenses for employment as drivers. Recall Franco, who successfully finished paying child support, but nonetheless struggled at times. At one point he had fallen into arrears while unemployed and received notice that his license was going to be suspended. He went to court to explain that he was looking for work in his profession as a commercial driver, and that he needed his license to do so. Although he thought the judge was going to be lenient, his license was ultimately suspended. Michael, another working-poor father, whom we profile in the Appendix, was in a similar situation, and felt the same frustration with the child support system. He did not understand how a system could penalize him for not working and paying child support, but then prevent him from working.

> So if I'm not working they penalize me. You know, and suspend my driver's license and all this kind of stuff so I'm in a no win situation because I, you know, everyday I'm looking for work but my driver's license is key for the type of work that I do and I will probably need my license when I, when I, you know, when I do start working because I, you know, the type I do will require me to have a driver's license.

In Chautauqua, having a driver's license was even more crucial for employment, because nearly everyone needed a license for basic transportation, not just for driving jobs. Without his license, Andrew had limited employment options.

Transportation's a big must. If you can't get around, I don't know. Without transportation, it's—you're limited to what you can do, where you can go, you know. It limits me on, uh, the type of work I can look for. I've got to find something close that's walking distance, something in town. Like I couldn't go to [the next town over] to find a job in some of the factories out there.

FROZEN BANK ACCOUNTS AND DAMAGED CREDIT:
FINANCIAL ENFORCEMENT

While suspending driver's licenses seems to have a fairly direct impact on economic security by limiting employment options, freezing bank accounts and other financial enforcement measures have a more subtle impact on economic security. They drive fathers away from formal financial institutions that could be used to promote asset building.

For example, as a result of previously having an account frozen, or fear that an account could be closed, fathers may close existing accounts or refuse to use bank accounts altogether. Michael has had bank accounts in the past, but closes them as soon as he is out of work because he knows he will accumulate arrears when he is not working, and that child support could then freeze his account.

> No, I refuse to open a bank account...as soon as you open a bank account and you owe child support, they freeze your account. I had an account when I was paying, you know, when, when, when I'm working. You know, I'm, I'm, you know, I may get an account but if I'm not, as soon as I'm not working I close it. I don't want to leave no money in there cause they'll freeze it.

When asked where he keeps his money now, Michael replied, "in my pocket."

Another common financial enforcement measure was reporting child support arrears to the credit bureau. Although most fathers had not experienced any negative consequences thus far as a result of damaged credit reports, some fathers feared that it could soon become problematic because more and more employers were examining credit reports. Antonio, a 32-year-old Puerto Rican father with an 11-year-old daughter and a 7-year-old son, whom we profile in Chapter 6, said this:

> And it's kind of crappy when, um, you know, you have that hanging over your head, uh, especially in today's day and age that a background check is more than just checking where you used to work. You know, now they check are you in debt, now they check how much you're in debt for. Um, I'm afraid that that's going to bite me in the butt if I don't get out of debt soon, because

I know potential employers are looking at things far beyond the criminal history now, and debt is one of them.

Because it is so difficult for many laid-off working-poor fathers to find regular work, the practice of reporting child support debt to the credit bureau may lengthen the duration of unemployment among vulnerable fathers who surely need a regular work.

"IF I KNEW I WAS GETTING MONEY BACK, I WOULD FILE":
SEIZURE OF TAX REFUNDS

In addition to reporting arrears to the credit bureau and freezing bank accounts, seizing tax refunds is another common financial enforcement measure. Some fathers approve of having their tax refunds applied to their child support arrears because doing so reduces their total debt. However, others alter their tax filing behavior in both subtle and direct ways that may ultimately undermine economic security or deter the accumulation of assets. Antonio no longer uses professional tax services, such as H&R Block, because of the $120 cost for filing, just to have his refund offset by child support; he now pays his brother $20 to file his taxes with Turbo Tax.

> This particular year, my brother. My brother did them for me personally. Uh, normally I go H&R Block, but since I have gotten accustom to my refund being offset, why am I going to pay H&R Block $120 to give me a rapid refund that is not as rapid as I would hope, because I'm not going to receive it anyway. So it took—it took me a few times bumping my head, but I figured it out this year. I give my brother $20. He does it on the computer with his Turbo Tax thing, and that's it. It's simple. I don't see it, so why go ahead and pay $120, because the hopes that they might send it to me. No, it's not happening. I've come to terms with that already.

Although these alternative means of tax filing are not necessarily problematic in and of themselves, they could impede a father's access to the Non-Custodial Parent EITC. It is likely that independent tax preparers would be best equipped to file straightforward federal and state returns, and that they would be less likely to be knowledgeable about credits requiring additional forms, such as the Non-Custodial Parent EITC. Recall that New York State launched the Non-Custodial Parent Earned Income Tax Credit in 2006 to supplement the earnings of economically vulnerable nonresident fathers.

However, to apply for the credit, applicants must complete a supplemental form for their state income taxes, must work in the regular economy, and must pay child support in full. To the extent that tax intercepts discourage the use of tax filing services that complete the required forms, it follows that vulnerable fathers will not have access to this credit. In extreme cases, the knowledge that tax refunds will be seized to cover child support arrears may cause fathers to avoid filing taxes altogether.

"WHY DO YOU KEEP TRYING TO LOCK ME UP?": ENFORCEMENT THROUGH INCARCERATION

When in *Making Fathers Pay*, D. L. Chambers celebrated the use of incarceration to enforce child support in Genesee County, Michigan, he could not have known that the earnings of most men of childbearing age would remain stagnant or decline for the next three decades.[44] Nor did he know that incarceration, or the threat of incarceration, would become so routine in the child support enforcement community over this period. However, some legal advocates are convinced that the adverse effects of state efforts to criminalize nonpayment of child support are concentrated on low-income fathers, their families, and communities. One public defender, who has advocated for many fathers in this circumstance, worries that: "the current system of aggressive support enforcement against incarcerated parents serves as a *de facto* civil sanction in many jurisdictions, creating yet another collateral consequence of incarceration."

As a result, the legal community has taken special aim at the routine practice of incarcerating fathers for their child support non-compliance. Patterson argues that there are at least two grounds for a legal challenge to this practice.[45] First, fathers are often deprived of their freedom before other options for securing child support payments have been exhausted. Second, fathers may not have the ability to take advantage of the one option offered by the court to prevent incarceration. This option is the immediate satisfaction of a payment on some portion of the fathers' child support obligation, usually recommended by the child support enforcement agency. This amount, known as a "purge payment," could include penalties and interest on top of the arrears arising from the original child support order. Often, especially when there is an unmarried birth, the child support enforcement agencies and the courts do not have information about the father's earnings and therefore assume that fathers are capable of earning what they earned on their previous job. Alternatively, they assume that fathers are capable of earning what a worker would earn if he worked full-time and full-year at the minimum wage. Thus, the child support order is based on the father's imputed income rather than his actual earnings. If the purge payment, including penalties and interest, is derived from this erroneous amount, the father will also be unable to pay this amount immediately. In sum, Patterson argues, "[f]laws in the child support enforcement system create a substantial likelihood that an obligor charged with contempt may lack the means to comply with either or both child-support order and the purge condition." She goes on to suggest that unless these flaws are addressed, "low-income child-support obligors will continue to be incarcerated for the offense of being poor" (p. 141).

One would presume that the most severe form of child support enforcement, incarceration, would be reserved for the worst offenses of willful non-payment of child support. On closer examination, however, it seems that the advocates are right. Among the fathers we interviewed, chronically unemployed fathers who were the least able to pay were at the greatest risk of incarceration. Dwight, a chronically unemployed father whom we will meet in Chapter 4, spent a week in jail for owing $145, or the equivalent of about three months of payments, for one of his two child support cases. He could not understand why he would be incarcerated for owing such a relatively small sum, while plenty of other fathers owe far greater amounts. "I know I owe money, but why you throwing me in jail, there's people out there that owe like sixty grand dude. You know what I mean? You're throwing me in jail for a hundred and fifty bucks. . . . So, I got lucky and was out within a few days. But just, eh, it's stupid, the—the way the courts are."

More recently, Dwight, who again owes around $150 in arrears, was given the option of attending a fatherhood program or going to jail. Two of the other fathers from Chautauqua, both of whom were also chronically unemployed, mentioned that their program attendance was court mandated as the only alternative to jail. One owes $7,000 and the other owes $1,500. Although regional factors may be at play, as the Chautauqua fathers were both disproportionately chronically unemployed and more likely to experience incarceration for non-payment, the association between being chronically unemployed and the risk of incarceration is nonetheless worth noting. How effective an enforcement measure is incarceration in motivating payment from fathers who are already impoverished, unemployed, and struggling to gain traction in the labor market?

The trouble with current methods of child support enforcement is their premise that fathers are willfully avoiding paying child support, and that punitive enforcement measures are necessary to motivate them to pay. While this premise may be true for some, there are many, especially economically vulnerable fathers, for whom it is not. As we have seen, these fathers are willing to pay child support in proportion to their ability to do so, and few owe exorbitant amounts of arrears. The largest group of fathers has low to medium orders and low to medium arrears.

Arrears tend to accumulate over time during periods of unemployment when orders are not modified to accommodate changes in employment and earnings. By applying punitive measures to fathers who are unable, rather than unwilling, to pay, the child support enforcement system reduces vulnerable fathers' economic security and undermines their ability to financially support their children.

Is this the view widely shared? And, if so, what is being done to change the system? We turn to these questions in Chapter 6.

Ernest's Story

Ernest is a 42-year-old African American father. He currently lives in what he has referred to as a three-quarter house, sharing a room with three other men. He has been living there since leaving a residential treatment program for substance abuse. Ernest is currently unemployed but hopes his joblessness will end soon, as he has recently completed a program in environmental response training. He had previously worked in a number of different jobs; however, most had been short-term or seasonal work. His last job was in the construction industry, but his boss was a heavy drinker and Ernest wanted to stay away from situations that might threaten his sobriety. Construction was also seasonal and, as a result, he faced unemployment during the winter months. He was just not making enough money to support both himself and his children. Training for a job in a different field offered a new beginning, a career rather than a job, so he could support his family comfortably. "In my opinion, my decision to spend time and take my children out is I didn't have that with my father a lot, because he worked two jobs, so that also goes back to having a career versus just a job, so that I can actually have one job and have more time for my children. And knowing how important it was for me as a child, I know how important it is for them."

Ernest has two children, a girl who is 11 years old and a boy who is 7. Both children live with their mother. He has a close relationship with both children and with their mother, who lived with Ernest for 11 years. She allows him open-ended access to their children, even allowing him to stay over in her home. However, the family lives four and a half hours away, which is a long and expensive commute for Ernest. As a result, Ernest sees his children about once or twice a month, not nearly as often as he would like, but he does speak to both children on the phone daily. Ernest sees his role as a father to be present and available to his children, something he never had with his own father.

The second youngest of six boys, Ernest did well in school. Both parents worked two jobs and were rarely available. Because Ernest was seen as "the one we don't have to worry about," he felt his parents did not pay much attention to him. Later, his father drifted into alcoholism and his parents divorced. Ernest felt that he missed the show of love and affection that children need when growing up, something he wants to make sure his own children receive. "So that's the one thing I love about my relationship with them more than anything else is that they're just really, really affectionate, and I've been so affectionate with them over the years."

In 1998, Ernest had been in graphic design as a silkscreen press operator. He made a good salary and had been promoted within the company. However, a little over a year later, while fixing his car, the fan blade in the engine hit Ernest in the eye, severely injuring him. He tried to return to his job several times, but his eye continually became infected, and finally, the tear duct stopped working. Though his employer held his position during his recuperation period, Ernest realized that he could no longer work at a job where perfect vision was required. Over a three-year time period, he subsequently lost his vision in the eye and then the eye itself. The sudden physical and financial hardship as a result of the accident left him depressed.

During this time, he was unable to work and was receiving disability payments. However, one night, after seeing a commercial on television about a career training school for computer repair, he enrolled. Ernest thought this might offer a new beginning since he had always been interested in computers and was mechanically adept. However, two months into the program, the school declared bankruptcy and immediately closed its doors. Ernest and the other students were literally left out in the cold. And he still had to repay the money he had borrowed to cover the tuition cost. The financial stress of living day to day and not knowing if he would have enough money for the next week took its toll. Ernest turned to drugs and alcohol. "So with those pressures on me I just, you know, I'm not saying that relying on drugs and alcohol is a good thing, because it's not, but it was what I was raised with, my father was an alcoholic, so it kind of—it looked normal in my home when I was growing up, so it seemed like a normal thing to do, because the people I respected and looked up to the most early on in my life did exactly the same thing."

The health, depression, and substance abuse problems took a tool on his marriage and ultimately led to divorce. Ernest has a child support order for both children, obtained when their mother applied for Medicaid and food stamps. When Ernest went into treatment, he was able to suspend his child support payments. He had the suspension extended so he could return to school to complete the program for environmental response training. However, even with the suspension and modifications, he currently owes $7,000 in arrears.

Despite this debt, Ernest feels that the child support system has been willing to work with him and has accommodated his unique circumstances. However, he is working hard to try to find a good paying job. He wants to support his children; he wants to be there for both of them to help them navigate life. "And I just want my kids to make the right choices, because even though a path may be laid for us, there's always an option—there's always a choice to make. So I want them to be able to make the right choices, and the only way I can impart that to them is to really show them that the right choices are to stick with school, get your education, and think about what you want to do with the rest of your life."

Ernest feels that most nonresident fathers do want to support their children but that sometimes events in their lives occur that make that impossible.

I mean yeah, there are some noncustodial parents that just will avoid their responsibilities, but there are many more of us, and I met quite a few good gentlemen in the fatherhood program that I'm in that have just hit some bad luck. You know, they may have had struggles like my own with addiction that prevented them from doing the right thing although they wanted to. So there are so many of us that want to do the right thing, that want to take care of our children, that want to be a part of our children's lives, and for the most part it seems like society views us as fathers who don't want to do anything. And like I said, it's usually not the case.

4 The Roles Nonresident Fathers Play

DAVID BLANKENHORN, DAVID Popenoe, and others have viewed with alarm the growing number of households in which the father no longer lives with his family.[1] Referred to as father absence, they hold that real harm can occur when fathers live apart from their children.[2] In response, an alternative view has emerged. According to a team from the University of Pennsylvania (Kane, Gadsden, and Armorer), children who do not live with their fathers desire and need their fathers' presence and experience social, academic, emotional, and financial benefits when their fathers are involved.[3] This alternate perspective, called father presence, considers the father-absence view too limited. Instead, it focuses on the complexities of father roles and how they are associated with family functioning and child outcomes.

For example, Waldo Johnson, a professor from the University of Chicago, has studied low-income, nonresident fathers in Chicago. He has found that links between father-child relationships and child well-being extend beyond residential boundaries, or even beyond the amount of time that fathers spend with their children.[4] Instead, these links often depend on the level of a father's emotional and functional involvement. Child development experts Natasha Cabrera, Catherine Tamis-LeMonda, and their colleagues, who have studied father-child interactions in early childhood education programs, found that continued contact with nonresident fathers who are loving, supportive, and nurturing supports children's cognitive and emotional development.[5]

Traditionally, the role of the father within the family has been that of the breadwinner, an arena in which vulnerable nonresident fathers operate at a disadvantage. Steven Nock, a sociologist who studied the role of marriage, found that men who father children in non-marital relationships, including cohabitation, earn lower wages, complete fewer years of schooling, and have higher rates of poverty than married fathers.[6] The same was true of men who divorced when compared to men who stayed married, and resident fathers when compared to nonresident fathers.[7] These comparisons are important because higher income accounted for about half the advantage enjoyed by children with resident fathers.[8]

Although they could not, or chose not, to provide as much financial support to their children as residential fathers, child support payments from nonresident fathers did help. Elaine Sorensen showed that financial support, mostly in the form of child support payments, accounted for a quarter of the incomes of families headed by women who were fortunate enough to receive such support.[9] Further, D. R. Meyer and his colleague at University of Wisconsin's Institute for Research on Poverty showed that such financial support lifts six-to-seven percent of single-mother families out of poverty.[10] Finally, child development experts, such as Columbia and Princeton professor Jeannie Brooks-Gunn and her colleagues, have shown that some children who received such support experienced improved cognitive development and school achievement, if child support agreements were cooperative and there was not too much conflict.[11]

The Breadwinner Role: Strain and Regret

Alice Eagly of Northwestern University hypothesized that our societal expectations reinforce the breadwinner role as the most important fatherhood role, providing an explanation about why fathers who fail to provide financially are disparaged.[12] Two predominant views have emerged when discussing vulnerable nonresident fathers and their inability to fulfill the provider role. Some hold negative images and these have a long tradition. As we saw in Chapter 3, D. L. Chambers popularized the "deadbeat dad" stereotype, a father who is unwilling to support his children and is uninvolved in their lives.[13] Others espouse more sympathetic views about the vulnerable father's financial shortcomings. McAdoo, Bowman, and their colleagues believe that the failed attempts of vulnerable fathers to conform to the breadwinner norm, which they have internalized, results in stress and anxiety, called "provider role strain."[14] This may explain why many fathers who suffer from long-term unemployment tend to withdraw from their children when they fail to meet the financial demands of being the family breadwinner.[15]

Those who support father presence have argued that vulnerable nonresident fathers who fail to fulfill the breadwinner role do not necessarily withdraw. Rather, they are often highly motivated to be involved in their children's lives in other meaningful ways. Some studies have found evidence that economically vulnerable fathers attempt to redirect provider role strain by rewriting fatherhood expectations. Jennifer Hamer and Kevin Roy conducted independent qualitative studies of low-income or unemployed nonresident fathers. They found that the fathers believed that other forms of emotional involvement and support were more important than the breadwinner role.[16] Other similar studies by Roy, Waller, and Marsiglio have shown that nurturing children and providing love and guidance through emotional support take precedence over financial support when vulnerable fathers think about their roles.[17] The vulnerable nonresident fathers interviewed by Hamer, Hammond, and their colleagues emphasized the importance of "being there" or "spending time" with their children, so that they could provide discipline and be both a friend and role model.[18]

STRAIN

Similar to the findings of other researchers, our findings revealed that the fathers we interviewed deflected provider role strain by emphasizing the importance of being present in the lives of their children. This was true for men who had been chronically unemployed as well as for working-poor fathers who found themselves working at lower wages, if at all, because of the recession. Born out of their current circumstances, these fathers realized the impact created by some of their earlier decisions, notably schooling, and wanted to prevent their own children from experiencing a similar situation by encouraging their education. Despite their inability to fulfill the provider role, the fathers were well aware of the advantages that financial support offered their children, and understood that their children relied on them financially. Though they tried to support their children financially and listed formal child support payments among their top two expenditures, as we saw in Chapter 2, unemployment and underemployment limited their capacity as breadwinners, and they had a difficult time financially. In Chapter 3, we noted that most of the fathers were behind on their child support payments. Many also knew and regretted that the financial support they provided for their children, either formally and informally, was not enough to meet all of their children's needs. As a result of their inability to fully meet the financial expectations held by themselves, their families, and their communities, the fathers experienced enormous pressures.

Despite this provider role strain, fathers generally did not abandon their responsibilities entirely. Instead, they expressed a commitment to meeting those needs, listing informal support for their children among their top three expenses. For example, José, a 48-year-old unemployed Latino father with two sons living elsewhere, had child support arrears of $14,000 and his driver's license had been suspended as a result. He graduated from high school but explained that both the recession and some physical and mental health challenges left his employment and financial situation in "dire straits." Nonetheless, he was seeing his children every other weekend and enjoyed a good relationship with both of them. He explained that he buys things that his children need, but that his lawyer scolded him for not meeting child support payments.

> She kept telling me, you know, "the coat, the things you're buying, the receipts, you know, you can show everything, but it doesn't mean anything. What it means is that you're not obliging by paying your child support, you're obliging by buying them what they need." And I said, "well, you know what, they need it." I mean, I will sacrifice. Yeah, well, the child support payments I can't make, I'll get—I'll get what they need.

The breadwinner role was an important part of the way these fathers thought about being present in their children's lives, and despite being "broke," they were often doing the best they could to provide for their children.

EDUCATIONAL REGRET

Interestingly, the fathers we interviewed highly valued education, with many expressing a belief that additional schooling could improve multiple facets of their lives, including the ability to fulfill their role as breadwinner. Similarly, Vivian Gadsden and Phillip Bowman found that young, low-income, African American fathers who experienced provider role strain wanted to reinvent themselves through education, and to transfer the gains of increased education to their children.[19] The fathers we interviewed experienced feelings of disappointment or regret for getting derailed from their educational paths. In the past, most of these fathers pushed aside education in favor of making money, but many now believed that they could have made more money had they remained in school, or if they returned to school. Whether high school dropouts or college graduates, most of the fathers we interviewed wanted to return to school because they believed that another degree would improve their earnings and employment stability. Fathers learned this lesson the hard way, and overwhelmingly wished to save their children from making the same mistakes. Fathers hoped, mostly in vain, to invest in their children's education by saving for their college education. Financial constraints motivated them to reframe their roles as fathers.

Similarly, Michael Lamb and Kevin Roy[20] argued that the ways men define themselves as fathers shape their motivation and behavior as parents. Failure as a breadwinner can lead some fathers to disengage from their children.[21] Dana Bauman and her colleague found that some fathers became more confident in their abilities as fathers as a result of their involvement in their children's educational activities, and they began to believe in their roles as "agents for change" in their children's lives.[22] Among the fathers we interviewed, educational regret and provider role strain motivated the ways in which nonresident fathers engaged with their children and fulfilled both economic and non-economic fathering roles.

For example, Ricardo, a 25-year-old Latino father, explained that in early adolescence, he "didn't care" about school and "wanted to do what I wanted to do." When his parents punished him for "messing up" in school by taking away "everything he wanted," he turned to the streets.

> I dropped out of school to stay on the streets selling drugs. I regret that, because now I'm older, and I'm feeling it. It ain't too late, but I'm regretting it. . . . I just finished the eighth. I didn't even make it ninth. I went to school to ninth grade one day, and didn't go back. Because I was too into—I was too into the streets.

Ricardo had child support orders for his two daughters, ages two and five, and was at risk of being kicked out of his apartment for not paying his rent. Now, Ricardo knew he needed his GED but he needed a job first, presenting the cyclical problem of needing education to earn more money, but also finding limited schooling a financial obstacle in and of itself. He was especially concerned with keeping his children engaged in school. He stated,

> I talk to them about school, because I want them to, like that's always — I'm like what's your score? If not, I'll give them a test, like spell this out. Like what I do, I keep, like I keep them occupied, because what I didn't do, I want them to do. I didn't finish school. I want them to finish school.

While reflecting on their educational histories, fathers often expressed deep frustration over what could have been. Many spoke about how having a child made them realize just how important education was for financial security. The added responsibility of providing for their children added to the regret of not going to school when it was more feasible. They wished they could go back in time and be "good" students so that they would be better prepared to provide for their children.

In the United States, gender accounts for much of the variation in school experience, behavior, and attainment. Fathers are already less likely to attain degrees in higher education than mothers. The National Center for Education Statistics reports that between 1980 and 2001, the number of men enrolled in degree-awarding institutions increased by 20 percent (from approximately 5 million in 1980 to 6 million in 2001), whereas the number of women enrolled increased by 41 percent (from roughly 5.5 million to 7.7 million).[23] According to the 2013 Census data, 21,715,000 adult women held college degrees as compared to 19,860,000 men.[24] Many researchers point to gender disparities in discipline that serve to push boys out of school. A study of over 11,000 urban students in the United States revealed that boys are almost always more likely than girls to be referred to the office for disciplinary problems and to be suspended, expelled, or subjected to corporal punishment. These disparities in office referrals and disciplinary sanctions remain even after controlling for socioeconomic status.[25] More than 30 percent of sophomores who drop out of school have been suspended—a rate three times that of peers who stay in school.[26] But in spite of these institutional realities, fathers still blame themselves for their educational failures.

The belief that working hard in school will pay off permeates US culture and society and has become known in the research literature as the "achievement ideology." Jay MacLeod examined the aspirations and attainment of young men in a low-income US city and found evidence of this ideology that states, "[e]ducation is viewed as the remedy for the problem of social inequality; schooling makes the race for prestigious jobs and wealth an even one" (p. 98).[27] If one accepts this line of reasoning, then those who fail to achieve or "make it" have only themselves to blame. The educational regret experienced by the fathers we spoke to stems from the belief that they could have the middle class life they imagined for themselves, if only they had the merit and ambition to achieve a college degree. As we learned in Chapter 2, for their parents' generation, this regret is accurate. If they attained more education, their earnings would be higher. However, according to Northwestern University labor economist Andrew Sum and his colleagues, in 2009, only those fathers who achieved a master's degree would have found improvements in earnings over their parents. Less educated males are finding it more difficult to obtain any type of employment and they earn considerably less when they do.[28] Nonetheless, education was viewed as an important pathway to success and fathers blamed themselves for allowing immediate financial needs, or the lure of the street, to pull them away from their educational priorities.

Although going back to school offered the possibility of higher earnings, fathers were unable to put aside their financial responsibilities and return to school. Education was considered a luxury when compared to the basic needs that had to be met, like housing and the financial needs of their children. Most fathers concluded that they needed to be more situated, further delaying their educational goals. A few, like Kelly, whom we met in Chapter 2, went back to school in order to be able to provide more for themselves and their children. To create time for study, they reduced their hours or took lower wage jobs, only to discover that such deliberate reductions in their income were not sufficient grounds for a downward modification of their child support orders. This may help to explain why a recent study using the fragile families data found that the proportion of community college students who are fathers is quite low[29]. Nevertheless, educational regret and a desire to prevent their children from experiencing the same hardships and regrets motivated these fathers to remain present in their children's lives as teachers, friends, advisors, and disciplinarians.

Non Financial Roles: Staying Present as Teachers, Friends, Advisors and Disciplinarians

TEACHERS: PROVIDING EDUCATIONAL SUPPORT

Many of the fathers we interviewed discussed the importance of both encouraging their children to stay in school, and helping them to meet their educational goals. Fathers participated in a variety of educational activities with their children that included academic supports for school-age children and day-to-day learning for younger children. Some fathers helped with homework; others used their visitation days to teach concrete skills; while others focused on literacy by reading or writing with their children.

Ernest, whose profile ended Chapter 3, spent a great deal of time reading to his children when they were young. Now that his daughter is in school, he helps her with math.

> You know, I would do the long division for her first, or show her how to do the variables and show her each step, and once she saw that first problem, and she made a few mistakes with the next couple of problems, but once

she realized the mistakes that she had made, you know, she was ecstatic about learning something new. And I was enjoying just seeing her because that's the way I was when I was younger. I was always ecstatic about learning something new.

Like Ernest, many fathers believed they were making a difference in the lives of their children, as evidenced by their enthusiasm for learning something new. For many, this was the best part of being a father. Chaska, a 36-year-old father of three children ranging in age from 5 to 13, has struggled to meet his child support obligations for many years. At the time of the interviews, he was in the process of being evicted, but school and learning activities still remained a priority.

My daughter, she likes when she learns new words. She likes to tell me, daddy, I can spell this, or I can spell that. I'll be smarter, because that's good. She still remembers the things that I taught her, and that shows me that they still keep that in their head. So that's what makes me happy.

The teacher role offered Chaska satisfaction and a connection to his daughter.

In a qualitative study with unmarried, low-income parents conducted by Maureen Waller of Cornell University, mothers agreed that fathers should be involved in their children's schoolwork. One mother, Debra, explained that a father should "help them with their homework and encourage them to do good things. Even if they're not doing good, encourage them anyway, 'cause I do. Encourage them and just be there" (p. 58).[30]

The fathers we interviewed provided examples of helping with homework, or engaging their children in conversations about school. They hoped, as a result, that their children would be less vulnerable to recessions like the one that had displaced so many of them. Many studies have shown that when parents are actively involved in the education of their children, they establish an invaluable bridge between school and home. This link promotes academic achievement, positive expectations for the future, higher educational aspirations, and improved educational attainment, as compared to the outcomes among children who lack similar parental supports. For example, Stanford University professor Russell Rumberger and his colleagues found that inner-city high school students were less likely to drop out of school when parents helped with decisions about proper behavior, monitored and helped with homework, attended school conferences and functions, and provided a supportive learning environment.[31]

However, very few of the fathers we interviewed reported meeting with their children's teachers or engaging in their children's school events, activities that several studies have shown are important for children's academic achievement.[32] For example, Nord and her colleagues found that students are 39 percent more likely to get mostly As and are 45 percent less likely to repeat a grade if their nonresident fathers have moderate to high involvement in their schools.[33] Amato and Gilbreth conducted a meta-analysis of 63 studies examining the well-being of children of nonresident fathers. Their results showed that fathering activities such as monitoring school performance, attending school functions, and helping with homework were some of the most consistent predictors of children's academic and psycho-social outcomes—more consistent than contact, closeness, or even child support. When nonresident fathers had some involvement in their children's schools, their children had the most positive outcomes. They were more likely to achieve higher grades and to go further in school, and were less likely to have ever repeated a grade, or to have ever been suspended or expelled.[34] These findings suggest that when nonresident fathers extend their role as teacher, and remain engaged in their children's schools, they will have the far reaching effects on their children's educational outcomes that they hope for.

FRIENDS: FORMING EMOTIONAL BONDS

To establish the emotional connection they needed to carry out more influential fathering roles, a majority of the fathers we interviewed stressed the importance of having fun with their children. For example, many fathers formed emotional bonds by watching movies together with their children, playing video games at home, or talking on the phone. Ernest recounted that when he and his children watched movies together, both would fight for a seat on his lap:

> I mean she still wants to sit on my lap when I come over and we watch a movie, or she still wants me to pick her up. And so when she sits on this leg, my son has to sit on the other leg. They just have to have equal time with me. So that's the one thing I love about my relationship with them more than anything else is that they're just really, really affectionate, and I've been so affectionate with them over the years.

Ernest emphasized that the activities didn't need to be expensive or complex to be fun and memorable.

> A lot of times I just take them to the park. I made them some kites out of garbage bags last year, just to show them it doesn't matter what you got around you, you can always make something out of nothing. And you know

my son loved that kite. Out of all the toys in the house, he loves that kite, him and his sister, so we go to the park and sometimes we just run up and down the park, you know, kick the ball around or simple little things.

Researchers, like Furstenberg and his colleague, often suggest that such activities are the most common but least valuable type of fathering role by nonresident parents.[35] However, the fathers we interviewed used such activities to establish the intimacy they felt was needed to undertake other fathering roles. For example, Antonio knew that he needed to connect with his two children on a more friendly and loving level before he would be able to play the role of disciplinarian. "I was out of their life for so long and, you know, I want to take that firm stance and be able to discipline them, but also have that balance that they know that they're loved, so I think that's a struggle I'm having right now."

Like many fathers we interviewed, Antonio was conscious of demonstrating sensitivity to his children's needs so that he could correct and mold his children effectively. When Antonio was with his children, he reported that he was always thinking about "what's next, what's new, what can we do that we haven't done before." They watched movies, rode bikes, and went to the park. He took both children to an amusement park together, and has taken his son to a Yankees game. He took his daughter to the mall because she liked shopping for her favorite toys. These types of activities promoted feelings of closeness between nonresident fathers and their children, and several studies have shown that closeness predicts positive behavioral and academic outcomes for children.[36]

ADVISORS: IMPARTING VALUES AND LIFE LESSONS

Almost two-thirds of the fathers we interviewed described themselves as advisors to their children. Fathers not only viewed advising as a responsibility, they viewed it as a privilege, with some believing it was the best part about being a father. Fathers not only identified a general desire to use their knowledge and experience to advise, guide and direct their children, but also identified specific values and lessons that they felt were important for their children to learn. The importance of education was especially reinforced through this role. For example, José, whom we met earlier in this chapter and who spoke about his financial situation as being in "dire straits," believed that he needed to make certain that his children understood the value of school, and believed that conveying this message was a vital part of his role as a parent.

You know, the things that I'm trying to establish with my kids now and inject it—embed it in their mind—you know, you have to graduate from college. . . . As long as I'm alive, I'm going to make sure that's established. And whatever it takes, if I have to work 18, 19 hours to make sure that they go to NYU, or they go to Yale, or they go to Harvard, or whatever school. . . . That's part of being a parent. But to make sure that this actually happens—not just to say it but actually happens—so whatever it is that I need to do.

Unlike most of the fathers in our study, José did more than just talk about staying in school, he maintained relationships with his son's teachers and described the pride he felt at his last parent-teacher conference ". . . like going and hitting the lotto." Staying involved in his son's education gave José the feeling of closeness that he could not experience with his son at home. Because fathers believed that education was the pathway to greater financial stability and self-sufficiency, they frequently utilized this advisor role to remind their children that education was important to their future. Fathers hoped this advice and support would enable their children to make educational decisions that would have a positive impact on their well-being.

In addition to encouraging their children to stay in school, there were two other notable features about the advising role. The first was unique to boys, and involved fathers' efforts to keep their sons out of trouble. This was similar to Kevin Roy's findings about the advice that vulnerable nonresident fathers gave their children, with the specific goal of preventing their children from making the same mistakes that they did, such as being pulled into "street culture."[37] The second feature applied to promoting open communication with both their sons and daughters, but with different emphases. Fathers wanted their children to feel comfortable talking to them about problems that were troubling them. For example, Ernest was particularly concerned about his son's fighting at school. He wanted to help him learn self-control, and encouraged him to talk to people, rather than fight, when he was upset. He told his son, "You can't overreact to certain situations, there's a certain way of doing things. If you're upset at somebody for something they did to you, there's always someone you can bring it to or whatever without always getting violent about it."

Ernest also understood that his pre-adolescent daughter needed an outlet to discuss her development. He became that outlet:

She talks to me a lot. She doesn't talk to her mother as much, which kind of bothers me some, because her mother's the one that's there all the time.

But we talk every day on the phone, so I do know that—knowing that she's so much like me, I always try to give her an outlet, because it's really, especially—she's 11 now—she's starting to develop, so she really needs someone to talk to about what's going on.

Many of the fathers we interviewed practiced authoritative parenting—a combination of control, communication, and warmth—when advising their children. In doing so, they followed the advice of child development experts such as Diana Baumrind, who identified authoritative parenting as the parenting style that yields consistently positive outcomes in children.[38]

DISCIPLINARIANS: CORRECTING AND MOLDING

Some of the fathers we interviewed saw their role as the disciplinarian, as the parent to correct and mold their children. They hoped to promote future success and prevent the types of problems that plagued so many children and adolescents, such as being seduced by street life or dropping out of school. For example, Terry, a 32-year-old unemployed African American father, explained that he hoped to secure a job so that he might help his son go to college. Terry also disciplined his son for not doing his homework. Terry wanted his son to succeed and used the disciplinarian role to emphasize the importance of education.

> I was like "teacher say you didn't do your homework, where's all your homework?" I said, "son, you went out to school without doing your homework. You went it's like for a whole week without homework." So I sat down and I was just grilling him you can't do that, you can't do that. How you supposed to be a football player, a dancer, a wrestler if you not doing your homework.

Similarly, Alberto, a 33-year-old Latino father, conveyed the importance of education by contributing some of his limited means to his son's Catholic school tuition and by rewarding his son for good performance in school. Alberto dropped out of high school, never received his GED, and had been unemployed for the past 13 months. He hoped to keep his son engaged in school through a disciplinary tactic of rewards and punishments.

> His grades, I put conditions on him. There was a time when his grades were very low and I told him if he continues with those grades there won't be

any nice things for you. If your grades are better, more nice things for you. So, I tell him that he has to pay attention to the teacher. So he brought his grades up.

The fathers we interviewed often disciplined their children by linking behaviors with consequences, set boundaries without being so stern that they would push their children away. Again, fathers were utilizing what is known as "authoritative parenting," which sets clear limits, but also offers communication, warmth, and nurturance.[39] Children and adolescents reared in such family environments experience more self-confidence, stronger academic performance, and higher self-esteem with fewer behavioral problems than children reared in more permissive or controlling environments.[40]

If Not the Breadwinner, Then What?

The vulnerable nonresident fathers that we spoke to regretted that leaving school prematurely was making it impossible for them to adequately meet their children's financial needs. Still, they often spoke about playing other roles in the lives of their children. First, to ensure that their children did not make the same mistakes, fathers became their children's teachers. They provided direct educational support, though few fathers worked directly with teachers or attended school functions. Fathers also maintained friendly relationships with their children that facilitated other roles that they played, advised their children about school and other matters, and used rewards and punishments for good behavior and performance in school. Whether substituting other roles for the breadwinner role is an effective strategy is an important question. Put differently, do children benefit when vulnerable nonresident fathers, who cannot play the breadwinner role well, play other roles instead?

To answer this question, quantitative researchers try to measure what fathers actually do when they perform various roles and whether these activities actually benefit children. Answering this question for the breadwinner role is fairly straightforward. When fathers play the breadwinner role, they work, so the amount of money they earn is a pretty good measure of how effectively they play the breadwinner role. Further, the effect of the fathers' earnings, or (formal or informal) financial support for children, tells us the importance of this role. Measuring what fathers do when they play other roles (such as teacher, friend, advisor, and disciplinarian) is more difficult. And, as we shall see, even when researchers are able to measure what fathers do in these other roles, measuring the effects on children is extremely difficult.

Quality Engagement Matters: It's Not Just About Time and Money

Psychologist Michael Lamb has been studying the role of fathers in child development. With colleagues, he established the most widely used typology of father involvement.[41] One category of father involvement is *responsibility*, by which Lamb means the extent to which fathers are involved in essential decisions involving the child. These may include decisions about healthcare, the school the child attends, and other important activities that affect the child. Another, called *availability*, refers to the ease with which fathers and children have access to one another. For example, residential fathers have greater access to their children than nonresident fathers, and nonresident fathers who visit their children at least once a week are more available to their children than nonresident fathers who visit their children only once a year. Finally, *engagement* refers to the kinds of activities that fathers undertake with their children when they are present. These might include reading books, playing games, and watching television, among other activities.

A team of Swedish and Australian scholars searched academic journals published in several countries and several academic fields for studies about the effects of father engagement on child well-being.[42] In this meta-analysis, they identified 63 such studies, from which they selected 24 that were based on sequential observations of families and children over time. Sequential observations help researchers establish which is the cart and which is the horse among the factors being examined. Such cause-and-effect relationships are much more difficult to establish using surveys involving simultaneous observations of factors. For example, suppose we found that children with the worst report cards in the 4th grade had fathers who attended their child's 4th-grade parent-teacher conferences most frequently. Do we conclude that the father's presence reduced children's academic performance? Another possible conclusion is that children's poor performance during the 4th grade motivated fathers to monitor their child's performance in school more carefully throughout the year. It is hard to say which conclusion is correct. On one hand, if we knew which fathers attended their child's parent-teacher conferences in the 2nd grade, it would be much easier to establish a causal link between father involvement and children's academic performance in the 4th grade. After all, the first could cause the second, but not the other way around. This is the reason the European research team focused only on studies using sequential survey data. They also focused on studies using good measures of father involvement.

Several of the 24 studies reviewed by the European research team were based on a 51-year follow-up survey of people born in a particular week in 1958. With this survey, researchers can follow the physical, educational, and social development of a birth cohort throughout its life span. Researchers can also track the effects of parental involvement into a child's adult years. Regrettably, no such resource exists in the United States, although after 15 years, the Fragile Families and Child Well-Being Survey is an early deposit on such a resource.

In all, the European team analyzed the results of 14,000 data sets from three national longitudinal surveys in Israel, the United States, and Great Britain, and a small study on premature infants. Of 17 studies that controlled for income or other measures of socioeconomic status, all but one showed that father engagement positively affected child outcomes. The authors of this systematic review concluded that father's engagement has a positive effect on child behavior, school achievement, and overall child well-being. The review was drawn from a wide range of disciplines, across different countries, and broadly defined fathers to include social and biological fathers, as well as resident and nonresident fathers. Among the population of nonresident fathers, the study included those who were also economically vulnerable.

Although the review was quite general in concluding that various forms of engagement have positive effects on children, several of the British studies that focused on the outcomes of children over five years old consistently identified the benefits of reading to children and father engagement with children's education. This finding was echoed by a similarly comprehensive meta-analysis of 63 studies examining the well-being of children with nonresident fathers by US researchers Paul Amato and Joan Gilbreth. They found that children who had more contact with their nonresident fathers were not necessarily better off.[43] What fathers actually did when they were with their children was important. When nonresident fathers offered advice, monitored school performance, and helped with homework, their children fared better in terms of their academic success and well-being. These qualities were the most consistent predictors of children's outcomes—more consistent than contact and closeness. Students were most successful in school, in terms of their academic and behavioral performance, when their nonresident fathers were both in contact with them *and* were actively involved in their schools.

According to a study conducted by the US Department of Education, when nonresident fathers have some involvement in their children's schools, their children are more likely to get higher grades and to go further in school. They are also less likely to have ever repeated a grade, or to have been suspended or expelled.[44] School involvement can include attending a school meeting, a parent-teacher conference, or another school event. Similar results were found when fathers participated in Head Start, a program for low-income children. Temple University professor Jay Fagan and his colleague found that children of fathers who participated in a Head Start father involvement program were better prepared for school in general, and better prepared for math in particular, regardless of the father's residential status.[45] Despite these benefits, researchers from the Department of Education concluded that "the majority of nonresident fathers who maintained contact with their children were not involved in their children's schools."[46]

Jones and Mosher found similar results in their study of father engagement using the 2006–2010 National Survey of Family Growth.[47] Resident fathers of children under the age of five were six times more likely than nonresident fathers to have read to their children daily. Sixteen percent of resident fathers and 52 percent of nonresident fathers had not read to their young children at all in the four weeks prior to the survey. For fathers with children ages 5–18, 30 percent of resident fathers compared to 6 percent of nonresident fathers had helped their children with homework, or checked that their children had done their homework every day. Sixty-nine percent of nonresident fathers had not helped their children with homework at all in the four weeks prior to the survey. However, as we saw in Chapter 1, some nonresident fathers in the National Survey of Family Growth are economically vulnerable; others are not.

A recent study based on Fragile Family Survey data examined nonresident and resident father engagement in activities that might affect their children's schooling.[48] Again, most nonresident fathers in this survey were economically vulnerable. The study focused on father engagement with nine-year-old children in reading and other aspects of children's education, using the most recent and age-appropriate measures available. In the Fragile Families data, 2 of every 11 fathers were divorced or separated from the mothers of their children by the time their children were nine years old. The other fathers never married, although some cohabited with the mothers of their children when their children were younger. Although resident fathers were more available to their children than nonresident fathers, two of three nonresident fathers still maintained some contact with their nine-year-old children. Remember, however, that children did not benefit merely by having their fathers present. Instead, the benefits of father involvement depended upon how fathers and children engaged with one another when fathers were available.

In a study of low-income nonresident African American fathers, Northwestern University professor Tim Nelson and his colleagues also showed that "fathers who felt that they had not accomplished all that they had hoped during their own adolescence and adulthood looked to their children to fulfill those dreams" (p. 551).[49] However, Nelson and colleagues found that fathers did not always match their idealized images of fatherhood and failed to actually engage in their children's education in concrete or meaningful ways.

As we have seen, activities related to education have proven benefits even before children reach adulthood.[50] However, both nonresident and resident fathers spend less time engaged in activities related to their children's education than in other activities. Nonresident fathers spend even less time in activities related to education than resident fathers. For example, in the Fragile Families study, two out of five resident fathers attended more than one open house or back-to-school night at their child's school each year, but less than one out of eight nonresident fathers attended as many meetings during the year. A third of resident fathers attended parent-teacher conferences frequently, while only one out of nine nonresident fathers did so. Finally, roughly one-third of resident fathers had never attended their children's school events, while two-thirds of nonresident fathers were similarly disengaged. Nonresident fathers were also less engaged in reading to their children, checking or helping their children with homework, and other activities related to their children's education.[51]

In his book *Fatherless America*, David Blankenhorn, president of the Institute for American Values, is one of the most vocal proponents of the traditional family. He maligns nonresident fathers by saying "the end of co-residency in the rupture of the paternal alliance means nothing less than the collapse of paternal authority" (p. 157).[52] The studies just reviewed send a similar, if less inflammatory, message—namely, that nonresident fathers spend so little time engaged in the kinds of activities known to improve child well-being that it is hard to see how they could have any effect at all.

Some qualitative studies showed that fathers who were ill-equipped to fulfill the breadwinner role were re-writing fatherhood expectations and emphasizing other roles. The fathers we interviewed believed that more schooling would have placed them in a better position to support their children. This belief inspired them to emphasize the value of education to their children. However, it appears that as a group, vulnerable nonresident fathers are much less engaged in their children's education than resident fathers. The former may want to play an important role in their children's education, but compared with resident fathers, they do very little. This means that vulnerable nonresident fathers are probably doing little to close the widening gap between the academic achievement of their children, and the achievement of children in married families.[53] Because of their day-to-day struggles to make ends meet, which we saw in Chapter 2, nonresident fathers may not succeed as the "agents for change" that they wish to be. The next chapter will explore some of the challenges to father involvement, and Chapter 6 will explore policy ideas that can help

Dewight's Story

Dewight, is a White 27-year-old father who currently lives with his girlfriend and her younger sister in her mother's home. He has two children by two different mothers, a boy who is three and a six-year-old girl, neither of whom lives with him. Dewight has a very strained relationship with both mothers. The mother of his daughter was a woman Dewight knew as a teenager, and their time together was short lived. Mother and daughter now live about 45 miles away, but since Dewight does not have a driver's license, the distance is insurmountable. Dewight has a poor relationship with his son's mother; in fact, she has denied him access to his child until he is up to date on his support. Currently, his son lives with his grandmother, who successfully sued for custody. As a result, Dewight has seen his son a few times and has visited his daughter even less. Though he doesn't have a relationship with either child, that doesn't stop him from wanting one.

Dewight's own childhood had little stability and was spent "bouncing back and forth between parents," his mother in New York and his father in Arkansas. He attended school, at times in New York while at other times in Arkansas, though Dewight described himself as "being from the backwoods, in the middle of nowhere." Both parents were alcoholics, but his father was also a certified bomb expert. On his large, 120-acre property, Dewight and his father used to "blow stuff up". With friends, Dewight lived the country life, shooting guns, hunting, and riding dirt bikes. Dewight also "borrowed" cars from neighbors, never getting into any real trouble for his antics. However, similar behavior in New York led to his first arrest, where he was sent to a juvenile detention center at the age of 13.

As a teenager Dewight loved wrestling and boxing; however, his mother was opposed to letting him wrestle. Only by agreeing to maintain a good grade point average did she ultimately relent, allowing him to continue boxing in school. Dewight had his second interaction with law enforcement when he was arrested at the age of 15 or 16 for being a public nuisance, and was sent to a group home. While there, he severely injured another boy during a fight and was convicted of a felony assault and sentenced to 18 months in a juvenile facility.

The years after his release were difficult and frustrating. Dewight wanted to join the military and follow in his father's footsteps, but his felony conviction made that impossible. Despite these setbacks, Dewight enrolled in college, focusing on business administration, but remained only a few weeks. His penchant for violence once again interrupted his plans. At a party held at his home, one of the guests hit Dewight's girlfriend. Again, Dewight found himself unable to control his anger. After the ensuing fight, he was charged with second-degree assault. Though the charge was eventually dropped, he spent a short time in jail and was ordered to pay restitution of $900. Dewight found a part-time job to enable him to make restitution payments, but the combination of working and jail time made remaining in school more difficult, and he fell further behind in his classes. It was impossible to catch up, so Dewight quit school.

It was at this time that two life-changing events occurred. Dewight was involved in an accident, getting hit by a car. He was unable to work due to the injuries sustained from the accident. Then, his girlfriend became pregnant. With a second child on the way, money became a focus, and Dewight turned to the drug trade. Though he eventually found a job off the books in construction, he continued selling drugs, resulting in his girlfriend's addiction and ultimately the end of their relationship. Dewight quickly moved into another relationship while continuing to sell drugs but was arrested, convicted of a felony drug charge, and sent to prison for a year. When he was released in 2006 with a five-year probationary period, his record impacted his ability to find work, making things even more difficult. "So like, I come out and I'm all like, yeah, I'm gonna get a job, but I knew what I was in for. I'm gonna be labeled a felon. I know it's going to be hard for me to get a job."

Dewight persisted in his job search and finally located work at Little Caesar's. But he did not like the job. "I'm standing there holding this little sign, 'hi,' you know, I was like I'm not gonna do this uhhh, no more man, I can't do it." He quickly applied for a position at a Subway sandwich shop and was hired. Dewight and his girlfriend moved in together, and with the shared expenses, Dewight was able to catch up on his bills and restitution payments. He became current on his bills and began looking for a better paying job, eventually finding employment at a cleaning company. Dewight lost this job due to widespread layoffs. When the couple broke up, Dewight found himself homeless, at one point living in a tent. Throughout this period, Dewight and his girlfriend remained friendly. She gave him a place to sleep during bad weather, access to her kitchen and shower, and a place to wash his laundry. Eventually, the couple reconciled.

To supplement his minimum wage earnings, Dewight worked off the books, painting houses. He acknowledged that once you start to earn extra money through off-the-books work, it's very easy to get used to the additional income and much more difficult to go back. Off-the-books work generated the extra money to pay bills, to have a social life, to purchase things. Dewight also felt compelled to seek off-the-books work because he needed to stay current on his child support obligation. If he were to fall behind, he risked a warrant for his arrest for failure to pay support, resulting in a violation on his probation, putting him at risk for returning to prison. Dwight had to continually balance his child support obligations, his expenses at home with his girlfriend, and his earnings. Off-the-books work offered a way out of his dilemma. "I've painted houses and stuff like that, but then all the money went to child support. That's the only way I put it, you know what I mean like, cause if they—they put a warrant in child support plus a warrant out for my arrest, then I violate my—my felony probation. So I'm constantly struggling to keep the child support, you know what I mean, away from me."

In moments of reflection, Dwight believed that his unorthodox upbringing was the cause of many of the problems that still plague him. Neither parent ever taught him a work ethic or really any life lessons. Instead, he had to learn them on his own, often not successfully. His multiple prison sentences ended his military career before it began and severely limited employment prospects, creating a sense of frustration. "I turned into a hellion, who didn't care about anybody." Dwight was confined to low wage jobs and turned to the underground economy to augment his income. He didn't see any other way.

5 The Challenges of Nonresident Fatherhood

AS THE NUMBER of nonresident fathers has increased over time, so, too, has their involvement with their children. We know this from different studies, particularly the work of University of Pennsylvania sociologist Paul Amato, who has been following nonresident father involvement with children for decades. In a recent study, Amato and his colleagues used surveys of nonresident children born in three different periods. They found that more recent cohorts of nonresident fathers were more involved with their children than their predecessors.[1]

Besides this "cohort effect," involvement by nonresident fathers changes as their children age. Until recently, the prevailing view was that nonresident father-child contact typically declined as children got older. However, another study by Amato and his colleagues showed this not to be the case, after examining visitation patterns from four national surveys over a 12-year period, beginning with the year the fathers first became nonresident.[2] About a third of the fathers maintained a high and consistent level of involvement over the entire period. Another third were barely involved with their children in the beginning, and this pattern of low involvement remained stable over the 12-year period. Only about a quarter of nonresident fathers showed the expected pattern of high levels of father involvement in the beginning, and a decline over time. Finally, the remaining fathers, one out of every 13, barely saw the children at all in the beginning, but their involvement grew as the children got older.

Still, children with nonresident fathers have far less contact with their fathers than children with resident fathers. For example, when we looked at mothers' reports of nonresident father involvement in the Fragile Families and Well-Being Survey, most of whom were vulnerable by our definition, we found that two out of three nonresident fathers still had some contact with their nine-year-old children. But, they saw their children only seven days out of a typical month, mostly through overnight visits, while resident fathers saw their children every day. Only 11 percent of nonresident fathers spent time with their children every day, while 82 percent of resident fathers spent time with their children daily. Still, about one-fifth of nonresident fathers spent time with their children several days per week, and another fifth saw them several days per month.

One obvious reason for their lower level of involvement was that nonresident fathers did not live with their children. When a father lives with the mother, he sees his child daily, a fact about which sociologists have given much thought. Though some divorced fathers saw their children much more frequently than others, University of Pennsylvania sociologist Frank Furstenberg and his colleagues emphasized a general pattern of declining father's involvement with children following divorce. They argued that father involvement was a byproduct of the relationship between fathers and mothers, which could be more easily assessed by marital status or cohabitation.[3] More specifically, Furstenberg reasoned that a father's involvement with his child was a consequence of a "package deal." As long as the relationship between the parents remained intact, the father had maximum contact with his children. Once the father divorced and formed a new family, which might include stepchildren, he changed his allegiance from his first child(ren) to his new family, and over time, involvement with his first child(ren) declined.

As this suggests, explanations were heavily influenced by researchers' attempts to assess blame—or at least, motivations of fathers or mothers—that resulted in the observed pattern of visitation. In Furstenberg's version of the package deal, fathers were clearly to blame, as they swapped old families for new ones. The focus of early studies on divorced parents made it easy for researchers to blame fathers for the decline in visitation as children got older. Studies had shown that divorced men tended to remarry more frequently than divorced women.[4] What's more, using a snapshot of nonresident fathers with children of different ages, Furstenberg and a colleague showed that nonresident fathers with younger children from a previous marriage visited more frequently than nonresident fathers with older children from a previous marriage.[5]

A careful study by a team by sociologists from Bowling Green University and the University of Michigan re-examined the family-swapping claim. However, instead of a snapshot of fathers with children of different ages, they used a sample drawn from a nationally representative survey of men, including nonresident fathers, whose contact with their nonresident children could be measured at two points: after they broke up with their wives or cohabiting partners, and again after five years.[6] Like Amato above, Wendy Manning and Pamela Smock showed that visitation patterns of nonresident fathers varied widely. After the breakup, some rarely visited their children at all. Some saw their children more as they got older, and still others visited less. The declining pattern predicted by the package deal was dominant, but this was associated with neither remarriage alone, nor remarriage with stepchildren. Instead, it was the number of new children, especially new biological children that reduced a father's visits with their nonresident children. While some regarded this explanation as splitting hairs, it suggested that new responsibilities, rather than shifted loyalties, forced fathers to make tough choices about how they would spend their time. Divorced fathers also had to make difficult choices about how they spent their money, because a companion study by the same research team showed that the children born to men and their new wives also resulted in reduced child support payments to children from a previous marriage.[7]

As we shall see, this distinction may be very important for the kinds of policies we adopt for the growing number of nonresident fathers who have children in more than one household. Shifting loyalties may be the reason that fathers see their children from prior relationships less often. If so, government may want to insist that fathers maintain their obligations to previous children if they choose to form new families, especially if taxpayers have to pick up the tab. However, if fathers simply do not have the time or the means to support the children they have in old and new relationships, it may simply be infeasible to require them to do so, even if children born in old or in new relationships are shortchanged as a result.

Births to unmarried parents also fueled the growth in nonresident fatherhood, as we explored in the previous chapter. So, more recent explanations have adapted the package deal idea to accommodate visitation by unmarried nonresident fathers. Linda Laughlin at the Census Bureau and her colleagues pointed out that unmarried parents were likely to break up, re-partner, and have children by new partners more rapidly than married parents.[8] But, they argued, unmarried cohabiting fathers held less traditional values about gender roles than married fathers. Therefore, unmarried cohabiting fathers were more likely to be engaged in childrearing than married fathers, even after they ended the relationship with the mothers of their children. After examining visitation by formerly married fathers and cohabiting fathers, using data from the Fragile Families and Child Well-Being Study when children were three years old, Laughlin and her colleagues showed that formerly unmarried but cohabiting fathers visited their children more than divorced fathers.

Mother–Father Relationships: It's Not Just about Fathers and Children

Other studies that extended the package deal to unmarried fathers focused on nonresident fathers who never lived with the mothers of their children. Interestingly, in these studies the mother's role in the decline in visitation among nonresident fathers becomes prominent, providing insights about what many (divorced, formerly cohabiting, and formerly non-cohabiting) fathers claimed was the most important barrier they faced in their efforts to remain involved in the lives of their children.

Katherine Guzzo, a colleague and sometime collaborator of Furstenberg, argued that because never-resident fathers were much less likely to interact with their children than formerly married or cohabiting fathers, the former were much less secure about their abilities as parents.[9] The former also relied much more heavily than formerly resident fathers on mothers to teach them to hold, feed, and care for their children, and to reassure them about how important they were to their children. Unfortunately, Guzzo argued, unmarried mothers would stop coaching, reassuring, and providing other types of co-parenting support to these fathers after a breakup. As a result, never-resident fathers gradually disengaged from parenting after breaking up with the mothers of their children. What's more, if the mother formed a new romantic relationship or had children with other men, the never-resident father's identity and involvement declined even further. By contrast, Guzzo reasoned that the package deal placed a firm foundation under the fathering identity of married and cohabiting fathers. When these fathers broke up with the mothers of their children, they switched their allegiance to new children, much as Furstenberg predicted. Though involvement with their children would fall as a result, it would not drop as drastically or rapidly as involvement between children and never-resident fathers.

Harvard University sociologist Katheryn Edin and her colleagues reasoned that visitation by unmarried nonresident fathers declined as children got older because the child's age coincided with how long it had been since the unmarried parents stop living together.[10] Though never as influential as Furstenberg's idea of swapping families, this simple explanation had also been used to account for the decline in visitation by divorced fathers. For example, Judith Seltzer and Suzanne Bianchi at the University of Wisconsin reasoned that "[t]he amount of time biological parents and children have been separated is a proxy for the number of opportunities they have had to encounter obstacles to continued contact. The longer their separation, the fewer common experiences they share and more likely parents are to have remarried, had additional children, or moved to a new geographical region" (p. 655).[11] Taking account of the time since the couple was last living together or were romantically involved might, therefore, diminish the relationship between the child's age and the frequency of nonresident father visitation. Further, they reasoned that after forming new romantic relationships, or having children with another man, a mother would actively try to reduce involvement by the father of her child. She would do this in the hope of recreating an ideal family (i.e., a new package deal), when the new man in their life would become a surrogate father to her children from a previous relationship. This would be easier, we reasoned, if the father of her children was out of the picture. Therefore, unmarried mothers would use a variety of "gatekeeping" strategies to discourage visitation by nonresident fathers.

Generally, studies based on the Fragile Families and Child Well-Being Survey, which includes mostly vulnerable fathers, found support for these new ideas about the package deal and visitation by unmarried nonresident fathers, including new evidence about the mother's role. Edin and her colleagues, who examined visitation trends until children were five years old, showed that nonresident father visitation fell steadily as time passed since the unmarried parents had been romantically involved, and after taking account of this, the child's age was no longer associated with nonresident father visitation. They also showed that re-partnering and new children by the mother and father further reduced visitation by nonresident fathers. Guzzo showed that if the mothers of their children formed unstable relationships with new romantic partners, nonresident fathers were more likely to visit their children less when children were three years old than they visited their children at 12 months old. If the mothers of their children formed stable relationships with new romantic partners, nonresident fathers were much more likely to have reduced the amount of contact with their children between the ages of one and three years, and were much less likely to have seen their children at all. Generally, the reduction in father-child contact was greater when the new romantic partnership was a cohabiting one. Fathers were also less likely to have seen their nonresident children at all if they were living with a new romantic partner by the time their nonresident children were three years old. So, both fathers and mothers were to blame for the decline in nonresident father visitation.

In the spirit of Furstenberg's package deal, all of these studies of nonresident father visitation focused on involvement of nonresident fathers after parents broke up. But what about involvement of nonresident fathers who were still romantically involved, but not cohabiting with, the mothers of their children? A research team from Princeton University and Columbia University noted that it was quite common for unmarried, romantically involved, African American parents to have children even though they did not live together, while unmarried

White parents were much more likely than their African American counterparts to have children while cohabiting.[12] Therefore, in studies that focused only on what happens after parents broke up, some visitation by romantically involved nonresident fathers might be "hiding in plain sight." So, they updated the previous study by Edin and her colleagues, and added visitation by nonresident fathers who were still romantically involved with the mothers of their children. We found that a nonresident father who was still romantically involved with the mother of his child saw his child almost as much as an unmarried father who lived with the mother and child.

Thus, there is no shortage of evidence that the romantic relationships between mothers and fathers are key determinants of nonresident fathers' involvement with children, whether or not the fathers ever married or lived with the mothers of their children. But what about the co-parenting relationships that nonresident fathers maintained with the mothers of their children when they were no longer romantically involved?

Co-Parenting: After the Love Is Gone

Co-parenting, defined as how effectively parents work together to raise their children, has been of particular interest to sociologists and social workers concerned about child well-being. One such team of sociologists at the University of Notre Dame and Pennsylvania State University examined co-parental relationships and nonresident father involvement with their teenaged children, using a nationally representative sample of mostly divorced parents.[13] They found that nonresident fathers who maintained positive co-parenting relationships with the mothers of their children visited their teenaged children more frequently than nonresident fathers who were unable to maintain such relationships. Furthermore, higher levels of visitation probably also made them more responsive fathers and improved their relationships with their children.

Another team of sociologists and social workers at Princeton University and Columbia University considered co-parenting and involvement of unmarried nonresident fathers.[14] Using data on vulnerable nonresident fathers from the Fragile Families and Child Well-Being Survey, they found that nonresident fathers who received more positive co-parenting support were more likely to have some contact with their preschool-aged children than nonresident fathers who received less positive support. What's more, among nonresident fathers with some contact, the frequency of visitation was also higher for those who received more co-parenting support from the mothers of their children.

Finally, a team at Temple University and the University of Delaware studied co-parenting and father involvement among resident and nonresident fathers, some of whom were in romantic relationships with the mothers of their pre-school children.[15] They found that nonresident fathers who received positive co-parenting support from the mothers of their children were more likely to be engaged with their preschool children. Further, co-parenting support and father engagement were more strongly related for nonresident fathers who were *no longer* romantically involved with the mothers of their children. There was no difference between the importance of co-parenting support for romantically involved fathers who resided with the mothers of their children and those who did not.

GATEKEEPING : "YOU SHOULDN'T USE THE CHILD AS YOUR WAY TO GET BACK AT ME"

When one parent has primary custody of a child, that parent necessarily plays a large role in determining the other parent's access to the child. This phenomenon is so widely recognized that the term "gatekeeper syndrome" was coined to describe it.[16] In fact, the quality of the relationship between the father and mother is one of the primary factors impacting nonresident fathers' level of involvement with their children.

Among the fathers we interviewed, co-parenting relationship quality ran along a continuum. When the quality of the relationship and parents' capacity for co-parenting were high, fathers felt comfortable visiting their children at almost any time, and their level of involvement was high. When the quality of the co-parenting relationship was poor, whether the parents were simply "not meant for each other," or whether other factors such as new partners created tension, the gatekeeper had less motivation to provide access to the child. Some nonresident fathers in this situation felt they had to limit contact with their children to avoid conflict with their children's mothers, or they felt that mothers deliberately denied visitation, leaving them struggling to maintain a relationship with their children. Others fathers remained involved in the lives of their children within the limitations created by mothers or unobstructed by mothers. These fathers often remained involved through what Waller and Swisher called parallel parenting.[17] Here fathers established and maintained separate relationships with their children, but did not attempt to coordinate their parenting efforts with mothers. This occurred through extended visits with their children during the summer, or more frequent visits in the father's place of residence, or in the home of the paternal grandmother.

Sometimes, relationships simply don't work out. For example, Kevin, whom we profile in the Appendix, felt as though he made a great deal of sacrifices that his ex-wife never appreciated. He thought "we both had a plan together," but then discovered that she did not want to be a part of the plan. They experienced financial difficulties, ultimately leading to bankruptcy, and he felt as though he was unfairly asked to shoulder the burden of their debt. Kevin was also frustrated because he thought that they had agreed not to involve the courts over child support and visitation, but instead the courts did become involved. Summarizing his sentiments about the current status of their relationship, Kevin emphasized that he and his ex-wife were "not meant for each other" and that he no longer respected or trusted her.

> I'm not saying his mother is a bad person, I'm just saying his mother and I, we're just not meant for each other is what I realized.... I won't teach my son to disrespect his mother or anybody else. But I have no respect for her number one and I, don't trust her you know?

Although he will not speak negatively of his ex-wife to his son, interactions between Kevin and his ex-wife are tense, particularly regarding their son. For example, Kevin related a detailed anecdote of a time when his ex-wife had agreed to drive their son down from upstate New York to visit, but then canceled at the last minute. He interpreted her abrupt cancellation as a deliberate attempt to make his life difficult, as he then had to make the drive on short notice after a long day of work. Along a co-parenting relationship quality scale, Kevin's relationship with his ex-wife would fall somewhere in the middle. The relationship ended, they separated and were getting a divorce. Interactions were stressful and they both harbored some negative views of each other. Nevertheless, they worked out a formal visitation system, albeit less frequently than Kevin would like, and were able to act civilly toward one other.

In contrast, Antonio's relationships with the mothers of his two children, which are detailed at the end of Chapter 6, would fall on polar opposite ends of a co-parenting relationship quality scale. Antonio has maintained an agreeable co-parenting relationship with his daughter's mother, and as a result, her mother was willing to allow their daughter to visit him. On the other hand, his son's mother "has a lot of pent up anger" toward him, that he believes she takes out through controlling access to their son. "You hurt me, I'm going to hurt you—I'm going to use your son against you." Before he established visitation, she would let him see their son at some times, but then at other times would make him wait for months for a visit. He understood that she was upset, but did not agree with her behavior. "You know, I've made a lot of mistakes, but I think that you shouldn't use the child as your way to get back at me. If you have something to say, you know, say it to me."

Re-partnering and Multipartner Fertility: Competing Responsibilities

As shown by more recent studies of visitation trajectories over time, re-partnering by mothers and fathers reduces father involvement with and without new children.[18] This is probably because re-partnering and multipartner fertility create competing priorities in ways that lead to co-parenting problems and gatekeeping. Multipartner fertility was the most common family structure among the fathers we interviewed, with 23 out of 43 fathers, or 53 percent, having children with more than one mother. Of those 23, 11 currently had partners (48 percent), and of the 11 with partners, 8 had a child with their current partner (73 percent).

For example, Claudio, whom we profile in the Appendix, had hoped to "work things out" with his sons' mother, but then she married his best friend. Navigating such complex relationships proved difficult for all involved. Claudio wanted to be involved in his sons' lives, but their mother's new husband did not even want him talking on the phone with them. One can only imagine how difficult it was for Claudio to accept being told not to speak to his own children, particularly by someone who was formerly his best friend. "For a while her boyfriend got real jealous, and he didn't want us talking, and he felt the kids were relaying messages to her so, it was hard for me to have somebody tell me I couldn't speak to my kids, you know? He got attitude problem, he said he was gonna fight with me, like it got very abusive, verbally."

As a result of the conflict with the new partner, Claudio initially lost touch with his sons for some time. However, more recently he has been able to institute a system of regular phone calls.

As opposed to the direct confrontations that Claudio experienced, Kelly, whom we profiled at the end of Chapter 2, perceived more indirect effects. The father of a nine-year-old girl, Kelly felt that her mother's current boyfriend had been trying to influence the family. According to Kelly, her mother has had "a few" boyfriends since their daughter was born. Two of the boyfriends had a significant impact, not only on Kelly's relationship with his daughter's mother, but also on his access to his daughter. He states that he and his daughter's mother "got along" until she acquired a new boyfriend when their daughter was two years old. From Kelly's perspective, the new boyfriend did not want her to maintain a relationship with him, and so encouraged her to take him to court and formalize their informal child support arrangement. Before the court order, she and Kelly communicated openly about their daughter's needs—financial support seemed like a team effort. The court order ended their collaboration, and turned financial support into an antagonistic issue.

Her mother and I, when she was born, had always gotten along. And when [daughter's name] turned about two, she started dating a guy who decided that it wasn't good for us to get along, and that we needed to have everything on paper, and we should go through the courts, and basically talked her into, you know, doing everything as far as through the courts. At first, uh, there was no official child support order or anything. Just we would talk about what her needs were, you know, whatever, and we actually sat down and figured out the cost of things like formula, food, yada yada, and I would just help her with those things.

Turning child support into a court issue also turned visitation into a court issue. Although the mother of Kelly's daughter no longer dates the boyfriend who encouraged her to initiate the court order, she now lives with a different boyfriend who Kelly believes encouraged her to reduce his visitation. Before this relationship, Kelly saw his daughter two days a week after school—the school bus would drop her off at his house. Now he only sees her every other weekend. He believes that her mother filed a petition to reduce his visitation because her new boyfriend wanted her to do so. "And that's when her mom had it [visitation] changed through the courts that that didn't happen anymore, so [So she changed the visitation, or—] Yeah, for a guy. He didn't like it. [He thought—he thought you were seeing her too much?] Too much, yeah."

The influence of new boyfriends and the involvement of the courts caused Kelly's relationship with his daughter's mother to deteriorate from one in which they were "getting along", to one in which they barely seemed able to work together. Kelly identified the hardest part of being a father as depending on "someone who is unwilling to work with you" for access to his daughter. Furthermore, he felt as though the courts had no interest in protecting his right to visitation, thereby enabling her to use their daughter "to manipulate me and to make things harder." At one point, he claimed that she prohibited him from seeing their daughter for four months. Even though he took her to court for violating visitation, the court did not impose any penalties or attempt to enforce visitation.

It doesn't matter how hard you try. If you have a kid with someone who is unwilling to work with you, or who wants to drag you to court every year for—to change one word on a visitation or whatever, that can happen. There's nothing in the courts that says that she can't. And actually I've—I— she kept my daughter from me for a while. It was like a four-month period that she just wasn't letting me have my visitation, and she wasn't returning my phone calls. I would show up and nobody would be there. So I violated her, and—through the courts or whatever, and they didn't—nothing happened to her. They just—we came into court and they said, "hey, there's an order, make sure that's what you're doing," and that was the end of it. So there was no repercussion for her whatsoever. And that, I don't know, at least in my situation, it gives her the ability to think that she's God as far as, you know, using my daughter to manipulate me and to make things harder. And it shouldn't be that. It should just be about raising a kid.

In Kelly's situation, the courts placed stress on a relationship already being strained by the introduction of new romantic partners, deepening Kelly's frustration with both the courts and with his daughter's mother, and ultimately leading to fewer visits with his daughter.

Domestic Violence: The Deal Breaker

Nationally, the incidence of intimate partner violence for women in marital or cohabiting relationships across the general population is approximately 20 percent.[19] After Claudio, who is profiled in the Appendix, had lost his girlfriend and sons to his former best friend, he felt isolated and angry. His former girlfriend had asked Claudio to relinquish his parental rights as a father and later had involved the family court system. Though this made Claudio upset, since he believed he was doing the best he could for his sons, he could understand her reasoning. During one very emotional moment, Claudio had threatened her.

> ...She needed to feel safeguarded cause I did, you know, threaten her one time and I was upset, uh, I was very emotional and I did threaten her and, um, you know. She took somebody's advice and she involved us in the, um, family court system so there could be some type of, you know, record, um, and, um, you know, for those purposes....

Ronald, also profiled in the Appendix, had been involved in a fight with his girlfriend as a teenager. He had been dating another woman secretly and she found out. When the fight between them escalated and he tried to leave in his truck, she put her hand in the way so he could not close the door. He pushed her hand away to shut the door and left. She later contacted the police and told them he threw her to the ground, though Ronald claimed it didn't happen.

...I was like 18 the next time I got in trouble and that was, that was just for arguing with one of my girlfriends, found out about another woman, whatever. She came at my truck, I couldn't get my door shut, she tried to put her hand in the way so I pushed her back, shut the door, and left. She told the police I threw her down, nah, that don't happen.

Domestic violence is not limited to male perpetrators. Sometimes, the abuser can be a woman. Ronald's wife has a history of mental illness and has been abusive, both to her husband and to their three children. In one incident, Ronald left his wife and children when her anger escalated, and he phoned the police and child protective services to report the situation at his home. As a former convicted felon, he did not want to be present when police arrived. He later discovered that all three children had been removed and placed in foster care. As a result, both Ronald and his wife must now complete substance abuse classes, parenting classes, and anger management. The event spurred changes for both parents. Ronald has done a lot of "soul searching" and maturing, and feels he has come a long way in the months preceding the event. His wife has received additional help, improving her mental health issues and anger problems.

Waller and Swisher found that domestic violence was usually a deal breaker. Mothers who were victims of domestic violence broke up with the fathers of their children. To keep themselves and their children safe from fathers who wanted to maintain contact, they obtained restraining orders, or required that fathers visit their children in the homes of relatives, especially the maternal or paternal grandmother.

Distance and Limited Visitation: "Our Time is Not as Much as I Would Like"

Besides strained co-parenting or barely functioning parallel parenting relationships with their children's mothers, vulnerable nonresident fathers faced additional barriers of time and distance that undermined their hopes of being involved with their children. However, this did not imply that their children were not a priority, or that the fathers were uninvolved. Instead, the fathers were not achieving their family and fatherhood goals, and therefore experienced disappointment over their level of involvement with their children. Nonetheless, many were deeply committed to being as active a presence in their children's lives as possible, given their situations.

Not living together in and of itself becomes a challenge to involvement by imposing a physical barrier between fathers and their children, whether the distance is a two-hour commute on public transportation across town, or 1,000 miles across the country. This physical distance often dictates how frequently fathers are able to see their children. The greater the distance between fathers and their children, the more prohibitive the time and expense associated with visits become. This is particularly true for fathers whose children live out of state.

The importance of distance as a barrier to visitation has a long track record. Older studies that relied on court-based samples of divorced fathers repeatedly observed the importance of distance. For example, a team of University of Wisconsin sociologists analyzed data from a small random telephone survey of divorced parents from their home state, and found that fathers who lived in the state were more likely to visit their children than fathers who lived out of state.[20] A similar study of divorced fathers in two Virginia counties by Arditti and Keith found that "distance from their children had a strong negative affect on the frequency of visitation" (p. 706).[21] Using mother reports from a much larger, nationally representative survey, Linda Stevens of the University of Washington found that divorced fathers who lived further away from their children were less likely to either see or have telephone conversations with their children.[22] Using reports of divorced and never married nonresident fathers in a more recent wave of the same survey, Cooksey and Craig found that the further away nonresident fathers lived from their children, the less likely they were to frequently see their children, or to speak with their children by telephone.[23] Studies focusing exclusively on unmarried fathers provided little evidence of the importance of distance for nonresident father visitation. However, in a qualitative study of low-income, unmarried, African American fathers, Jennifer Hamer found that fathers who saw their children rarely, if at all, reported that "physical distance from the children was a primary hindrance to their fathering" (p. 124).[24]

Ernest, who we profiled at the end of Chapter 3, has not seen his 11-year-old daughter and 7-year-old son in three weeks. Part of the reason he has not seen them more recently is the amount of time it takes to make the visit. He hopes to find an apartment closer to where his children live once he finds a job, so that he will be able to visit them more frequently. "I'll move a little closer... so that the trip to see my kids isn't too great. Right now, I have to travel for four-and-a-half hours on public transportation when I go see them..."

Antonio, who has been profiled at the end of Chapter 6, is a 32-year-old father of an 11-year-old daughter who lives in Pennsylvania, and a 7-year-old son who lives in New York City. He married his daughter's mother when he was only 17 years old, and they remained married for seven years. Antonio lived with his daughter for the first four years of her life, but then did not see her at all for six years. He has since reunited with his daughter, but because she lives in Pennsylvania, he only sees her during school vacations, although she has stayed with him for up to a month at a time during the summer. Antonio never married his son's mother, but lived with his son for the first two years of his life. After those first two years, he did not see his son for three years. He has also reunited with his son, whom he currently sees every Saturday.

Even when distance is not an issue, court-ordered visitation requirements may restrict the amount of time nonresident fathers are allowed to spend with their children, with some orders set as low as six hours a week, or one day every other week. If the father wants more than the standard custody and visitation order, and the mother objects, he must pay for additional legal consultation to get it. Joint custody is one such possibility; however, the potential legal fees may present a barrier for vulnerable fathers. Joint custody may refer to either shared legal custody, or physical custody. Shared legal custody specifies the rights of both parents to make legal decisions on behalf of the child, regardless of where the child resides. Shared physical custody refers to the residence and care of the child, to be shared equally or unequally between the parents.[25] Unequally shared custody allows for increased visitation for the parent who does not have primary custody, which can vary from little more than traditional visitation to just less than equal time for each parent.[26] Equally shared custody, on the other hand, shares time equally between both the parents. Regardless of whether custody is equal or unequal, shared physical custody implies that the child lives in two residences, something that may not be feasible for working-poor fathers. Among the Wisconsin divorces studied by Maria Cancian and Daniel Meyer, shared physical custody was more likely among higher income parents. Furthermore, many of vulnerable fathers we interviewed were doubling-up with relatives or (present or former) girlfriends, at least until they found better paying regular jobs.[27] Vulnerable nonresident fathers, who may be limited to the more traditional custody options, feel pressure to accomplish all that they would like to do with their children in the limited time they have. Antonio, who sees his son every Saturday, but only for the day, finds the limited time he has with his son challenging. "Yeah, since our time is not as much as I would like, I try to fit as much as I can into those 6, 10, 12 hours that I have with him."

Fathers who previously lived with their children, as Antonio did, cannot help but contrast the comparatively brief contact they now have with the constant involvement they formerly had and feel disappointment.

Fathers who have only ever known their children through visitation may experience a different kind of disappointment, recognizing that they cannot have the same relationship with their children through visitation as they would through living together as a family. Never having lived with his daughter, Kelly now finds it challenging to develop and maintain a relationship with her within the confines of his weekend visitation. "It's—it's hard because it's hard to form a personal relationship with someone in a two-and-a-half-day weekend real quick." In addition, when he does see her, he is always conscious of the brevity of their time together, and makes concerted efforts to keep busy. "And when I do see her, I guess, because, you know, I haven't seen her already in two weeks, um, just try and keep busy. We play outside. She has a large sandbox and swing set and a big pool, and just kid stuff."

Personal Battles: Substance Abuse, Incarceration and Street Life

In addition to the separation imposed by physical distance and low visitation orders, fathers also identify their own personal struggles, particularly with domestic violence, incarceration, substance abuse, and street life, as factors that make it difficult for them to establish or sustain contact with their children. A few recent studies have shown how much these personal challenges matter for father involvement. One of the most important was undertaken by Cornell University sociologists Maureen Waller and Raymond Swisher, who used the Fragile Families and Child Well-Being Survey to examine how the personal challenges of nonresident *and* resident fathers affected their relationships with the mothers of their children, and their involvement with their children. Almost half of the fathers in their study had at least one of the following personal challenges: had an episode of violence involving the mother of their child, had struggled with drug or alcohol abuse, or had spent some time in prison or jail. Just over 3 of 10 of the fathers in their sample suffered from just one these issues. About 13.2 percent of the fathers in the Swisher and Waller study suffered from two of these issues. Finally, about four percent of fathers in the Swisher and Waller study had all three problems.

Despite their use of strategies, which Waller and Swisher refer to as protective gatekeeping, mothers usually allowed fathers with personal challenges to have some contact with their children. Fathers responded differently to mothers' protective gatekeeping strategies. Some simply did not follow through on the restricted opportunities the mothers provided for them to see their children.

Others responded to a mother's attempt to restrict access, particularly after a breakup, by simply walking away from the mother and child.

SUBSTANCE ABUSE: "LIVING IN AN UNDERGROUND TOMB"

According to Waller and Swisher, substance abuse reduced the prospects that fathers saw their children in the past month. This also occurred among the fathers we interviewed. For example, after a difficult life growing up without either biological parent, Antonio, whom we discussed earlier, found himself turning to the same coping mechanisms used by those around him—alcohol and drugs.

> You know, my—my own personal issues, you know, still dealing with a lot of the things of the past—my abandonment issues, XYZ. Uh, it–it–it flooded over so to speak into my personal life—into my personal relationships. All of these things, and the only way I knew how to cope was through what I'd always seen—addiction, alcoholism, drug use.

After his marriage with his daughter's mother ended, his son was born out of wedlock, during the height of his addiction. In large part due to his addiction, the relationship with his son's mother did not work out either, and they separated when their son was around age two. After the separation, he distanced himself from her and from their son, as well as from his daughter, for quite a number of years. "Unfortunately, I abandoned my children too due to my addiction. Ultimately that's what happened—both of my children. You know, and, uh, but although I was gone out of my daughter's life, I hadn't seen my daughter—the last time I had seen my daughter, she was four years old. And I'd seen her again for the first time six years later. . . ."

Antonio describes the years when he was lost to addiction and out of his children's lives as "living like in an underground tomb, you know, the walking dead so to speak."

Many fathers in Waller and Swisher's study responded to the concerns that their substance abuse raised for mothers by attempting to get help for their problem. Interestingly, Caldwell and her colleagues developed an intervention, called Fathers and Sons, which attempted to engage nonresident fathers in the lives of children with the mother's support and permission.[28] They noted that a byproduct of the intervention was the father's increased awareness of the debilitating effects of substance abuse on their children, which resulted in an increased effort by fathers to get help with their substance abuse problems.

When fathers had substance abuse problems, they sought treatment. Often mothers arranged for supervised visitation or made other arrangements if they believed that substance abuse made fathers poor or untrustworthy parents. For example, Ernest was receiving substance abuse treatment while living in transitional housing. Despite their divorce, Ernest's wife allowed him to stay over in her home, so that he can maintain a close relationship with his children. Antonio became a substance abuse counselor, after undergoing treatments for his own substance abuse problems. After his recovery, he has been working to rebuild his relationships with his children. In this effort, Antonio has received support from his daughter's mother; however, the road to recovery for his son's mother has been more uncertain.

INCARCERATION: FORGOTTEN AND ABANDONED

Incarceration was the most common challenge among the fathers in Waller and Swisher's study. This was not surprising because almost half of the fathers in the overall Fragile Families and Child Well-Being Survey had been in prison or jail by the time their child was five years old.[29] Our own estimates show that by the time their child was nine years old this proportion had risen to 60 percent.[30]

Recall from Chapter 1 that nearly all the chronically unemployed fathers we interviewed had felony convictions. For example, the timing of Claudio's descent into addiction, which we detail in the Appendix, corresponds with the beginning of his spells of incarceration, which continued off and on for most of his twenties. Claudio's attempts to reestablish a relationship with his sons' mother after his first incarceration were halted by his re-incarceration. She did not keep in touch with him while he was incarcerated, and rarely brought their sons to visit, causing Claudio to feel "forgotten" and "abandoned."

> Well, that's the whole thing, uh, I would see them like briefly once in awhile until me and the mother—cause when I came out of prison me and the mother, uh, we were in talks—this was in 2001 and, um, we, we're trying to like reestablish, you know, some type of relationship but during my incarceration she never wrote me, probably wrote me twice, brought my kids maybe twice to see me prior to, you know, 2002. So, you know, I felt like I was forgotten, like I was abandoned and I held resentment against her....

Now, Claudio is in some ways just as abandoned out of jail as he was in it. Due to parole restrictions that prohibit him from leaving the state, he cannot even visit his sons: "It's outta my control. I mean they're in Florida, I'm out here I'm on parole. It's not like I can just go out there, you understand? It's outta my jurisdiction. So I can't do nothing about it anyway so I just like kinda leave it in God's hands."

The combination of parole restrictions and his sons' mother unwillingness to bring or send the boys to visit now leaves Claudio feeling fatalistic about his opportunity for direct contact with his sons.

Similarly, Waller and Swisher found that nonresident fathers who never went to prison or jail were much more likely to see their children than nonresident fathers who had spent some time in prison or jail after their child's birth, and more likely to see their children than fathers who had been in prison or jail before the birth of their child. Among resident and nonresident fathers, those who had been incarcerated after the birth of their child also spent fewer days in the child-related activities we reviewed in Chapter 4, such as playing, providing direct care, and showing affection, among other activities. Interestingly, alcohol and substance abuse did not appear to reduce the amount of time fathers spent in these types of activities with their children.

Because incarceration was so common, Waller and Swisher speculated that it presented a different kind of barrier to father involvement. Mothers were less concerned about their (or their child's) safety, and the competence or trustworthiness of incarcerated fathers. Instead, the physical distance and logistical and other obstacles associated with prisons and jails made visitation difficult. Incarceration, which often comes along with substance abuse problems, was a common challenge among the fathers we interviewed.

In the long run, however, incarceration fractured package deals between resident fathers and the mothers of their children. Afterward, barriers to father involvement by incarcerated fathers were mainly logistical. Another study, by Yale University sociologists Turney and Wilderman, claimed that upon close examination, incarceration was a barrier to father involvement only among fathers who formerly lived with the mothers of their children.[31] They found that the effects of incarceration on involvement by fathers who never lived with their children disappeared once they accounted for other personal problems, such as substance abuse, impulsive behavior, and other similar behaviors, which were also linked to incarceration. We suspect this conclusion may have gone too far.

Waller and Swisher showed that the physical distance or logistical obstacles created by incarceration did hinder mothers and fathers from executing the parallel or co-parenting strategies they might otherwise have undertaken with fathers, whether or not they ever resided with their children. For example, to see their children, currently incarcerated fathers relied heavily upon the co-parenting support of their children's mothers. If she did not take the child to prison or jail, direct contact with a father in prison was impossible. However, few mothers were willing to take their children to prisons, because the experience was traumatic for both the father and the child. If she did not permit the child to receive the fathers' letters, or accept his collect calls, indirect contact with the child was also impossible. While most prisons allow fathers to call their family members collect, the costs of such calls were extremely high and were paid by mothers.[32] In the face of these obstacles, many incarcerated fathers gradually withdrew from their children. Re-establishing contact after release was also difficult and equally dependent upon the mothers' co-parenting support.

Interestingly, in a follow-up study, the Cornell University team reasoned that incarceration would be less of a barrier for visitation by Black and Latino, than for White nonresident fathers, because these race and ethnic groups attached different meaning to incarceration.[33] Knowing that Black and Latino men are the primary targets of mass incarceration policies, they reasoned that Black and Latino mothers would interpret the incarceration as evidence of victimization of their communities by a hostile legal system. By contrast, White mothers whose partners, male neighbors, and family members are much less likely to be incarcerated, would interpret incarceration as a sanction of the fathers' illegal behavior, which might place the mother and her child at risk. Consistent with this thinking, they found that past incarceration reduced contact between White nonresident fathers and children much more than past incarceration reduced contact between Black and Latino nonresident fathers and their children. Moreover, incarceration was strongly associated with mothers' distrust of White fathers, whereas Black and Latino mothers were no less likely to trust fathers with a history of imprisonment.

STREET LIFE: GETTING CAUGHT UP IN THE GAME

In addition to substance abuse problems, being on the streets or hanging out with friends who participated in a variety of undesirable activities, perhaps while using harmful substances, was also a concern for mothers. In some cases, fathers' turnaround strategies also involved breaking ties with the streets and with associates who might place the father and their children at risk. Unfortunately for Kevin, the lesson came too late.

Unlike Claudio, Kevin had never been to jail. However, his prior involvement with street life was so great that it proved just as destructive a force as incarceration in pulling him away from his children. Kevin was so consumed by "hustling and getting caught up in the game" as a young man that he was largely absent from his older, now adult, children's lives while they were growing up. Later in his life, after he had abandoned the game, he attempted to reach out to his children. He had to learn to accept the fact that it was too late, and that they no longer desired an active relationship.

> When I was growing up um, I fell off the track. As far as hustling and getting caught up in the game as they say. I've never been to jail, but it brought distance between us [Kevin and his older children] you know what I'm saying? And I was the kind of individual who believes in honesty so when I turned around and told the older kids, cuz they were old enough to understand exactly what happened, they had a choice. They could be bothered or not.

Although Kevin has some contact with his older children now and knows where they are and what they are doing, they are not close.

That Empty Loneliness Feeling

Regardless of how frequently they saw their children or what type of barriers stood between them, nearly all of the fathers we interviewed wished they were more involved with their children and were disappointed that they were not. Fathers who previously lived with their children and had the experience of constant daily involvement felt this disappointment even more keenly.

Kevin states that the hardest part of being a father is "being separated from him." He contrasts the previous experience of living with his son, and his own parents' experience raising him, with his current situation, expressing a deep sense of loss.

> Not seeing him around me like when I get off of work and stuff like that. Having him with me on the weekends and then watching him go to his mother's, you know what I'm saying? I get that empty, loneliness feeling. Look, my motto was, I'll deal with all the bullshit in the world, everything. My mom and dad did it, you know what I'm saying, to raise us. But at the end of the day they got to see us. When I used to come home from work, my son would, dad's home, and when I turned the key he was like, dad let's wrestle. It just left all that other stuff outside, you know what I'm saying? Regardless of what was going on in the house but, so that's the **hardest** thing. Not being around him as much, you now what I'm saying?

Claudio struggles with not being the father he wants to be. He states that the hardest part of being a father is "wanting to be there for them and not being able to." When asked what he would like to change about himself, he replied simply: "Honestly the only thing I would like to do is just see my kids." Claudio had a clear vision of his ideal family life, including kids, "the picket fence," and a stable job to support a family, but now fears he will never be able to obtain it.

Antonio hopes for increased visitation with his son, including overnight visits, and has a court date for visitation scheduled in a couple of months. He and his present wife, who also has children from a previous relationship, wish one day to live together with all of their children.

> The divorce rates are pretty high amongst Hispanic families. A typical family isn't mother, father and son anymore. It's mother and son, or just the single father and a son and a daughter, um, so we're trying to break that as far as our family's concerned. We're sort of like your Brady Bunch so to speak now. You know, two different people, we both have our own kids—but little by little we're trying to bring them all together. You know, all the children want to come live with us.

However, their current situation will not allow them to create the Brady Bunch family they desire.

As we saw, however, more than half of the fathers we interviewed had children by more than one mother. As we saw in Chapter 2, more than 40 percent of vulnerable nonresident fathers also have resident children with a new partner, or are the surrogate fathers for their partner's children. Finally, in the Fragile Families and Child Well-Being Study, between 25 and 33 percent of fathers had children by more than one partner.[34] Could this mean that fathers are resolving their disappointments about the older children with whom they have inadequate contact by having new children in new relationships?

The Father Merry-Go-Round

When Kevin's girlfriend became pregnant 20 years after his first child was born, he viewed it as an opportunity to become the father for his new child that he wished he could have been for his older children. He married his girlfriend in an effort to "make a family out of it."

> I don't have much contact with my older children, but um, um, with my young one now before he came into the world. . . . I was going to make a

family out of it. I was going to give it my best shot. I was going to be a stand up guy....Now come on. I got a baby coming 20 years later.

Ultimately, Kevin's effort to "make a family out of it" failed and he separated from his wife. This was not surprising. As Paul Amato from Pennsylvania State University has noted, "Second (and higher order) marriages, however, have an even greater likelihood of dissolution than first marriages" (p. 1269).[35] Kevin, however, was still determined to have a second chance to experience a close relationship with his child, even as a nonresident father. Remorse for his earlier lack of involvement compelled him "to be there" for his younger son. He did not want his young son to experience what his older children did.

I need to be there for my son. That's all it is. I just need to be there for my son....I don't ever want nobody to turn around and say well I did this! No one will ever have that, no one will ever have that over me, my two prior children, they went through that you know what I'm saying. They can say that because I take no credit for them.

For many of the fathers, the experience of having grown up without an involved father themselves enhanced the importance of family and fatherhood. These fathers desired to provide for their own children what their own fathers failed to provide. Claudio grew up in Brooklyn with his mother and two siblings. He described himself as a child as "ignorant" and "full of a lot of pain." Without a father at home, he felt as though he were left "learning on my own." Now as a father himself, he identified with a child's need for a male figure to offer guidance, love and, protection. "But being that I knew what it was like to always want to have a male figure to talk to, you know? Um, someone to protect me, someone to look up to, uh, someone to hug, someone to tell me I love you, you know, son, I'm proud of you."

Similar to Claudio, Antonio's desire to be an active presence in his children's life was driven by a void in his own. Antonio grew up without either of his biological parents, and was instead raised by another family member. He directly attributes his decision to marry at the young age of 17 and his desire to create a family to growing up without one. The experience of being raised without a father compelled him to try to provide for his children what he lacked. "Not having a father myself, um, I try to do everything that I would have liked my father to do with me."

Previous qualitative studies with nonresident fathers have found a similar relationship between men's histories with their own fathers and their motivations for assuming various fatherhood roles with their children.[36] So, it appears that even when fathers are not living up to their fatherhood goals, the memory of what they lacked from their own fathers can be a powerful motivating force that encourages them to keep trying. For some fathers, like Claudio, this means trying to provide for their own children what their fathers failed to provide them. For other fathers, like Kevin, this means doing better with their second set of children than with their first. For still other fathers, like Antonio, this means both. This adds an additional dimension to the problem of serial fatherhood, which Edin and Nelson highlight.[37] However, doing the best that they can for their next children might be unnecessary if they had more help achieving goals for fatherhood and family their first time around. Helping them do so is the topic of the next and closing chapter.

Willie's Story

Willie is a 31-year-old African American man, born in the Bronx, New York, but raised in Harlem. He has been unemployed for two months and cannot find work, though he looks for it every day. To help make ends meet, a friend offered him work as a porter, substituting when the regular porter was off duty. Willie earned only $1,500 last year, but even that has now ended. The recession has made a difficult job search impossible, and so Willie resorted to working small, private jobs off the books, just to make ends meet. He cuts hair, hands out flyers, does small jobs, and demolition, whatever he can do to earn money. Willie makes more money off the books because, as he admits, it's cash and he doesn't pay taxes, but he would like the consistency of a job and a steady income rather than hustling.

> I mean the full time job. The consistency, you know, consistently having a income on the job and, you know, I don't need a g—I don't need no more gigs. I'm tired of just being over-broke, being outta work, not having no income is, you know, just being on the grind, hustling. I mean it's not even surviving right now but I am surviving.

He wants to work, even filling out five or six applications at McDonalds, but he did not receive one telephone call from them. Willie doesn't want a handout, he just wants to work and live a middle class life. But work is more than just a job— it will make him a man. He wants to live in his own apartment and support his children properly, something he is now unable to do. As he reflected,

> until I get my GED or get a consistent job it's like I'm just feeling like, um, like a–a guy that going from being a boy to a man and I haven't become that

man yet until I financially—I'm financially fit, I'm stability fit with shelter, not living in my mom's house, and I'm able to do for my kids and make sure they alright.

Willie was raised by his mother and stepfather, having no relationship with his biological father. Willie credits his stepfather with teaching him carpentry skills and, really, all of his skills. He was the youngest of three children; he had an older sister and brother. His brother had cancer as a child and lost his leg to the illness; later, he drifted into addiction. But Willie said his brother has turned his life around. Willie desperately wants to turn his life around, too.

When Willie was 13, he helped his mother with her job by running small errands, sorting mail, or packaging. He was very athletic and dreamed of a basketball career, but at 14, he was shot multiple times. He was no longer able to attend school and was tutored at home. He later returned to high school and remained until the 10th grade. He was home schooled until he reached the 11th grade, when he stopped attending school. Willie tried school again, this time attending a local community college for a business management degree and a GED, but only remained a year and left without a degree or a GED. In 1997, Willie took the GED but did not pass it, and is now pursuing it again through a local university. This will be his third attempt, and he really wants to be successful this time. Though Willie said his mother attended college, neither Willie nor his siblings have a college education.

Willie is also the father of four girls, though presently none of his children live with him. His oldest daughter, who is 17, has a daughter of her own, making Willie a grandfather. Willie himself became a father at 14, and fathered three other children with a different mother. His daughters range in age from 10 to 17. Willie tries to see his three girls about once a month and recently took his daughters to the new Martin Lawrence movie. He wanted his oldest daughter to join them but she did not. The mother of his youngest daughters does not want them to be exposed to their older half sibling. She is very concerned about keeping her daughters from becoming pregnant and feels she is a bad influence, though Willie doesn't feel that 17 is a bad age to have kids. Willie really doesn't see his daughters as much as he'd like and acknowledged that he will probably see them less often now that their mother has a new baby and the girls have started the new school year.

Willie was convicted of a crime he did not commit. Prior to his arrest, he had never been sent to jail. Five years earlier, Willie had been arrested for marijuana possession, though it had not resulted in a prison sentence. Willie had been working at a bank, sorting mail and inputting data. Though it was not well paid, it was a steady job. However, in 2006, he was arrested and charged with second-degree murder. He was incarcerated for the crime. Eleven months later, with little explanation, he was released and the charges against him were dropped. "Um, they say I—I killed somebody. They locked me up for a murder two. Yeah, something that I didn't do and just, um, 11-months later after that they let me out." However, his wrongful incarceration created a cascade of other events. Willie had a support order for his first child of $508 per month, more than he earned at any of his prior jobs. "I have never sent a payment of $508 cause I never made that much—McDonald's only paid you $140 a week. I never made the $508 a month that this judge enforced." He did pay what he could, but it was always much less than owed, and the amount continued to accrue. When he was incarcerated, Willie was unable to pay any money and he now owed over $38,000 in arrears, with the amount increasing due to penalties. He does not have any support orders for his other children although he wants very much to support them, buy them presents, and give them money when he is able.

Willie dreams of continuing his education and wants to attend college. He wants to be able to support his children, but at the moment, he can't even support himself. To help with expenses, Willie lives with his mother and his girlfriend. Though his mother has been retired for a year, his girlfriend has a full-time job. Willie acknowledged the benefit of family support, reflecting "I think if it wasn't for my moms and my girlfriend her having a job, a full-time job, that, you know, I would really just be messed up." He would like to help his mother with her bills but can only help with food by using his food stamps. But Willie still worries about his financial situation. Sometimes, he goes to a soup kitchen to eat because he doesn't want to take from his mother, even though the family is supportive of one another. Willie wants very much to be able to contribute financially but he has very little. The only money he has to his name is one dollar, kept in a Chase Bank savings account. But Willie looks forward to his pending lawsuit. Currently, he has a suit filed through a lawyer for wrongful incarceration, with the hope he can win a large financial settlement. Then, he wants to buy his mother a house and give his girls a college education and maybe start a small business, perhaps a barbershop or a tattoo parlor.

6 Policy Reforms to Help Vulnerable Fathers

Why So Rough?

The rationale for so many punitive sanctions in the child support enforcement program becomes clearer when we understand how relief systems and family law developed in the United States.[1] According to D. D. Hansen, a legal historian, our current child support enforcement policies derived from efforts to reduce the burden on taxpayers for poor children who were abandoned by their fathers.[2] Family law and relief systems were adapted by the American colonies from the English poor laws, which did not establish a legal obligation for fathers to support their children.

By the mid-1800s, however, local relief systems became overwhelmed by children and their mothers who had been abandoned by married and unmarried fathers. Though publicly funded relief efforts were operated by private charity organizations, they lobbied for state laws making it a criminal offense for fathers to abandon their children. The original goal of child support, therefore, was to deter fathers from abandoning their children on the threat of criminal sanctions, including fines and jail time.

In his classic treatment of the history of relief systems in the United States, Michael Katz shows that in the ensuing decades, states also established cash assistance programs to improve the well-being of children in single-mother families.[3]

Since most of the mothers of these children were widows, the first state laws were known as "widows' pensions." These widows' (and later, mothers') pensions were incorporated into the Social Security Act in the mid-1930s, when President Franklin Roosevelt established the Aid to Dependent Children Program.

As divorce and non-marital births grew over the next four and a half decades, the predominant recipients of cash assistance became the children of divorcees and unmarried mothers, not the children of widows. This change in the composition of children receiving cash assistance and the sheer growth of expenditures on cash assistance prompted a backlash against welfare in the early 1980s. Five years earlier, Senator Russell Long observed that the cost of cash assistance, two-thirds of which was paid by the federal government, was being thrust upon the public because fathers had abandoned their children. To recover these costs, Senator Long sponsored legislation to establish the federal child support enforcement program. The goal of the cash assistance program was to improve living standards for children in mother-only families. Despite this link, the punitive nature of the child support program remained.

Can We All Get Along?

As this brief history illustrates, the child support enforcement that families experience on the ground involves a complex arrangement of federal, state, and local policy, and financing. Family law is the purview of the states, whose rights are protected by the Constitution. In exchange for assistance in funding their child support (cash assistance and other relief) programs, states allow the federal government to encroach upon their state policymaking authority. However, unless federal legislation specifically regulates an issue, states are free to determine the issue on their own.

Senator Long's legislation made the federal Office of Child Support Enforcement responsible for locating absent parents, establishing paternity, establishing child support orders, and collecting support. The federal office monitors states' efforts to achieve these goals. The office also uses discretionary funds to undertake basic research as well as demonstration research intended to improve child support enforcement programs. The office monitors the findings of this (and other sponsored) research occurring all around the country and uses the results to provide guidance to the states on best practice.

Because of these complex arrangements between federal and state policy and financing, child support enforcement policy evolves in the following way. Ideas about improving child support enforcement are tested on an experimental basis, and if successful, these ideas spread among advocates, researchers, policymakers, child support staff and administrators, and other stakeholders. Eventually, a consensus develops about the ideas that work and ideas that do not. Often, this involves similar experiments in several states. Proven ideas, which we call present innovations, are adopted by members of Congress into federal law, usually in the form of amendments to section IV D of the Social Security Act. This section directs and funds the activities of the federal Office of Child Support Enforcement and its state counterparts. However, if Congress fails to act, states that may want to implement these present innovations must use their own money to do so. Unfortunately, state funds represent only one-third of the cost of operating state child support programs. The rest comes from the federal government and can be used only to implement the child support provisions in federal law. Federal child support administrators contribute much to the development of new ideas directly and indirectly.

Besides present innovations, there are also future innovations: ideas about improving child support enforcement, which, though promising, have not been proven by research. The ideas emerge from the experience of child support enforcement administrators at the federal, state, or local level. Advocates for mothers and fathers with child support cases also contribute to these ideas. Finally, ideas also come from policy analysts and researchers, who analyze data on the determinants of outcomes of the child support caseload. These are the types of ideas that the federal Office of Child Support Enforcement might encourage and incentivize states to test, or ideas that states might try on their own. These ideas are untested, so no consensus exists about how well they work.

But as these ideas are circulated, some policymakers, experts in the field, or private donors are persuaded of the potential value of these ideas, and begin to examine them in experiments. Often, the federal Office of Child Support Enforcement funds the experiments. Until that time, however, these ideas remain in a very developmental stage. However, when child support administrators are effective, they move the most promising ideas through the process by disseminating information about their efficacy to the states, encouraging states to experiment with these ideas on their own, and build consensus among the relevant stakeholders so that these ideas become present innovations and, ultimately, current law.

An easier way to imagine this complex interplay is to picture a train with three cars: the engine car, the carriage car, and the caboose. The engine represents federal law, and state child support enforcement programs receive federal funding for carrying out this law. However, there are other policies and practices with demonstrated effectiveness and the support of experts and stakeholders. These policies and practices, representing present innovations, sit in the carriage car, waiting to move up to the engine car to become federal law. The Office of Child Support Enforcement can inform states about these present innovations and can encourage their adoption through discretionary funding, but states are not required to adopt the innovation, nor can they be compensated with federal funds for doing so. Finally, ideas that have not yet been tested, or those that do not yet have the support of experts in the field, sit in the caboose. They may one day move to the carriage car, or even to the engine car, but that cannot happen until they have additional support and the necessary research.

Because of the 1996 welfare reform that made child support immediate and inescapable, our train is speeding down the track out of control, with vulnerable fathers onboard. As we have seen in Chapter 3, many are falling into arrears because they are unable to meet their child support obligations and have difficulty modifying their child support orders. Before the Great Recession, most vulnerable fathers experiencing such difficulties (i.e., on the train) were chronically unemployed. Since late 2007, when layoffs among working-poor vulnerable fathers began to grow, they have boarded the train as well. Fortunately, there are changes in the child support enforcement system that might help. They are like "heroes," such as the Lone Ranger or Indiana Jones, on a horse, in full gallop chasing after the train. Nostrils flaring and frothing at the mouth, the horse finally catches up to the caboose, and our hero leaps off the horse onto the train. He scrambles into the caboose. As the train rumbles down the tracks, our hero stumbles at times, falling onto vulnerable nonresident fathers, who urge him on as he makes his way forward from the caboose toward the engine, where the engineer lays unconscious. If our hero can only get into the engine, before the train derails, he can take hold of the throttle, bring the train under control, and rescue his helpless passengers.

The speed with which our hero moves through the system (from the caboose to the carriage car to the engine) depends upon new knowledge, knowledge consensus, policy consensus, leadership, and money. New knowledge tells us that something we believe about the underlying forces generating child and family poverty has changed. Signs of the change might be apparent to many stakeholders, but someone must clearly identify the change and make it apparent to all stakeholders. Once that occurs, some general consensus that the new knowledge is in fact true must emerge before it can be acted upon. Even after consensus has developed, there will be different views about how to respond.

After some knowledge and policy consensus has been achieved, it still takes leadership to persuade key stakeholders at various levels of government to act. In this case, the president and members of Congress must act on key federal legislation that would enable states to use federal funds to move present innovations in child support enforcement from the carriage car to the engine. Barring that, states must be persuaded to use their own funds (or discretionary funds dispensed by the federal Office of Child Support Enforcement) to adopt these policy innovations. Put differently, without changes in federal legislation, the present innovations remain in the carriage car. States can adopt them if they choose, but for the most part, they must pay for them with their own funds.

Hence, the final step in the policy reform process involves money. Without money at the state level, even policy innovations that have been tested and whose effectiveness is affirmed by consensus remain in the carriage car. As we shall see, many future innovations have become present innovations over the last 20 years; however, these have not found their way into current law. For good or ill, most policies related to vulnerable fathers are debated in the context of welfare and child support reform. Like its sister issue, welfare reform, child support reform has fallen off the top of the policy agenda. In their place, Congress and Presidents George W. Bush and Barack Obama have been preoccupied with tax relief, homeland security, wars in Iraq and Afghanistan, Wall Street bailouts, healthcare reform, and fiscal stimulus needed to help the economy recover from the Great Recession. In the course of these policy battles, the federal budget has gone from unprecedented surpluses at the beginning of the Bush administration to unprecedented deficits today. The partisan political rancor in Washington has also slowed the process. In addition, federal funds for the child support program have been cut in recent years because of budget battles ending in sequestration. As a result, states barely have sufficient resources to cover their responsibilities under the existing federal law, and they cannot use federal money to implement ideas still stuck in the carriage car.

Finally, because of declining revenues and increased expenditures during the Great Recession, most states still find themselves with tight budgets. They are loath to adopt any policy changes that involve new state expenditures or reductions in state revenues. For these reasons, there is a backlog of present innovations that many believe would help states require and enable vulnerable fathers to be more involved with their children, financially and otherwise, which are simply stuck in the carriage car. There are also future innovations that some stakeholders believe would help to achieve the same goals, which are languishing in the caboose. What are these present and future innovations?

Oops!

Child support is a tool used to ensure that fathers continue to support their children after their parents separate, or to recover the cost of public benefits that replace what fathers should have provided. The federal child support program gave states access to federal money to carry out punitive approaches to achieve these goals. Although these policies were strengthened over the intervening years, the 1996 welfare reform stepped up the effort to make child support automatic and inescapable. As a result, fathers with and without the means to support their children were exposed to a range of tough and highly coordinated enforcement tools.

According to Harvard University economist Richard Freeman and his colleague Jane Waldfogel, the number of new children with child support orders rose dramatically. Unfortunately, overall collection rates did not, because children of economically vulnerable mothers and fathers were responsible for much of the growth, and their fathers had limited ability to pay. For these fathers, the reforms backfired. Arrears grew in place of collections, and the performance of child support programs suffered.

To address the problem, Congress passed the 1998 Child Support Performance and Incentive Act, which distributed incentive funds to states on a competitive basis, depending upon how well they performed on five measures: (1) paternity establishment, (2) establishment of support orders, (3) collections on current support, (4) collections on arrears, and (5) cost effectiveness. Before these changes could take full effect, the economic wave on which the country had been riding for almost a decade reached its peak. As a result of a mild recession in 2001, a jobless recovery until late 2007, and the Great Recession, many working-poor fathers experienced employment interruptions, which exposed them to the new child support enforcement system.

As we saw in Chapter 3, some vulnerable fathers struggled under the new automated, but now performance-based, system. Sometimes, courts set orders that vulnerable fathers believed were unreasonable, given their income. In other cases, the father may have had a reasonable order to begin with, but circumstances changed. A father may have lost his job, gone to prison, or returned to school to make more money so that he could better support his children (and himself). If the original order did not reflect these changes, but the order was difficult for the father to modify, he might be unable to pay the order in full. A flexible enforcement system might have been able to accommodate these fathers, but an automated system could not.

There has been no major change in federal laws governing how states spend federal subsidies for their child support programs since 1998. However, federal and state child support administrators (and a wide array of stakeholders) have learned much about the effects of child support enforcement on vulnerable fathers. For the most part, these lessons are circulating from one state to another in the carriage car. What are some of the most important lessons?

SETTING THE ORDER

With primarily children of divorcing parents in mind, child support orders are designed to prevent children from suffering a loss of support after their parents decide to separate.[4] To prevent children in the same circumstances from having widely different levels of support from their nonresident fathers, federal law requires states to use specific guidelines in setting child support orders. Judges or child support administrators involved in setting child support orders generally follow these guidelines, which are based on estimates of what the typical American families spend on their children.

States can choose among three different formulas for these guidelines. In some states, the formula is based upon the income of the nonresident parent alone; other states use a formula that depends upon the income of both the mother and father. Because the incomes of low-income families are lower than the incomes of the "typical" American family, all the formulas require low-income fathers to pay a higher proportion of their income in child support than fathers who earn more. As we saw in Chapter 3, if the father thinks the order is unreasonable, he is unlikely to pay. To avoid this, most states try to balance the needs of the child with the ability of the parent to pay by making adjustments to guidelines at the lower end of incomes.

SELF-SUPPORT RESERVE, LOW-INCOME STANDARDS, AND MINIMUM
ORDERS: WHAT'S THE DIFFERENCE?

Self-support reserves, low-income standards, and minimum orders are tools that many states use to depart from the normal child support guidelines for fathers with low income. However, these tools operate in very different ways, with self-support reserves and low-income standards usually resulting in lower orders for vulnerable fathers.

A self-support reserve, which is based on the poverty line, takes the father's basic needs into account prior to ordering child support payments. Thirty-seven states use a self-support reserve to depart from the guidelines. Some states deduct basic living expenses from the father's income before comparing the result to the relevant measure of poverty. If the father's adjusted income is below the self-support reserve, his child support order is set at a low amount, usually between $25 and $50 per month for each child. If his adjusted income is greater than the self-support reserve, the child support order is set on the amount of income that remains after deducting the self-support reserve from his adjusted income. The purpose is to ensure that the father's basic needs are covered before paying child support. Brustin, a legal advocate, points out that this policy ensures that the father has a minimal standard of living, but thrusts the major cost of caring for children onto mothers, many of whom are no longer receiving cash assistance, but are instead working at low wages.[5] While this criticism is true, this argument ignores the Federal Earned Income Tax Credit, which provides about $3,000 to a single mother with one child and over $5,000 to a single mother with two children. Extending a similar credit to vulnerable fathers is one of the future innovations, located in the caboose, which we will discuss below.

Thirty-seven states use a self-support reserve to depart from the guidelines. Only poor or near poor fathers can take advantage of it, and states have been slow to increase the self-support reserves, despite increases in the cost of living. Nevertheless, depending upon the kinds of expenses that states use in calculating adjusted income, fathers with earnings approaching $20,000 could be eligible for the self-support reserve.[6] This means that under 40 percent of employed men, if they were fathers, could qualify for the self-support reserve. So, many vulnerable fathers who are eligible for the self-support reserve are completely unaware of it.

Even states without a self-support reserve sometimes use a low-income standard to ensure that fathers can meet their basic needs before being ordered to pay child support. If the father's adjusted income is below this standard, judges or child support administrators are given discretion to set a child support order at a level the father is more likely to be able to afford.

Finally, when other states seek to provide relief from guidelines that would make the child support orders of low-income fathers unreasonable, they use a standard designed to ensure child needs rather than protecting the fathers' ability to pay. These states set a minimum order for the father, which is based on a standard of need, often based on the state's cash assistance (TANF) grant. However, as Sorensen and her colleagues have observed, this can translate into a fairly consequential sum, well above the means of many vulnerable fathers.

GETTING IT RIGHT IN THE FIRST PLACE

To use the guidelines, judges and child support administrators must be able to determine the fathers' income. This information is usually available in a divorce proceeding, but when married couples separate without a legal divorce or parents are never married, information about the father's income may be unavailable. This is especially likely for vulnerable fathers who are more likely to separate without a legal decree or to be unmarried fathers. As we also saw in Chapter 3, both parents may prefer an informal arrangement for support in these cases, but often the father's informal payments diminish over time. In such cases, the mother may turn to the court, or to a local child support enforcement agency, to petition for a child support order. Alternatively, the child support agency may petition on behalf of the state if the mother applies for public assistance.[7]

To obtain the required information about income, the court will subpoena the father to appear. However, many chronically unemployed fathers do not respond to these notices. They may be living someplace other than the "last known address" to which the court mails the subpoena. They may be unable to understand the "legalese" in which these documents are typically written, or be intimidated by such notices, given their past unfavorable experiences with the legal system.

Sorensen and her colleagues have shown that states with the largest arrears established the majority of the child support orders by default. Confirmation of these findings in other studies has moved "avoiding default orders" from the caboose into the carriage car. Because default orders increase the number of cases on which the state collects no child support or arrears, such orders make it harder for states to achieve three of the five performance standards established in the performance act. Therefore, the federal Office of Child Support Enforcement has advised states to avoid such orders.

Paul Legler is the former Clinton administration official who likened the certainty of child support collections to "death and taxes." More recently, he tracked how states are trying to undo the harmful results of the sweeping child support provisions in the welfare reform law, including increased reliance on default orders.[8] He noted that some states were simplifying the language used in legal documents to make them more accessible to fathers with lower levels of education, and less threatening to fathers unfamiliar with the judicial system. Other states were reducing filing fees, which created a barrier for fathers who needed a modification of their child support order, or who wanted to challenge a determination of legal paternity or other aspects of the child support order. Even requiring additional notifications before a default order could be issued helped to reduce default orders by giving fathers additional opportunities to participate in court proceedings.

Working-poor fathers were more likely to receive and respond to the subpoenas, but they may be unable to document their current income. This was likely to occur if they were recently laid off, but had not applied for or received unemployment insurance, or if they did not qualify for unemployment insurance. So, whether the father failed to appear or lacked adequate documentation of his earnings, the court was under pressure to establish a child support order so that the child's needs were met, to recover the cost of public benefits paid on behalf of the child, or to help the state satisfy one of the five performance measures. In the absence of verification of the father's income, the court "guessed" (technically, imputed) how much the father was able to pay.

IMPUTING INCOME

When the court or child support enforcement administrators lacked information about the father's income, most states simply responded by making assumptions about the father's ability to pay. Just before the Great Recession, the federal Office of Child Support Enforcement surveyed 14 representative states to determine the most frequently used source of information to impute income. All of the states used the father's last reported wage most often. The second most frequently used method for imputing income was to assume that the father was capable of earning what a worker would earn if he were employed full-time and full-year at the minimum wage.

Research has shown that in cases where the income was imputed, child support was less likely to be paid. Since this can also reduce state rankings on the performance standards, orders with imputed income can also impact federal funding to states for their child support programs. Even before the recession, avoiding these methods of income imputation had also begun to move from the caboose into the carriage car. For example, researchers who have studied the harmful effects of many child support policies on low-income fathers have suggested that using actual income to set an order may require more staff and time, but child support administrators can consult state records or tax returns to get more accurate information about ability to pay.[9]

But as we saw in Chapter 3, imputing income based on last known earnings or using full-time, full-year employment at the minimum wage can go terribly wrong when there is mass incarceration, high unemployment, and long unemployment spells. Therefore, the federal Office of Child Support Enforcement has issued new advice discouraging states from using the minimum wage to impute income for ex-offenders, who are over-represented among our chronically unemployed fathers. More generally, the federal Office of Child Support Enforcement has also recently advised states to use actual income to establish child support orders and to use income imputation only sparingly.[10]

Making a Bad Situation Worse

RETROACTIVE SUPPORT

Recall that many fathers enter the formal child support enforcement system only gradually as their informal arrangements for providing financial support for their children break down. For unmarried parents this may take up to three years, but it may also happen when married parents separate without a legal proceeding.

After such an informal separation, which we used to call desertion, the father may or may not provide for his child informally. If the mother seeks help from child support enforcement or seeks public benefits, local child support enforcement becomes involved. When this occurs, the court can back date the child support order to the birth of the child, the date the case was filed, or the date the father stopped living with the mother and child. This is called a retroactive order, and it is not all that vulnerable fathers have to fear. The state may incur costs (e.g., court and paternity testing costs) in establishing the order, which it can add to the child support order. Finally, for unmarried fathers, like Ronald, birthing costs can top off these amounts. So, before the father leaves the courtroom, a child support order that was within his reach can quickly explode into an order that he finds unreasonable.

Advocates of retroactive support believe that the responsibilities of fatherhood begin at birth. From a more practical standpoint, states benefit from the additional money to help recover the cost of public assistance programs. However, a government survey of state child support practices found that fathers with orders established long before the court date are less likely to pay anything on their orders.[11] So the federal Office of Child Support Enforcement advises states to establish orders as soon as possible and, where possible, to use discretion in determining the amount of retroactive orders. For example, if the father was not actively avoiding the child support orders, retroactive support should be minimal. Similarly, in states where birth costs are not prescribed by law, these should not be routinely included in retroactive orders

MODIFICATION

Modification refers to the process of adjusting a child support order that the mother or father believes no longer reflects their circumstances. Sometimes, modification is necessary because the initial award was set too high. This is often the result of using imputed income, when actual income was not available to the court at the time the court issued a default order, a common problem for vulnerable fathers. Sometimes, an order needs to be modified as a result of changing financial circumstances, sometimes for the better or sometimes for the worse.

Modifications have a very important role to play in times of economic turmoil, like the recession from which the country has just emerged. Though the recession is over, the aftermath and its impact on workers remains. An order that may have been set within the father's ability to pay can become unreasonable, after a long spell of unemployment or after he accepts a job at lower wages.

Recall that some child support cases are enforced by state child support enforcement programs. For brevity we shall refer to these as cases in the public system and shall refer to all others as cases in the private system. About three of four cases are in the public system. Further, in the public system there are two kinds of cases: those for mothers who are (or were) receiving public benefits, and those for mothers who have asked for help. Cases related to public benefits are primarily for mothers with limited financial resources; however, among those who have entered the system voluntarily, there is greater income diversity.

There currently exists no trigger for modification in the private system. Either parent may request a review, but to obtain one, the change in circumstances must be substantial. In some states it must also be permanent. The procedure differs for cases in the public system. Federal law can trigger a review and possible modification of child support orders in the public system every three years. The law requires a review and, if warranted, modification of orders related to public benefits every three years. However, reviews of other cases in the public system are not required. Instead, child support enforcement agencies must notify the parents every three years that they can request a review. Only if the change in circumstances is substantial will the review and modification occur.

Whatever the circumstances, financial changes need to be addressed in a timely manner. This can be problematic for fathers in the private system. Federal law does not require regular review of their orders, so they do not receive periodic reminders of the opportunity for a modification. Vulnerable fathers with cases in the public system at the mothers' request may not respond to notices about their right to request a review and modification, or they may not need one when the notice arrives. But circumstances can change swiftly. Relying as it does on a client-initiated process for modifying child support orders—which, as we saw in Chapter 4, can be costly, uncertain, and time-consuming—means that vulnerable fathers cannot get a modification when they need one.

One consequence of the increase in defaults on child support orders is that states are responding to the problem. Some states are setting up automated processes that parents can initiate online. Others are providing for temporary modifications. Still others are undertaking special outreach efforts to encourage parents to apply for modifications and simplifying the process for doing so. Finally, other states are taking a more proactive role by using unemployment insurance claims to identify vulnerable fathers who are at risk of missing their child support payments, developing simplified forms and procedures to expedite petitions for modification, and facilitating conferences between parents so that some modifications can be approved without a court hearing.[12] Child support agencies that are prepared to rapidly respond can help secure ongoing payments to mothers and children, and can help fathers avoid accumulating arrears and improve their performance on child support collections.

SANCTIONS

Once the court sets the child support order, the father must pay in monthly or bimonthly installments. Sanctions come into play only when fathers fail to pay the required amount. Perhaps the three most important sanctions are license revocation, financial penalties, and incarceration.

License Revocation

States initially adopted the automated case-processing techniques required by the 1996 welfare reform in a straightforward way, much like the stages of the workplace disciplinary process. The first offense triggered a verbal warning, the second offense a written warning, the third offense triggered mandatory training, and the fourth offense dismissal. Here the offense would be the number of missed payments. So, the first missed payment might trigger a letter indicating the various sanctions that would follow should the father miss subsequent payments. Prolonged delinquency would usually trigger a hearing in which the father would be ordered to make payment, if he could offer no suitable reason for his failure to pay. Subsequent missed payments would place the father in contempt of court, and driver's license suspension without further notice could follow shortly. This seems to have been the sequence that Franco experienced.

States have found driver's license suspensions to be a very effective enforcement tool. Even so, some have begun to delay the use of such suspensions even after issuing a warning. One state has even found that sending driver's license suspension notices on pink, rather than white, paper increases compliance while reducing the number of licenses actually suspended.[13]

Incarceration

When the court found fathers to be in contempt of court for failing to pay child support, incarceration was the ultimate sanction. However, a 2011 Supreme Court decision, *Turner v. Rogers*, established that before implementing this sanction states had to ensure that fathers were represented by counsel. Alternatively, states had to provide procedural safeguards, including steps that ensured that fathers had the ability to pay both the original order and any purge payment the courts frequently required to avoid incarceration. The decision has severely limited the use of default orders, income imputation, and incarceration by child support enforcement agencies.[14]

Financial Penalties-Arrears

Between license suspensions and incarceration, financial penalties, mostly in the form of arrears, are another important sanction. While arrears may begin to accumulate slowly, like water dripping from a leaky faucet, they can accumulate quite rapidly, like water bursting from an opened dam, depending upon the father's income, the size of the order, and the way in which states treat unpaid child support. While child support enforcement cannot affect the size of the father's income, it can affect the size of the order and the factors we have reviewed thus far. So, states that lack self-support reserves or low-income adjustments, and states that make heavy use of practices such as default orders, income imputation, retroactive orders, or slow and expensive processes for modifying orders, all tend to have higher arrears.

In addition, Sorensen and her colleagues have noted that states that charge interest and penalties on overdue child support payments also tend to have higher arrears.[15] In a typical jurisdiction, fathers must pay their full current child support order plus an amount of child support that administrators apply to the father's current arrears. If the father's current payment is less than the amount required, the state decides how much of the payment goes toward current support and how much of the payment goes toward arrears. Assuming the father's payment is less than the total amount of arrears outstanding, arrears will grow if the jurisdiction charges penalties and interest on outstanding arrears. If the father fails to pay the full amount of his current child support order, the difference will also be added to arrears before the next cycle begins. As a result of this kind of interest compounding, arrears can grow rapidly.

Before the Great Recession, 18 states were charging interest on arrears on a regular basis, and an additional 18 states charged interest intermittently. However, the 1998 act rewards states for collecting a higher proportion of the amount of child support plus arrears owed. Since charging interest on arrears leads to unreasonably high child support orders, states should be charging interest on arrears primarily on cases where they believe fathers have the ability to pay. In addition, high rates of unemployment and child support non-compliance since the Great Recession have led the federal Office of Child Support Enforcement to encourage states to limit the practice of charging interest and penalties on arrears.[16] So charging no interest on arrears is the practice in carriage car. Whether states actually make use of this practice remains to be seen.

Sorensen and her colleagues also point out that arrears are concentrated among fathers with little or no income. Some of these fathers are capable of meeting their child support obligations, but they conceal their income through self-employment or taking irregular jobs. Charging penalties and interest on the arrears that these fathers owe will likely motivate compliance. Others fathers, like Willie, Kelly, and even Franco at one point, do not earn enough to meet their child support obligations. In addition, they are self-employed or working at irregular jobs because they cannot find regular work. Charging penalties and interest on the arrears that these fathers owe only builds up debt that these fathers may never be able to pay. The automated case-processing techniques that states were encouraged to adopt under the 1996 welfare reform make it difficult for child support administrators to distinguish between these two types of fathers. But this distinction is important, because of the results we reported in Chapter 3. When arrears are low relative to a father's overall earnings, fathers tend to work more hours per week, presumably to make more money so that they can pay off their child support debts. However, when arrears are high relative to a father's overall earnings, fathers tend to work fewer hours per week.[17]

This illustrates the dilemma for child support enforcement administrators. When using enforcement tools that influence arrears, administrators must strike a delicate balance. Some tools will encourage fathers to get caught up on their child support obligations by allowing arrears to grow. However, the same tools will discourage other fathers from working once the arrears reach a threshold that causes "sticker shock." Chronically unemployed fathers with low earnings can reach this threshold quickly. However, working-poor fathers can also reach this threshold if they have default orders reflecting imputed earnings, retroactive orders, or have had difficulty modifying their child support orders.

Plugging the Dike

Besides avoiding the practices that lead to arrears, states can also make it easier for fathers to plug up the dike. Some states are trying to do this using arrears abatement or management strategies. These strategies involve forgiving part or all of the arrears for fathers who are very unlikely to pay (e.g., offenders, ex-offenders, fathers on disability, and those with incomes below the poverty line). Other states are also gradually canceling arrears for fathers who are consistently keeping their current child support payments up to date.

However, child support agencies can only forgive debts for child support orders that have been signed over to the state in exchange for public benefits (about 60 percent of all cases in the public system). These cases are more likely to involve chronically unemployed fathers than working-poor fathers, so chronically unemployed fathers are more likely to see their arrears fall. Working-poor fathers with children who have not received public assistance owe child support (and any associated arrears) to mothers. These mothers may operate just like child support agencies before performance standards gave states incentives to eliminate arrears with low prospects of payment. That is, mothers may be content to watch the arrears owed by fathers grow, even though their chances of collecting on these arrears are slim. In an attempt to prevent future arrears, some states have arranged conferences to encourage mothers and fathers to expedite downward modifications in the face of declining earnings during the recession. However, there is no indication that mothers are encouraged to forgive some portion of past arrears. Since the actual monthly payments that fathers make include current support plus a portion toward arrears, decreasing the total amount of arrears owed would reduce a father's monthly obligation while increasing the likelihood that future support payments are made.

Arrears abatement and management programs grew out of research projects, like those conducted by Heinrich and her colleagues at the University of Wisconsin.[18] These projects showed that payments on current child support grew when fathers were given the opportunity to reduce state-owed arrears in exchange for consistently paying current support. After a series of replications, 44 states had adopted such programs by September 2011.[19] In other words, arrears abatement has moved from the caboose to the carriage car. To enable more working-poor fathers to participate in arrears management programs, perhaps it is time to undertake similar experiments—with mothers' permission of course—when the arrears are owed to mothers.

Getting Help

RESPONSIBLE FATHERHOOD PROGRAMS

Child support has become an automatic and inescapable enforcement system that can create great stress. To help vulnerable fathers cope, community-based responsible fatherhood programs have sprung up around the country. Though these programs have traditionally served chronically unemployed fathers, they have unfortunately had limited impact on the employment or earnings of most men, except for those who are the least job-ready. Nevertheless, several evaluations have shown that responsible fatherhood programs increase the fraction of participants who pay anything on their child support orders. However, because employment and earnings among participants generally do not rise, responsible fatherhood programs do not generally increase the amount of child support paid by participants.[20]

Vulnerable fathers may find local child support enforcement agencies intimidating places to seek help with their child support problems. By contrast, like many of the fathers we interviewed, they may regard local responsible fatherhood programs as good sources of information and assistance, which are much less intimidating. This may help to explain why responsible fatherhood programs can increase child support payments, even though they have no effect on employment or earnings. These programs help vulnerable fathers understand how to negotiate the child support enforcement system, including how they can modify their child support orders, seek orders reflecting the self-support reserve, and manage their child support obligations in other ways. Therefore, the federal Office of Child Support Enforcement encourages states to partner with local responsible fatherhood programs.

The federal Office of Child Support Enforcement continues to sponsor responsible fatherhood program demonstration grants in an ongoing effort to uncover strategies that will increase employment and earnings among chronically unemployed fathers. However, the discretionary funding available for these programs falls far short of the need, and local programs have found it difficult to leverage competitive federal funding with state, local, or private funding. This situation creates concerns about the long-term sustainability of the field.[21] Additional funding for these programs is definitely needed, or services that help vulnerable fathers understand how to work with the child support enforcement system should be more fully integrated with workforce development programs, which have much more stable funding.

ACCESS AND VISITATION PROGRAMS

Besides the help they need finding jobs and managing their child support orders, vulnerable fathers also need help gaining access to their children. Until now, it has been useful to view policy solutions that help working-poor fathers as part of the same solution used to assist chronically unemployed fathers. This argument is less convincing when we approach matters of custody and visitation, because chronically unemployed fathers are more likely to be unmarried, while working-poor fathers are more likely to be divorced. Whether never married or divorced, the vulnerable fathers we interviewed wanted to be more involved in the lives of their children, and the barriers they encountered, with the exception of incarceration, were similar. In particular, co-parenting problems with the mothers of their children were paramount for fathers, whether they were divorced or never married. Therefore, it is important to focus on policies to improve co-parenting skills, or at the very least, to mitigate some of the more adverse effects of poor co-parenting relationships. In turn, this might lessen gatekeeping behaviors of mothers.

The custody and visitation problems encountered by never-married vulnerable fathers are an extension of the custody and visitation problems encountered by their divorced counterparts. Though the divorce is an emotionally difficult transition, custody and visitation are part of the standard procedures, and are set at the same time as child support obligations are being established. This is not the case for a child born to unmarried parents. Even after paternity has been established, an unmarried father's rights regarding custody and visitation must be determined. This may require litigation, which is more or less onerous (and costly), depending upon state law. Because of these cost barriers, legal custody and visitation arrangements for unmarried fathers are uncommon. Without such arrangements in place, any one of a host of events that sours the relationship between unmarried parents can reduce access that the noncustodial parent, usually the father, has to the child. As we saw in the previous chapter, these events include the failure to pay informal child support, re-partnering by the mother or father, or a new child with the mother's or father's new partner. This helps to explain why visitation among some unmarried fathers declines over time. Married fathers also separate from their wives, sometimes without a legal divorce. They, too, lack legal visitation rights.

Finally, many divorced fathers also lack the access and visitation arrangements they want, because they could not afford the legal representation they needed to advocate for more favorable visitation arrangements. Therefore, gatekeeping by mothers, often provoked by concern for their own safety, or concerns about the quality of the fathers' parenting skills, can prevent fathers from seeing their children. Though child support enforcement agencies have long maintained that gatekeeping by mothers does not justify withholding financial support for children, Chapter 3 reviewed several studies showing that fathers that have contact with their children are more likely to provide financial support. Therefore, policymakers are taking a number of steps to promote access and visitation for vulnerable fathers.

The first step is to help all noncustodial parents (divorced, separated, or unmarried parents) to spend more time with their children. To this end, the Office of Child Support Enforcement has been making grants to state access and visitation programs across the country. These programs provide three types of services: mediation, parent education, and supervised visitation. Through facilitation by the mediators, mothers and fathers discuss parenting skills and visitation arrangements, and develop parenting plans face-to-face.[22] Parent education programs provide parents with information about child development, co-parenting, how to handle parenting conflicts, as well as other parenting skills. Supervised visitation allows fathers to meet with their children in the presence of a third party.

Evaluations of these programs show that all three types of services help to promote father involvement.[23] Fathers prefer mediation and parent education programs to supervised visitations. Because of the high cost of legal councel, most Americans negotiate the details of their divorce agreements without benefit of counsel, which often results in visitation arrangements that are less than satisfactory[24]. Some divorced fathers learn about their full visitation and custody options for the very first time as a result of participating in access and visitation programs (personal communication of David Levy, March 19, 2014). Therefore, with the help of mediators, many vulnerable nonresident fathers were able to reach agreements about visitation and to develop parenting plans with the mothers.

Access and visitation programs have served unmarried as well as divorcing parents. Participation in the programs has resulted in increased visitation and child support payments among unmarried parents, encouraging policymakers to take a second step. This involves facilitating the establishment of legal visitation rights for unmarried fathers. Through its Parenting Time and Opportunities Program (P-TOC), the federal Office of Child Support Enforcement supported the development and evaluation of state strategies to establish visitation (or parenting time) orders concurrently with the child support order for unmarried parents. Other than special safeguards for cases involving domestic violence, which are a part of all programs, there is considerable variation among approaches. Some programs involve pro bono legal assistance for parents seeking to establish parenting-time arrangements. Other programs provide a special court that issues financial support and parenting-time orders after parents attend co-parenting workshops and receive case management services. Still other programs establish guidelines for helping unmarried parents choose options for handling the most common issues that arise when negotiating parenting time, buttressed by other supports, such as mediation and supervised visitation that are usually provided by access and visitation programs. Finally, one state (Texas) has already standardized parenting time for unmarried parents by passing a state law, so that parenting-time orders become part of the initial child support order.

Although it will be several years until results of an evaluation of the P-TOC projects will be available, federal policymakers have already begun to take action. President Obama's most recent budget request contains a provision that will require states to include visitation (parenting-time) provisions at the same time the order is set, and to expand access and visitation programs.[25] The Senate is also considering a bill (S. 1877) with a similar provision to include voluntary visitation (or parenting-time) orders for unmarried noncustodial parents, once an initial child support order is established. This bill would also require state child support enforcement agencies to report about efforts to improve access and visitation for noncustodial parents.[26]

Recognizing that unmarried and divorced fathers who cannot afford legal representation have similar visitation and access problems, some advocates for fathers and children, such as David L. Levy, cofounder and president of the Children's Rights Council from 1985 to 2009, want unmarried and divorced fathers to join forces to push for more widespread adoption of joint custody (personal communication, March 19, 2014). Joint custody can refer to the physical custody of the child, or the shared legal decision-making by both parents on issues that affect their child. According to Joan Kelly, a psychologist, researcher, and mediator who has worked with divorcing parents for four and a half decades, in the 1960s, when divorce rates began to rise, courts initially presumed that mother-sole custody, with visitation rights granted to the father, was the living arrangement in the best interest of the child.[27] That most married women were full time homemakers and most married men, full-time workers in the 1960s was compelling evidence for this determination. Since then, labor force participation, especially among married women, has dramatically increased, and most states have removed references to gender from the language in their laws governing presumptive custody. Nevertheless, the maternal preference still dominates guidelines for custody decisions, so courts, attorneys, mediators, and divorcing parents, bargaining in the "shadow of the law," continue to use mother-sole custody as default living arrangement for divorcing parents. As a result, changing state laws to provide explicit language specifying more equal sharing of time and decision-making authority for divorcing mothers and fathers has been a major objective of groups representing divorced fathers since the early 1980s.

Meanwhile, researchers have been studying joint custody since 1979, when joint custody first became available in California. Braver, one of the most well-respected experts on the consequences of divorce, and his colleagues found that joint custody was relatively rare; only two to six percent of divorces in the United States were joint custody. Maria Cancian and Daniel Meyer of the University of Wisconsin found that while mother-sole custody remained the more likely arrangement in the Wisconsin divorces they studied, joint custody had slowly increased.[28] A meta-analysis that reviewed 33 studies found that, contrary to some critics, joint custody was not found to be harmful to child adjustment.[29]

A cross-national review of studies of joint custody found that children in these living arrangements had better communication with their parents than children from other family arrangements, and equal or better communication than children from intact families.[30]

In a small but very well-designed study, Braver and another colleague examined the effects of joint physical custody on elementary school children and their parents, after accounting for a host of characteristics, measured before divorce proceedings occurred, that might influence whether or not divorcing couples chose joint custody.[31] These characteristics included parents' age, race, income education, conflict, gatekeeping, religious affiliation, presence of new partners, and measures of parental mental health, including those likely to affect co-parenting relationship quality and child well-being. They found that although mothers with joint custody were less satisfied with the arrangement than those with mother-sole physical custody, the former were more likely to move on to new relationships with new partners. Mothers with joint custody were not more likely to receive child support payments, which was surprising in light of many other studies that found that joint custody and child support compliance were positively related. So, joint custody was a mixed blessing for mothers. The consequences for fathers and children were more straightforward. Children with joint custody were better adjusted than children with mother-sole custody, and enjoyed more visits with their fathers than children with mother-sole custody.

Despite these findings, the jury on joint custody is still out. In his review of the literature on joint custody, Amato, another highly respected expert on fathers, points out that joint custody is relatively new and that most studies have not examined long-term outcomes for children once they reach adulthood. This is important because the divorce process itself can be stressful, and this stress can increase the risks of negative outcomes for children when they have reached adulthood.[32] It is also clear that joint custody may not be an appropriate choice for families that have a parent with a history of physical abuse, or severe mental illness. Some critics also contend that in homes with high parental conflict, joint custody can expose children to increased levels of conflict, but others have found that joint custody lowers conflict and increases cooperation between parents. Finally, joint custody requires that both parents possess the financial resources for a large enough living space for children. These concerns reveal how the debate about pros and cons of joint custody for vulnerable fathers, their families, and children may differ from the pros and cons of joint custody for higher income fathers.

First, while joint physical custody would enable vulnerable nonresident fathers to be more involved in the lives of their children, many children would spend more than 20 percent of their time with their divorced fathers as a result.[33] In many states, fathers who have this level of contact with their children are allowed to pay less in child support. Therefore, advocates for women argue that joint custody can, in effect, harm mothers by reducing child support obligations. They also question whether fathers really will spend more time with their children.[34] Thus, vulnerable nonresident fathers are in a debate with mothers and fathers from higher income families, whose bargains over time with children in exchange for financial child support have been a subject of much academic research since the publication of Mnookin's classic study.[35] However, this bargaining takes place not only in individual divorce mediation sessions, but also in broader policy debates where the voices of vulnerable mothers and fathers are too often overlooked.

What's more, the resolution of the joint custody debate that might be satisfactory to some high-income fathers has entirely different implications for vulnerable fathers, their children, and families. Advocates for fathers claim that the default custody arrangement, mother-sole custody, reflects the gender bias of the courts. This may be true; however, it is also true that mother-sole custody reflects judicial concern for the best interest (of the child) standard, which has been enshrined in family law since before the Industrial Revolution. As Stephanie Coontz reminds us, in Colonial America, most men worked near their homes and had primary responsibility for childrearing, including teaching children a trade. Therefore, in cases of a divorce, presumptive custody went to the father. After the Industrial Revolution, when most men worked in factories, leaving mothers to take primary responsibility for caregiving at home, presumptive custody was diverted to mothers, so that divorce would not disrupt the childrearing arrangements to which the children had become accustomed. Thus, continuity, rather than gender bias, is an alternate justification for mother-sole custody as the default arrangement. To the extent that vulnerable fathers have more traditional ideas about gender roles, they are less likely to be involved in caregiving roles, prior to divorce, than higher income fathers. While their wives may be as likely to work as the wives of higher income fathers, the former are less likely to use paid child-care providers. Finally, vulnerable fathers are less likely than higher income fathers to have extended vacations, flex-time work options, and opportunities to work from home. For all these reasons they are less likely to be involved in caregiving than higher income fathers, before and after divorce. This means that a gender-neutral standard that recognizes the best interest of the child would be less advantageous for vulnerable fathers than for higher income fathers.

Finally, higher income fathers would be satisfied if the presumption of joint physical custody required courts to award joint physical custody on a fairly even basis in cases where custody was in dispute. This means that when the mediation processes that are available to divorcing couples in many states broke down, judges would be required to revert to joint custody as the default arrangement. In each of the few states where there is a presumption of joint custody, this type of guideline for judicial decision-making is the mechanism on which states rely. But since it is the expense of litigation that prevents many vulnerable nonresident fathers from getting the custody and visitation arrangements they want, presumptive guidelines for joint physical custody might not be enough. Instead, vulnerable fathers would need some kind of administrative presumptive custody, which would not require a court hearing to consider the appropriateness of joint custody on a case-by-case basis, at least not initially.[36] Such an administrative arrangement would almost certainly neglect the potential risks associated with providing custody, for one reason or other, to a parent who was an unreliable caretaker of the child. A good example would be a workaholic. Presumptive joint custody made available by an administrative process might require the child to spend a lot of time with a risky caretaker: an alcoholic, for example. Put differently, it would involve setting aside the best interest (of the child) standard in favor of the rights of one or both parents to remain involved in the lives of their child. Higher income parents might be able to avoid these risks by hiring a lawyer to reverse such an administrative outcome. However, economically vulnerable fathers (or mothers) might not be able to do so.

In short, joint physical custody is available in a very limited number of states, and it is more likely to be chosen by divorcing parents with higher incomes and more education. For this reason, we do not know how much visitation by vulnerable nonresident fathers would rise if joint custody became the default standard in more states. In addition, nonresident fathers lose more contact with their children with increases in the time since the end of their romantic relationships with the mothers of their children. So, the increases in father-child contact that we would expect to occur if joint physical custody were available would likely involve children who were three or five years old or more.[37] There is little evidence that increasing contact between nonresident fathers and children who are three or more years old increases child well-being.[38] The evidence that engagement of resident fathers improves child well-being may rest on the idea that such engagement compliments engagement by mothers. Children with resident parents can receive the benefits of parents at the same time, or fathers can care for children while mothers are working, sleeping, or engaged in other leisure or household activities. Joint custody, by contrast, may substitute the father's caregiving for the mother's caregiving, especially if it requires children to spend 20 to 30 percent of their time with fathers.

Unless arrangements could be made so that divorced parents learn how to provide complementary caregiving, joint custody feels more like a zero sum game. There is some doubt that this would occur naturally, because some mothers might view the increased engagement of fathers as a threat to the new relationships they are attempting to form with new partners. So, a wiser path may be to improve the co-parenting relationships between nonresident fathers and the mothers of their children. With or without new partners, increased father involvement should compliment, rather than reduce, the quantity and quality of parenting provided by mothers. This appears to be what needs to occur in the next generation of responsible fatherhood programs, as recommended by experts, such as Virginia Knox, who have worked with responsible fatherhood programs, and experts such as Phil Cowan and Carolyn Cowans,[39] who have begun to adapt marriage education programs for use by unmarried co-parents who are not romantically involved.

Future Directions

Making child support automatic and inescapable for fathers has hurt those who are vulnerable, but the child support enforcement system has made some adjustments since 1998 to reduce some of these harmful effects. Nevertheless, the long-term decline in wages for men without graduate degrees is likely to continue for some time to come. Further, instability will characterize the employment experience of many. Finally, there is nothing on the horizon that suggests that divorce or non-marital birth rates will fall in the near future, so that the proportion of these less-educated men who become nonresident fathers will also grow. What ideas are on the horizon to help us manage these worrisome trends?

SUPPLEMENTING THE EARNINGS OF VULNERABLE FATHERS

The Federal Earned Income Tax Credit is now the largest anti-poverty program in the United States providing payroll-tax relief and work incentives to thousands of families headed by low-wage workers. According to the Center on Budget and Policy Priorities, an influential advocacy organization focused on poverty alleviation, this credit lifted 6.6 million people out of poverty in 2009.[40] The maximum credit for a childless worker is a fraction of the maximum credit for a single mother with one child.[41] Under current federal law, even when vulnerable nonresident fathers pay child support, they are eligible for the same Earned Income Tax Credit as childless workers. In 2008, then Senator Barack Obama co-sponsored legislation to expand the Federal Earned Income Tax Credit to vulnerable nonresident fathers. This proposal, modeled on the Non-Custodial Parent Earned Income Tax Credit in New York State and Washington, DC, applied the same income requirements for nonresident parents as for all childless workers, but doubled the credit that vulnerable nonresident fathers would receive.

According to Sorensen and her colleagues, the New York State credit reached only a third of the eligible population in 2009, three years after it became available. We interviewed Franco, Willie, Kelly, and 40 other fathers to understand why participation was so low. We found that vulnerable nonresident fathers knew little about the tax credit, and almost none had applied. Even if the credit were better known, few of these fathers would have received it in 2009, because they had not paid their child support in full during the previous year, one of the key eligibility criteria in New York. Full compliance with child support was also an eligibility requirement in Washington, DC law and in the proposed federal legislation.

The basic purpose of the Federal Earned Income Tax Credit is to supplement the earnings of low-income workers who provide for children. To most legislators who have proposed legislation for a Non-Custodial Earned Income Tax Credit, this means that vulnerable nonresident fathers must pay their child support in full. However, if full compliance bars these fathers from taking advantage of the credit, it seems sensible to use mechanisms such as the self-support reserve to bring the full compliance criteria within their reach. This would provide the work and child support incentives that legislators intended.[42]

Finally, even though the New York State Non-Custodial Parent Earned Income Tax Credit doubled the credit available to vulnerable nonresident fathers under the current federal law, the work incentives available in the state program were still far smaller than the work incentives available to single mothers under the Federal Earned Income Tax Credit. According to estimates by Sorensen and her colleagues, increasing the credit by $100 would have modest but positive effects on employment and child support compliance by vulnerable nonresident fathers with low child support orders. To our knowledge, no new state Non-Custodial Earned Income Tax Credit had been introduced since 2009, nor has a federal bill been reintroduced since that year. Assuming no turnaround in the wage trends of vulnerable nonresident fathers, some additional experimentation and development of this idea is needed.

BUILDING HUMAN CAPITAL

In his book *Assets and the Poor*, Michael Sherraden makes a compelling case that antipoverty strategies should provide opportunities for low-income people to build assets.[43] Building assets better positions low-income people to respond to unpredictable circumstances, such as job loss, and to take advantage of opportunities to improve their well-being. Arguably, debt accumulation must have the opposite effect. For example, child support arrears magnify the harmful effects of unpredictable events on vulnerable fathers. Recall Dwight, in Chapter 4, who worked at irregular jobs because a layoff, resulting in a child support default, would land him back in jail. Similarly, debts also prevent vulnerable fathers from taking advantage of opportunities that might improve their long-term well-being, and that of their children. Policymakers should consider the implications of this asset framework for policies affecting vulnerable fathers.

Workforce development policy is one area where such reconsideration is desperately needed. Besides their traditional mission of educating students who eventually want to earn to a four-year degree, community colleges have become major centers for vocational training. They are especially attractive to prime-age adults who want to earn higher wages by upgrading their skills while working at their current, lower-paying jobs. The vocational training courses that community colleges offer are often designed in partnership with local businesses, so that the skills students acquire match local workforce needs. As degree-granting institutions, providing certificates for students who successfully complete vocational training programs is well within the processes already established at community colleges, and employers often value this certification.[44] For these reasons, community colleges have attracted increasing public financial support to retrain displaced workers, such as the working-poor fathers who lost higher-paying jobs during the recession. Examples include retraining for displaced workers under the Pell Grant Program, the Workforce Investment Act, and the Trade Adjustment Assistance Act.[45] As part of his strategy to support the middle class, President Obama's stimulus package in 2009 expanded upon the latter program through the Trade Adjustment Assistance Community College and Career Training (TAACCCT) Grants Program. This $2 billion program has been supporting capacity-building efforts by community colleges offering retraining programs lasting two years or less to manufacturing workers who were displaced as a result of plant closings or job loss due to competition from international firms.[46]

As we saw in Chapter 1, even before the recession, many vulnerable fathers who worked full-time and full-year were poor or near poor after meeting basic expenses and child support obligations. The situation is unlikely to change, unless these fathers can increase their earnings, generally requiring additional training or education. Several fathers we interviewed tried to combine work and coursework at community colleges. When this workload became too demanding, they took part-time jobs, believing that they could reduce their child support obligations temporarily. However, they were wrong. To our knowledge, no state currently grants downward modifications of child support orders to fathers who voluntary reduce their earnings, even over the short term, in pursuit of additional education in order to increase future earnings. In denying such modification requests, states are presumably placing the needs of children before the needs of fathers. However, such denials may actually be placing children's present needs above children's future needs. In view of the stagnant or declining earnings of men without post-secondary training or schooling, this may be shortsighted.

R. J. Lalonde has studied the effectiveness of a variety of workforce development programs over the years. Using a unique administrative database that matched courses taken by community college students in Washington State following the recession in early 1990s with employment and earnings data, he and his colleagues showed that "technically oriented vocational and academic math and science courses" (p. 272) had positive effects on the long-term earnings of displaced workers, including men. Most important, a companion study found that the effects of such courses were similar for younger men (29 years old on average) and older men (43 years old on average).[47] If downward modifications of child support orders were available to vulnerable fathers so that they could attend similar courses at community colleges, which had similar effects on their earnings, child support payments might increase over the long term as well. States with proven community college training programs should consider pilot testing this approach. Doing so might prove more successful than many efforts aimed at increasing the employment, earnings, and child support payments of chronically unemployed fathers.[48]

However, two-year, vocational training programs at community colleges are not the only strategy for building the human capital and increasing the long-term earnings of vulnerable fathers. Local businesses have also partnered with nonprofit, workforce development providers to create vocational training programs. Though participants can complete these vocational training programs in less time than students normally take to complete a one-semester course college, many participants receive certificates that qualify them for higher paying jobs. What's more, through career path strategies, participants can acquire higher, but related levels of skill, in "stackable" training programs.[49] This allows participants to mix periods of instruction with periods of work, at progressively higher wages. Because rigorous evaluations of such strategies are currently underway, we do not yet know how much such short-term training efforts affect the employment and earnings of experienced workers. However, during the recession the workforce providers who helped us recruit the vulnerable fathers we interviewed for this book saw a substantial increase in the proportion of their clients who were working-poor, rather than chronically unemployed, fathers. The change in client composition required providers to upgrade the kinds of employment assistance they provided their new clients, and to experiment with higher levels of skills training more suitable for experienced workers. Some of this experimentation involved partnerships with employers. As a result, providers were eager to participate in such efforts, and have experience on which policymakers can build.

Given the importance that vulnerable fathers attach to their children's education, policymakers should also consider testing a strategy that links payment of current support to a child savings account that subsidizes the savings of vulnerable fathers (and mothers) toward their children's education. Such asset-building programs, called Individual Development Accounts (IDAs), usually enable participants to save for a car, home, business, or education. Many vulnerable fathers would find the opportunity to retire debt and save for their children's education very attractive. Sherraden's studies show that even when parents contribute little to such accounts, children with child savings accounts go further in school than children lacking such accounts. A likely explanation is that once parents commit their own funds to increase the probability that their child has access to higher education, parents make the other sorts of investments, such as modifications of the child's home environment, and activities that promote academic achievement.

For example, many vulnerable fathers are anxious to reduce the arrears they accumulated since they were laid off during the Great Recession. States are able to do this for fathers with children who received public benefits, because the arrears belong to the state. It is much more difficult to do this for fathers with children who have not received public benefits, because the arrears are owed to the custodial mother. However, states might consider encouraging mothers and fathers whose children have never received public benefits to enter into an exchange in which the mother agrees to save a portion of the arrears the father pays toward the child's education. This exchange could be used as the parents' contribution to a traditional child savings account that is matched by a third-party donor. Though the cost to the father is no different from the cost he would incur without this commitment from the mother, the father's incentive to pay on arrears would be greater, because his arrears payments would leverage other funds for their child's education.

Many of these ideas are currently being tried in some states.[50] The Department of Health and Human Services encourages states to include families in the child support system in programs that help low-income families build assets. Through the Building Assets for Fathers and Families initiative (BAFF), families receive training in financial literacy and debt management, including how they can better manage child support payments and avoid arrears.[51] Families that receive this training are also eligible to have their savings in individual development accounts matched. Some programs match savings dollar for dollar, while other programs provide up to $8 for each dollar saved. The Department of Health and Human Services encourages states to provide incentives for custodial and noncustodial parents in the child support system to participate in Individual Development Accounts by entering "an agreement that trades reductions in arrearages for steady contributions to support payments and savings by noncustodial parents."[52]

Unfortunately, few fathers participating in the Building Assets for Fathers and Families program use the individual development accounts available to them. To be eligible for the matches, individuals must be in families with incomes no more than 200 percent of the poverty level, or they must be in families receiving welfare benefits. Most fathers with incomes this low have not yet established stable employment, or have earnings too low to take advantage of the available matches.[53] However, this focus on very low-income families ignores what we have found, namely: nonresident fathers with earnings as high as $40,000 remained poor or near poor after meeting their usual expenses and paying child support. Thus, raising the income limit for receiving the matches for vulnerable fathers could reduce poverty among children and families served by the child support system. Doing so would also enable such programs to reach vulnerable fathers who had stable employment histories prior to the recession, and who can be expected to have sufficient earnings to take advantage of the matches offered to IDA account holders as the nation returns to full employment.

Conclusion

A new vision for economically vulnerable nonresident fathers is needed: one that understands that these fathers are a much larger and more diverse population than most observers realize. What's more, the long-term social, economic, and demographic forces that have made vulnerable nonresident fathers more numerous and widespread show no signs of abating in the near future. If anything, the reverse is probably true. Nevertheless, there is reason for optimism. After a long and deep recession, the nation appears to be returning to full employment. As a result, strategies that can help chronically unemployed fathers enter the workforce, and lower their debts, become more feasible. Full employment also makes it easier to put working-poor fathers back to work, but on a pathway to the wages that afford them, their children, and families a decent standard of living. Even before the recession, there was a mandate to provide new pathways into the middle class. There was also a mandate to restore the quality of life that middle class families enjoyed in the United States. Heightened awareness that greater income inequality is a lingering wound of the recession makes these mandates stronger.

However, in response to these mandates, we must act on the knowledge we now have that many of the men whose economic prospects we want to improve have children living elsewhere. Providing a middle class standard of living for these men and their families means taking account of all the children for whom these men should be providing. This will require adjustments to our thinking, in the same way that reforming welfare nearly two decades ago required adjustments that acknowledged the special circumstances of the mothers who were moving from welfare to work. Besides work, these parents needed child-care services, reliable medical care for their children, and a subsidy to make work pay. So we radically altered the way employers, welfare agencies, workforce providers, and the tax code treated these parents. Equally radical changes, such as those suggested here, will be required to alter the way employers, workforce providers, community colleges, the financial sector, and the child support enforcement system treat working-poor parents with children living elsewhere.

Finally, some stakeholders will be concerned that focusing more attention on working-poor fathers, as we have done in this book, will result in reductions in supports for chronically unemployed fathers. This would be a mistake because chronically unemployed fathers face more serious barriers than working-poor fathers, and so many past efforts to remove these barriers have been found wanting. We share this concern, but we still believe that more attention must be paid to the working poor, for four reasons. First, recent studies show that upward mobility is harder for children if their parents divorce, than if their parents never marry. It is also difficult if their parents do not complete college.[54] Thus, continuing to ignore working-poor fathers forecloses opportunities to promote economic mobility. Second, because efforts to assist chronically unemployed fathers have been so disappointing for so long, we need some successes. These successes are more likely to occur among fathers with some prior work experience. The third reason is related. By focusing more attention on working-poor fathers, we can reframe the discussion about the American family from one that focuses on reducing poverty to one that focuses on reducing inequality. The latter framing will find common ground with a broader constituency. As a result, vulnerable fathers are more likely to receive public support.

The last reason became clear after a discussion with the chief executive of the workforce development agency that has been working with chronically unemployed men and fathers since the mid-1980s. He was asked: "Suppose you were able to take a chronically unemployed father, and move him into a job paying $30,000 a year. Would that represent a slam dunk?" Without hesitation he answered, "yes." We continued. "You mean on your best day, all you can do is move a father from the underground economy into the ranks of the working-poor?" His response was a knowing silence. Put differently, if we continue to ignore the working poor, what will the chronically unemployed have to look forward to?

Some readers would agree that such an achievement might be good enough for the fathers, families, and children of some disadvantaged group from whom we expect little. But things are not this simple, anymore. Half of all births to women under 30 are non-marital births, half of all marriages end in divorce, and 60 percent of all men earn $40,000 or less. So, economically vulnerable fathers are not strangers from communities that we watch on the nightly news. They are close to home for most of us: our neighbors, our nephews, or even, our sons.

Antonio's Story

Antonio is a 32-year-old Puerto Rican father of two children, both of whom live with their mothers. Antonio is divorced, but recently remarried several months earlier to a woman he had been seeing for the past two years. She has three children of her own, all teenagers, but none of whom currently live with the couple. Antonio's children are younger: his daughter is 11 and his son is 7. Though his son lives close by, in the Bronx, his daughter lives a distance away in Pennsylvania. He dreams of one day having a large, blended family with all of the children living together with him, but at this time, it will remain a wish. The couple does not have the space. Antonio has been unemployed for eight months and had to give up his apartment. He is currently living with the woman who raised him until he can get back on his feet financially.

Antonio grew up poor, without either biological parent, and was instead raised by another relative, a woman he refers to as his mother. "I hate to sound typical, but I guess I am going to sound pretty typical. I grew up in a relatively poverty stricken neighborhood in the Bronx—South Bronx—uh, mother and father not there, you know, raised by another family member who I ultimately came to see and call mom." Antonio regards his early marriage at 17, after completing high school, as an effort to construct a family, even though he now realizes that he got married for all of the wrong reasons. However, he also acknowledged that it pushed him to become the man he is today. During his marriage, Antonio obtained a two-year associate's degree; however, he accelerated his drinking and drug use, a problem that started in high school and also one that ran in his family.

Over the course of the marriage, he and his wife had a girl. Antonio lived with his daughter for the first four years of her life, prior to the marriage ending in divorce. He continued abusing drugs and alcohol. During this period, Antonio entered into another relationship, and he and his girlfriend gave birth to a boy. He remained for the first two years of his son's life, then the relationship ended. Though he had been a functioning addict, attending school and holding down well-paying jobs, things started to spin out of control. "I would say from '04 to '06—I had a little, you know, a downward spiral. And ultimately I had to go into treatment. I had no choice."

During the height of his drug use and subsequent treatment, he withdrew from both children. He did not see his daughter again for six years, or his son for three years. Recently, he has reunited with both children, and they each have a close relationship with Antonio. His daughter and former wife live in Pennsylvania. Antonio does not see his daughter as often as he would like, although she stays with him during school holidays and over the long summer vacations. Antonio and his former wife have maintained a good relationship, and work together for the sake of their daughter. However, the relationship with the mother of his son is a lot more difficult to navigate. His ex-girlfriend still holds a great deal of anger toward him. Before visitation was established, she would let him see his son at some times, but then, not at others. Currently, he sees his son every week, on Saturday. Antonio finds the limited time he spends with both children difficult, and tries to fit in as much as he can in a short amount of time. It is never enough.

Though his substance abuse complicated his personal life, it created less of a problem at work. Antonio was employed at a variety of jobs, beginning by working in construction. He also worked in retail, eventually managing a large grocery store. He earned a good living, which he feels might have had the perverse effect of increasing his drug use, finally pushing him over the edge. "When you give a 20-some-year-old a $60,000 paycheck a year, and you've got all these beautiful fringe benefits and all of the things, you know, things got pretty ugly pretty fast."

Antonio has a child support order for both children. During the time he was in treatment, his order in New York was suspended, though his order in Pennsylvania was not. Along with treatment, Antonio was assigned a caseworker and now attends bimonthly group classes that deal with child support issues and other issues that impact fathers. Some of the services that he is given are career support, to help locate employment. Antonio is very happy with the help he has been given, and feels he is very close to finally finding a job.

Child support for his daughter is taken out of his unemployment checks, but even so, he has fallen behind. Because he receives so little from unemployment, he has very little money, barely enough to pay his bills, but not enough to save any money. The order for his son has remained suspended until he finds work; however, when the order was in force, it was set at $50 per month, the self-support reserve. He expects it to remain the same. Because of the low support order, Antonio currently has no arrears for his son. Antonio wants to continue to build a relationship with both children. He lost time due to his addictions. He doesn't want to lose any more.

7 Resources

FORTUNATELY, THE LIST of organizations and agencies working to advance research, policy, and practice affecting economically vulnerable fathers and their families is growing every year. While the following list is selective, it includes the organizations on which we have relied and with which we have collaborated closely over the past 20 years. Interested readers who want additional information or who want to become involved can trust that these organizations have long-standing and proven expertise.

The Policy Community

- Federal Offices of Family Assistance and Child Support Enforcement; http://www.acf.hhs.gov/programs/css
- Administration for Children and Families: https://www.acf.hhs.gov/
- White House Domestic Policy Council: http://www.whitehouse.gov/administration/eop/dpc
- Office of Planning, Research, and Evaluation (OPRE): http://www.acf.hhs.gov/programs/opre
- The Income Security Subcommittee of the Ways and Means Committee:
- The Department of Labor : http://www.dol.gov/

- The Office of the Assistant Secretary for Planning and Evaluation (ASPE): http://aspe.hhs.gov/
- The Office of Faith Based and Neighborhood Partnerships: http://www.whitehouse.gov/administration/eop/ofbnp

The Research Community

- Brookings Institution, Center on Children and Families: http://www.brookings.edu/about/centers/ccf
- MDRC: http://www.mdrc.org/
- The Joint Center for Political and Economic Studies: http://www.jointcenter.org/
- The National Campaign to Prevent Teen and Unplanned Pregnancy: http://thenationalcampaign.org/
- John Hopkins University's Institute for Policy: http://ips.jhu.edu/
- Center for Policy Research (CPR): http://www.centerforpolicyresearch.org/
- The Urban Institute; http://www.urban.org/
- National Center for Children in Poverty, Columbia University: http://www.nccp.org/
- Fragile Families and Child Well-Being Study: Princeton University: Center for Research on Child Well-Being (CRCW) and Center for Health and Well-Being, the Columbia Population Research Center: http://www.fragilefamilies.princeton.edu/
- The National Center for Children and Families (NCCF) at Columbia University: http://policyforchildren.org/
- Institute for Research on Poverty, University of Wisconsin–Madison: http://www.irp.wisc.edu/index.htm

Selected Fatherhood Initiatives and Practitioners Active in Promoting the Responsible Fatherhood Field

- The Fathers and Families Coalition, Inc.: http://fathersandfamiliescoalition.org/
- The National Fatherhood Leaders Group (NFLG): http://www.nflgonline.org/

- The National Partnership for Community Leadership: http://www.npcl.org/
- Men's Health Network: http://www.menshealthnetwork.org/
- Father's Incorporated: http://www.fathersincorporated.com/
- National Responsible Fatherhood Clearinghouse: http://www.fatherhood.gov/
- Coalition on Human Needs: http://chn.org
- The National Council of La Raza: http://nclr.org
- National Fatherhood Initiative: http://www.fatherhood.org/
- The National Latino Fatherhood and Family Initiative: http://www.nationalcompadresnetwork.com/nlffi/nlffi.html
- NYC Dads: The Mayor's Fatherhood Initiative: http://www.nyc.gov/html/hra/nycdads/html/home/home.shtml
- Fathers Support Center: http://www.fatherssupportcenter.org/
- The New England Fathering Conference: http://www.nefatheringconference.org/
- National Center for Fathering: http://fathers.com/
- Fathers, Families, and Healthy Communities: http://www.ffhc.org/

Appendix

In-depth interviews with 39 economically vunerable nonresident fathers were an important source of information we gathered for this book. The interviews provided a means for fathers to make meaning of their: family background, current family composition and living situation, relationships with children, child support obligations, organizational involvement and support, employment history, educational attainment and goals, personal finances and expenses (current income, taxes, savings, and debt).

To analyze these interviews, we used an interpretive approach intended to reveal the lived experiences and contexts of the nonresident fathers who spoke to us.[1] First we read more than 500 pages of verbatim interview transcripts multiple times. From these readings we condensed the interview material into shorter narrative summaries, which captured the essence of the stories being told. Next, we divided the data in the transcripts according to the major themes that were revealed in the father's narrative summaries. Finally, we identified overlapping themes and patterns across transcripts and reported these themes and patterns throughout the chapters of this book, with illustrative quotes drawn from the interview transcripts staying true to the language of the participants.[2] We also discussed the ways in which the themes and patterns supported or extended previous literature about nonresident fathers.[3,4]

In the end we felt that this approach disembodied the themes from the fathers who lived them, which shortchanged both the fathers and our readers. Therefore, we concluded each chapter with a life story of one of the fathers whose experiences best illustrated the theme in the following chapter. In the end, it was hard to select the father whose experiences best illustrated the main themes in each chapter, so we included seven additional father stories here. We refer to these fathers throughout the book in the appropriate chapter, and hope our readers will take a moment to read these stories as well.

Claudio

Claudio is a 33-year-old Dominican father with two sons. Neither child lives with him; both live with their mother and her husband in Florida. Her husband was once a friend of Claudio's; however, they are no longer close, and the prior friendship has been a source of friction, making it difficult for Claudio to maintain a relationship with his children, something he very much wants. Claudio is currently employed in New York as a program assistant in AIDS services. It is a job that he loves, and one for which he feels real passion. For this reason, he is grateful for his period of incarceration, where he earned his certificate and was able to qualify for the job in the company where he currently works.

Claudio was raised in a single-parent household, one of four children. He was born in Central Islip but was raised in Brooklyn. Growing up without a father left an indelible impression. "To me it, it means like when I said that I meant like, you know, nobody ever really like sat down and explained to me the responsibility of being a man period. Or, you know, what it is to be a, a father. What is a good father? Nobody defined that to me." As a pre-adolescent, Claudio searched for a father figure, finding a man whom he believed he could trust. Instead, he molested Claudio in a church. Now a father himself, Claudio understands and identifies with a child's need for male guidance.

Just before he turned 20, Claudio searched for his father. When they met, Claudio found him to be very cold, someone who would treat him like a son one minute and a stranger the next. "You know, it got to a point where I asked him and I think that was his turning point and I just broke down in tears and asked him why did you bring me to this earth? Why? What was the, you know, I guess the look on my face, I—and with the energy I said it, you know, and I'll never forget the look on his face like, you know, it was like a look of, you know, shock." Father reached out to son and they began to get to know one another. However, Claudio's father was a drug addict, and Claudio began using drugs, too. Just when they had started to become close and soon after his oldest son was born, Claudio's father died. His death was very difficult for Claudio and left a great deal still unfinished.

Claudio does not want his children to suffer as he did and wants to be present in their lives; however, they live far away, in Florida, and he does not see them. He cannot, and the absence creates great sadness. The life he so wanted, he feels he cannot live.

> I always wanted to have like a family, kids, you know, the picket fence, the house, you know, just have a job, come home, and settle down and it's like for some reason I felt like my whole life I could never attain that. Like it, it wasn't meant for me. I feel something like Batman, you know, like the dark knight cause it's like I feel like it was meant for me to be alone cause I have a beautiful heart as I am told but yet I've been through so much in my life it's like I was forced to be, you know, cold.

Claudio is unable leave New York to visit his children in Florida, as it would violate the conditions of his parole. Most of his twenties were spent incarcerated. Now he feels the same sense of isolation and abandonment as when he was when in prison. "I mean they're in Florida, I'm out here I'm on parole. It's not like I can just go out there, you understand? It's outta my jurisdiction. So I can't do nothing about it anyway so I just like kinda leave it in God's hands." Claudio was sent to prison for a robbery. The crime was never committed, and he believes he was arrested because his friend, whom he trusted with his plan, contacted the police. When the incarceration occurred, his oldest son was one. His youngest

had not yet been born. His second incarceration occurred directly afterward, also for robbery. During his imprisonment, he did see his sons, albeit very infrequently, when Claudio's
mother brought them. Now, contact with his children is limited to care packages and telephone calls. His vision of an ideal family life is slowly slipping away.

Communication with his children has been limited because their mother married Claudio's
former friend who had initially contacted the police, leading to his arrest and incarceration.
It has created an obstacle that has been difficult to surmount. His friend became resentful,
and prohibited Claudio from speaking with his children, even on the telephone. As a result,
Claudio lost touch with his boys. However, recently, he has re-established contact and is
working with the courts to try to ensure that he remains a presence. The courts had not
been involved at the beginning. However, his former girlfriend and mother of both sons had
asked Claudio repeatedly to relinquish his parental rights. One night, he became very angry.
This led to a confrontation and he threatened her. As a result, she turned to the courts to
document the incident. Now, Claudio hopes the courts will also work with him, to modify
his child support order and help him so he can see his sons.

Claudio has support orders for both children and is currently in arrears of over $20,000.
Even though he is working, he has a great deal of money taken from his paychecks, making
it difficult for him to support himself with the little that remains. The arrears have left him
with a driver's license suspension and a frozen bank account. He has been working with
the courts to try to get his support situation under control since the initial order was set
by default, and the same order remains open in two counties. Claudio is currently sending the child support money voluntarily, because if it were automatically deducted from his
paycheck, his entire wages would be garnished. Claudio doesn't mind paying child support.
He feels that fathers should support their children, and he is not a deadbeat dad. But he also
understands that some situations are very complicated.

> I would like to say that, you know, um, there are good fathers out there and not
> every father that is not with their kids is not a bad father. Some circumstances are
> just very, very sensitive and there's more to it than just a father not being there for
> his child, and I more or less am starting to understand why my father wasn't really
> there so, you know, but then again there's, you know, if falls back to what I wish, if
> everybody could just be judged individually, that's it.

Charles

Charles is a 32-year-old African American father with a 15-month-old daughter. Currently,
he is unemployed and lives with his parents in his old bedroom. He is grateful that he has a
place to stay but considers his current situation temporary, until he can "get back on track."
He has a current support order for his daughter, established when her mother applied for
benefits. When he first received a letter from child support, he was very surprised because
he thought that when you had a child, an agreement was reached between the parents. He
never envisioned that anyone else would be involved.

> I didn't know what was really going on. So when I got the letter, I'm like wow, child
> support, what is this? I know what it means—what a child means and what support

means—but you put the two together, you know, you've got to support your child. I thought it was just between you and the mother, but I figured out the state—when you're on the system—the state plays a bigger role in wanting their money back for what they're giving for what you're supposed to be doing, so I understand what's going on.

At first, the order was set for $50 a month. Charles was able to pay this amount by cobbling together money made from his informal work. However, the rate was increased to $60 a week, when he missed his second court date. Charles failed to attend because he simply didn't realize it was necessary. The first time, he had received notification in the mail; however, this time he did not. His current employment situation makes his new order impossible to pay and he now has arrears of about $1,000. A new court date has been set.

Charles is the oldest of three boys. His parents are married. Charles grew up in New York and describes his childhood as "sheltered." His mother kept him in the house to try to keep him off the streets. Though both parents are high school graduates, Charles dropped out of high school in the 12th grade. "...I dropped out after twelfth—in the twelfth grade, one credit shy of graduating. I was chasing girls. I wanted to play hooky...." He is now working on his GED and has some college credits, with the goal of eventually getting a college degree. Because Charles now has a child, he recognizes that his first priority is taking care of his daughter. "If it's about me, I'll do what I want, but when you've got a child, it's not about you anymore. It about you doing for your child."

Charles feels strongly that fathers need to support their children. In fact, in addition to the support he pays, he also buys his daughter diapers, food, and clothing. "I just do what I—what I, you know, things that—as a father should do. Even if you're paying child support, I still feel you should still buy Pampers—buy milk if your daughter needs it. Why not?" Charles feels the little extras are necessary, especially given that his support money goes to the state to reimburse for TANF payments, rather than his daughter. He guesses he spends close to $100 each month to make sure his daughter has what she needs.

Charles sees his daughter every day. He feels that it is important for a father to spend time with his children. " I want to take her places. I take her to the park. She's too young to understand and fully grasp what's going on but, you know, just take her outside, take her—just spend time. Children just want to spend time with their parents, and when they act out, it's just because they're not spending enough time getting the attention they need."

Currently, Charles has been working informally, as a bouncer and in small security jobs. He doesn't mind informal work but would prefer the consistency and regular paychecks that formal employment offers; however, he has not worked at a regular job since 2004, when he suffered a knee injury. It took about a year before his injuries healed and he was able to walk again. During this period, he could not work. Charles received a sizable legal settlement from his injuries and lived off the money for some time, making a job less critical. But with a new daughter, money has become much more pressing and Charles wants to find a job. He has been preparing for his security license so he can return to the security field. Charles wants to make sure that this time, he is able to complete the goals he sets for himself—something he was unable to do when he was younger. He now has to consider another person, his daughter.

Yeah, that's the change, I mean, if a child can't change your life, then you—there's something that you're doing wrong, because children is the most beautiful thing in the world. To bring in—bring life to a child is changing—changing from doing what you used to do and make you want to be a man. It's made me want to be a man.

Just wishing I had the knowledge of what I know now earlier—much earlier, even before I had a child, so this way when I had a child, I would be, uh, better prepared. Even though I'm not doing bad now. My child is happy. I'm happy.

Jeffrey

Jeffrey is a 27-year-old African American father. He has one son who now lives with his mother, though he had been living with Jeffrey for the first four years. Jeffrey's relationship with the mother of his son is not ideal, and for two years, he had not been able to see his son at all because she moved without letting him know her new address. This left Jeffrey very upset. His high child support order did not allow for the luxury of a lawyer, and he turned to the courts for help. He now sees his son each Saturday for six hours, time he cherishes. "We talk about school, you know, and what he does in school, what he wants to be, you know, try and get him set early. And I just explain life to him. You know, that's what we do a lot, just try to explain life to him and play, you know, go outside and let him have his fun, and then do the educational stuff and, you know, try to jam it all into six hours, you know? That's the best I can do, so."

Now that his son no longer lives with him, Jeffrey has been paying child support. This arrangement began about the time he started working at Merrill Lynch; however, he is currently unemployed, having lost his job due to the crisis in the mortgage market. Though his job was not directly impacted, as he worked desktop support, the company lost a tremendous amount of money. Jeffrey survived the first round of layoffs but was not as fortunate the second time around. "I survived that first layoff, and then they said they were laying off more people, and I've only been there a year and a half, so I knew it was coming and, um, the way people act, you know the whole funny stuff. It was terrible, and I got laid off there." Though Jeffrey was able to find another job in his field, this time at the auction house, Sotheby's, he lost that job after a few months when Sotheby's began layoffs. He now works part-time for a foundation that helps urban youth by providing college credits, skills, and experience, a program from which Jeffrey graduated. It provided his entry to Merrill Lynch.

Jeffrey grew up in a single-parent household, the oldest of three children. He described the household as very poor and unstable. Though he had the opportunity to be a good student in school, he often had to provide for himself and his siblings while his mother pursued an education. Jeffrey started living on his own at 17 and never finished high school, acquiring a GED instead. Though he attended one semester of college, he had to drop out, but he also took some online courses from a local city university. Now, as an adult, he realizes the value of school and wants to return to finish his degree. He wishes he had known about things a lot earlier. "You know, I just wish I would have known the opportunities that were available to me, I wish I'd have known how to capitalize on certain things." But for now, a college degree has to wait; he needs to find a job first. Jeffrey is also interested in starting a nonprofit to help teenagers who have left home and are living on the streets. He has been studying proposal writing to try to get his ideas for the nonprofit off the ground. He is also trying his hand at writing a novel, to share some of his experiences with others. He keeps himself very busy.

Jeffrey enjoys the time he and his son spend together, but he doesn't see him as often as he would like, and he wants the limited time they spend together to be fun and memorable. Even though he is unemployed, Jeffrey buys him toys and equipment that they can play with together. Both father and son are very athletic and like to play sports. Jeffrey bought him some basketball outfits and sneakers to make it extra special time. But education is a priority. Each time they see each other, Jeffrey teaches his son new words, what he refers to as "big words," and explains their meaning and how and when to use them. He wants his son to value school and not miss opportunities, as he did. "I want him to take advantage of every opportunity available to him, so every grant—all the grants that's available out here and every, you know, learning what to gear yourself towards like as a career."

When Jeffrey lost his job, he was able to get a downward modification on his child support order from $1,600 a month to $532 a month. Even with the modification, it was hard to pay his child support order in full each month, but he managed to keep arrears very low, to just $400. Jeffrey has found some short-term work in addition to his part-time job, but in general, the salaries were much lower than he had earned previously. Even though things were very difficult for him, Jeffrey did not mind paying child support. He knew the laws. Jeffrey understood that once you have a child, things change. "So if you want something, it's your child and then you, you know." He had friends who were also fathers, and they didn't always understand that their children must come first, it's not a choice.

Jeffrey is earning some money, but after his child support payments, he is only left with about $600 a month, half of what he earns. This does not leave him with enough to live on his own, so for the time, he is living at home. He hopes this arrangement doesn't last long. What he does earn he spends on bills, with a small amount left over for his savings. But he wants things to be better for his son than they are for him.

> I just want my future to be all right and my son's future. You know, I don't want to be in the same type of situation I feel my father left me in, you know, where I have to worry about and take care of myself to—to, you know. I don't want my son to have to go through that where he has to struggle and work, work, work, just to take care of himself and not have anything, at least give him some relief, so that's my concern.

Kevin

Kevin is a 48-year-old African American father of a 5-year-old boy. He also has two adult children from prior relationships, a daughter who is 24 and a son who is 27. He and his wife got married when she learned she was pregnant. They have been married for over four years but were in the process of seeking a divorce. Their family home, located in upstate New York, is about one and a half hours outside New York City and was a long commute to the hospital where Kevin works as a phlebotomist. He has been doing that job, drawing blood from patients, for the past 12 years. After the separation, Kevin moved back to New York City, and his wife and son remained in upstate New York. Now, it is a shorter commute to the hospital but a very long way from his son.

Though at one time Kevin and his wife both had the same goals, this was no longer the case. Financial difficulties, ultimately resulting in bankruptcy, pulled the couple apart, with the burden of the financial debts falling on Kevin. He now feels frustrated that agreements they had once made together no longer seemed to matter. This is especially true regarding the issue of child support and visitation. Both parents had agreed to resolve these issues without the involvement of the courts, but suddenly, the courts were very much involved. But the hardest thing for Kevin has been the separation from his son. He was used to seeing him every day when he would return home from work. "Not seeing him around me like when I get off of work and stuff like that. Having him with me on the weekends and then watching him go to his mother's, you know what I'm saying? I get that empty, loneliness feeling."

Kevin has joint custody and sees his son every other weekend and during school holidays. However, he has limited contact with his two older children. When they were born, "hustling and getting caught up in the game" became seductive forces that pulled him away. More recently, Kevin has tried to reestablish contact with his two older children, but despite his efforts, they do not remain close. He has occasional contact with his son, who recently called to inform him that he was a grandfather. Kevin has not yet seen his grandson but is certain it will happen soon. His daughter is in college, continuing her education with post-graduate work. He is very proud of her achievements. Kevin has learned to accept the fact that his behavior created the distance, and now that his children are old enough to understand what happened, they can choose whether or not to resume the relationship. In light of this painful lesson, maintaining a close relationship with his young son has become a priority.

Kevin is one of five children. He has an older brother and sister, and a younger brother and sister. He is right in the middle. Though the family was from Virginia, they moved to the Bronx when Kevin was born, living in a high-rise housing project. As a child, Kevin had very severe asthma that impacted his life growing up, and on several occasions he was hospitalized for his condition. Both his mother and father were employed by hospitals; his father was a nutritionist and his mother worked in housekeeping. All was not always calm at home, as Kevin's father had a drinking problem. Though Kevin was shy as a child, he became less so as he got older and got into trouble. He never finished high school, dropping out in the 12th grade, preferring instead to earn money by working. However, in hindsight, he wishes he could have finished school and maybe gone to college. Instead, he got his GED on his first attempt and for now, that will have to be enough.

Kevin enjoys spending time with his son, and wants him to have the kind of childhood he never had because of his severe asthma. He wants him to have fun. Even though Kevin and his wife are getting divorced, his son seems to be happy, but there are moments when he'd like to protect him from everything that's happening. "But I mean, when you break home, you know what I'm saying.... I mean, some things trickle down. You know what I'm saying? Because he has asked me on occasions, Dad, are you and Mom going to get back together? I was like, son, that's not going to happen but Dad will always protect you and love you and always be there for you. He said, okay Dad."

Kevin has been more fortunate than most, he has had continuous employment. Though he doesn't make a lot of money, he paid support for his two oldest children until they aged out, and he has a support order for his youngest child. Prior to his current job, he had been out of work for eight years, and did have some hard times. But he took a course and found the job at the hospital, and has worked there ever since. The job also has health care benefits, which is important because Kevin is able to cover his son. Though he enjoys his job, he hopes one day to return to school and study respiratory therapy. It would allow him to remain in the same field but it pays more money, something that could really help since child support takes so much money out of his paychecks and he is left with very little. Sometimes, Kevin gets frustrated that fathers are not afforded the same flexibility and sympathy as mothers. Kevin doesn't want much; all he wants is to continue to see his son.

> ...Do you not see that us fathers hurt and bleed like women do? And I'm not, don't get me wrong....I can tolerate a lot of stuff I really can, but sometimes we can use a little help, you know what I'm saying, and I don't want to just go create another family. I just want to see my little one, I just want to be in his life. Now if you want to help me, help me stay in his life. Don't continuously just look at me as the one who doesn't show up or, because that is not the case.

Michael

Michael is a 39-year-old African American father. He has two children by two different mothers. His daughter is 14 years old and his son is 12. Neither of his children lives with him, and currently Michael does not have a close relationship with either child. Though he last lived in Georgia, Michael did not like the South and moved back to New York City, where he was raised. He lives with his mother until he is able to get back on his feet financially. Michael is attending school, hoping to earn his bachelor's degree in community human services so he can one day get a master's degree in social work, but that's a long way off. Right now, he is just trying to get his head above water. He needs a job.

Michael was one of four children, raised in a single-parent household by his mother. His father abandoned the family when Michael was only two years old. He had no relationship with his father when he was a child, but has re-established some limited contact now that he is an adult. Michael respects the fact that his mother "never took him for child support, never," even if the family struggled. He felt that his mother did the best she could. "She really did, she did a heck of a job with what the cards she was dealt she played her hand very well, um, it was okay."

Michael, too, doesn't mind hard work. However, he is embittered and frustrated from his experiences with the child support system.

> The system need to be revamped, somehow it has to be revamped because, yes, we need to take care of our kids, yes, we do, they need to live but we need to live also. Don't penalize me because I have a kid, you know what I'm saying? I just always felt like, you know, it's just a way to keep, to keep us down that's just my opinion, you know, and I don't, you know, I just felt like the system was designed to just keep us down, frustrated, angry, you know, and um, if we don't work then more penalties come, then they want to put us in jail, you know, and um, you know, that sort of thing, so I just feel like the system is designed to destroy us.

Michael has a support order for his daughter that was initiated when her mother applied for Medicaid and food stamps, directly after the birth. Mother and child live in New York, and although Michael felt he had a good relationship with his daughter earlier, he finds it difficult to interact with her now. "She was always a typical girl, you know, but with my daughter I feel like, um, I have to be very delicate, very gentle, you know, and I don't really know what to do." Michael last saw her several weeks ago at Easter. She asked him for some money, which he provided, and when he asked her about school, she informed him that she was doing okay, only failing two classes. "So I made a deal with her; you do better in school, show me your report card, tell me what you want as long as it, you know, um, within range, you know, as in sensible and I'll get it for you, but school has to be your number one priority and I stress that with both of my children." Father and daughter communicate primarily by telephone and text messages.

Michael has not seen his son in close to two years. Michael and the mother of his son were married. They lived as a family until his son was about six, when they separated acrimoniously. Child support was part of the divorce proceedings. After Michael moved to Georgia, his ex-wife also moved down South, about two hours away. They had arranged to meet in the middle, and she could drop off their son to visit; however, she reneged on the agreement. When they went to court, Michael felt she lied and left the judge with the impression that he did not want to see his son. Now, he does not even answer Michael's calls, nor will he speak to Michael's daughter, his half-sister.

Though Michael wants to support his children, he is having great difficulty given his financial circumstances. He has fallen $1,300 in arrears, an amount he believes is small. He feels this proves he has been paying child support, because after all, had he not been paying, his arrears would be much greater. Between the two orders, he owes just over $500 in support each month. Even when he was working and earning over $800 every two weeks with overtime, after child support took their money, he had little to show for his efforts. "Child support was taking all my money . . . could you imagine? You work for two weeks and get 295. Them people don't care man, they didn't care. If, if, I would have became homeless as long as they took they child support money." Michael did try to have his New York order modified, but it was denied. He was ordered to attend fatherhood classes, send whatever money he was able to afford, and return again to court in two months. He was sent to Strive, an experience he enjoys. He has made friends among the other fathers in similar situations.

Michael feels harassed by the system and wishes he could work off the books just to keep child support at bay. He is more than willing to accept the risk of being caught by the Internal Revenue Service if it would keep child support unaware of his earnings. "I, I tell you this, the way child support chase you I would rather work off the books sometimes cause I could care less about the income tax thing cause I don't get no money back anyway but to keep child support off me and just send them, just send them what I can and they don't have to know exactly what I make." But really, what Michael would like is a full-time job with benefits. He thinks that when you get older, benefits are important.

For the time being, Michael is afraid of even the most ordinary of things, like a bank account. Though he has had bank accounts in the past, he fears that child support might freeze his account. It's too great a risk because he is unemployed and will accumulate arrears since he has no paycheck. "No, I, I, I refuse to open a bank account . . . as soon as you open a bank account and you owe child support, they freeze your account. I had an account when I was paying, you know, when, when, when I'm working. You know, I'm I'm, you know, I may get an account but if I'm not, as soon as I'm not working I close it. I don't want to leave no money in there cause they'll freeze it." For Michael, he feels it's safer carrying his money in his pocket.

David

David is a White, 24-year old married father, currently living in a rental apartment with his wife, her 5-year-old son, and their 2-year-old daughter. Though he would prefer to live in a house, the apartment is not in a bad neighborhood and David describes himself as pretty happy. David has a second child, also a girl, and also two years old. By way of explanation, he says, "I won't get into the details. I was naughty but they are both two." David's stepson has started kindergarten, and he described him as a "little smart mouth." Though his other daughter lives with her mother, she and David remain close. She visits the household often, and is treated as a sister by the other children. David's wife works by providing child care in their apartment. Money is tight, but David loves his family and feels that right now, everyone has what they need.

David grew up close to where he currently resides, about 20 minutes away. He described his childhood home as idyllic, with acres upon acres of land, where his family went swimming and fishing. David was one of three brothers, all of whom share the same father but have different mothers. David and one brother lived with the family, while the other lived with his grandmother. His mother was a full-time homemaker and his father often worked extra shifts. Though money was tight, his father always seemed to provide for the family.

David appreciates being a father and feels he has a great relationship with all of his children. He finds the hardest part of being a parent disciplining his children when they misbehave. However, he loves spending time with his children, taking them to the park to play or other activities that they enjoy. David has a lot of fun with his stepson. They play football and watch wrestling together. David believes it is his responsibility to be a father to his stepson, because the child's biological father is currently incarcerated. David is also close to his daughter. She has become a real "daddy's girl" and enjoys hearing her father play music from his band, something her mother doesn't always appreciate. David has also maintained a close relationship with his other daughter. Although she lives with her mother, he sees her once a week and every weekend.

Though David has a good relationship with all of his children, he has traveled a very rough road with child support enforcement. He is required to pay child support for his one nonresident daughter, but must also pay birthing costs for both of his children since he was not married to either mother at the time his daughters were born. New York State is one of many states that recover birthing costs for non-marital children that were originally charged to Medicaid. When paternity tests revealed that David was the father, paternity was established and the court ordered him to pay birthing costs for both children, and child support for his nonresident daughter. At the time, he was working as a taxi driver and the employer failed to deduct child support payments automatically from his pay. David failed to realize the mistake and assumed, incorrectly, that as long as taxes were being withheld, so, too, were support payments. He discovered his error when he was summoned to the court to explain why he had not paid all of the child support due. Child support administrators did not find his explanation for the oversight reasonable, and ordered him to pay the birthing costs for both children, in addition to a nine percent penalty. Trying to modify the charges took some time, resulting in a loss of his driver's license for a short period, and the very real risk of incarceration. David does not mind paying child support. He feels it's his responsibility as a father. However, he is angry about the birthing costs, especially the costs for his wife, given that the payments have created hardship for the family.

David was last employed at Hope Windows, a firm that produced prison windows. He worked as a grinder, a job that required grinding down the welds on the windows before they were painted. The job appealed to his sense of aesthetics. He was able to see each window in its rough form as it reached his station and worked hard to create a perfectly finished surface. David really enjoyed the work, "it was like artwork to me. I mean it's like, that's what it looked like before it got to me, and that's what it looks like when I got done with it." The job gave him a sense of accomplishment. In addition to the work satisfaction, he received health insurance, vacation time, and later, a pay increase. However, after 14 months and without warning, David was laid off, along with many other employees. Prior to his job as a grinder, David had been driving a cab. He was paid by commission rather than an hourly wage and consequently made very little money. In past positions, he earned below minimum wage. None of the jobs had any fringe benefits.

David is currently unemployed. Though he does get unemployment benefits from his most recent position, it is not enough to pay all the bills. To make ends meet, the family needs to pool all of their resources. Bills are prioritized, with the most important ones paid first. Food stamps have helped to supplement their grocery budget. David also plays in a band, something he did for pleasure. Now, he admits, he needs the money he makes from performing, anywhere from $50 to $100. Everything must be carefully calculated. He also works off the books, something that also needs careful consideration, as he does not want to jeopardize his unemployment benefits. "Sometimes I'll get somebody to ask me to fix a—fix their car for them or something, you know, I'll do that. You know, I'll make a little extra there, but that don't happen too often." The family also receives additional income from the child-care services his wife provides in their home.

After the loss of his most current job, David was ordered to participate in a fatherhood program, where a case manager helped him to get a downward modification of his child support order based upon his unemployment insurance. Additionally, the judge suspended the penalties and interest accumulation during his period of unemployment. These changes have made his support payments manageable. However, David is concerned that this reprieve may be only temporary. To pay the penalties, David must find a high-paying job. Minimum wage will not be enough to pay what is owed. Lack of a college degree and experience have made his job search that much more difficult. However, a high-paying job will also increase his support obligations, perhaps making it even more difficult financially. The state also wants money up front for each case, money that David does not have. Because he is unable to pay the amount, a lien has been placed on his property, including his cars, drums, and guitar, all of which are necessary to earn a living. David has been left with very conflicted feelings about child support enforcement in New York: anger and frustration at the system, but also a sense that he is paying for the poor decisions he made prior to marrying.

Ronald

Ronald is a White, 27 year-old man. He is married, and a father of three children, the first of whom was born when Ronald was 20. The children, two boys and a girl, range in age from two to seven years old. Both boys have ongoing medical problems, with the youngest legally blind in one eye and the oldest needing medication to control his hyperactivity. At the moment, none of the children live with the family, as all three remain in foster care.

Ronald and his wife are currently taking a series of classes to try and have the children returned to them. This includes parenting classes, anger management, and drug and alcohol abuse treatments. Ronald admits it hasn't been easy for the family. Though they just moved into an apartment in August, prior to the move, they were forced to live in a van. They didn't have the money to be able to afford anything else.

Though Ronald has been unemployed, his wife has been working full time. This has been very difficult, as Ronald has watched his wife struggle to keep the family together under very trying times. His wife also battles mental illness, causing frequent mood swings and abusive behavior toward both Ronald and the children. After a particularly upsetting incident in which she threatened the family, Ronald left home and called the police and child protective services to intervene. Four days later, he was notified that his children had been placed in child protective services. When he attempted to remove his children and return them home, he was told his wife had informed police he was a drug dealer with a violent past. Although Ronald had a history of drug use and had been imprisoned, he had been released two years ago and has remained drug free for five years. Subsequently, the children have been in placed in foster care for the past seven months, during which time both parents have made a great deal of progress in meeting the conditions for reunification of the family. Despite these difficulties, Ronald and his wife have been together eight and a half years, although they only decided to marry recently.

Ronald grew up poor. His parents were dependent upon welfare, Medicaid, housing subsidies and food stamps to support the family. Ronald's impression was that they were lazy and survived by working the system, something that Ronald never wants to do. Although he admits that he is broke, Ronald feels proud that he is not like his parents, dependent upon government support. "I don't get no welfare, I may be broke but I'm not, I don't get no food stamps, I don't get no welfare, I don't get nothing." It has been difficult for him, though. Ronald did not graduate from high school, dropping out like his mother, and the lack of a high school degree has limited his employment options. Decades earlier, there were plenty of manufacturing jobs but those left long ago. Ronald did find a job working in a hotel, but was fired in 2001. He lost that position when the hotel had a management change, although he believed his obesity played a role in the decision to fire him. Ronald has had a weight problem much of his adult life, causing health concerns. However, he has recently lost weight, leading to improved health and energy. His weight loss has also improved his relationship with his children, as he is now able to play more actively with them, something he was unable to do when obese.

After Ronald lost his hotel job in 2001, he was able to scrape by with small jobs. However in 2002, with his first child on the way, Ronald felt a pressing need to earn more money and turned to the drug trade. He started selling cocaine.

> The felony charges were in 2002. I just turned 20 years old. My son was born February 21st. I just started selling cocaine before that to try and get some money together 'cause I couldn't do, you know, there ain't nothing here. This little Jamestown is the armpit of New York. There's, there's really nothing here.

Thirty-eight days after his son was born, Ronald was arrested and sentenced to prison. This was his third arrest. Ronald has been incarcerated three times over the course of his life, the first time for assault, when he was only 15 years old. He stabbed a young man at a festival in his hometown, because, he admitted, he didn't like the way he approached him. "I stabbed a guy in front of five thousand witnesses just because he came to me the wrong way. I was 15 when that happened." After his release, Ronald stayed out of trouble for two years.

However at 18, he got into a fight with his girlfriend over a girl he had been talking with at a party. The argument had escalated, and when she tried to keep him from leaving by standing between him and the door of his truck, he pushed her hand from the door and left. She accused Ronald of pushing her down, and reported the incident to the police.

Ronald has not had a full time job for almost nine years, despite performing well on his last regular job. His employment record, combined with his incarceration record, has made finding any job very difficult. In prison, Ronald's life stopped, although everything and everyone on the outside of the prison walls continued to grow and change. It left a large and painful impact on his life.

> Your whole world are so, so you quit growing and if anything you actually digress in life after it, cause when you come back out everything's got moved around in the world and, and, and technology and, and, and reality and everything is kept going but you been stuck right here.

After his release, the effect of prison continued to stalk him when he began searching for employment. All employers, even those for minimum wage jobs, do a background check, and a felony conviction is almost certain rejection. Ronald noted that "even at McDonalds, I find out, you know, they do the background check, boom, felony."

Off the books employment offered a way to earn money. Ronald collected scrap metal and sold it for cash. At the time, scrap metal prices were very high, and he was able to earn about $8,300.00 for seven months of work. His weekly earnings would range from an average low of $100.00 to a high of $1,500.00, however, unlike formal employment, it was difficult to anticipate how much he might earn from one week to the next. Scrap metal costs were high and he was able to earn enough money, however, the high prices drove others to also sell the metal, and it became harder to find with so many competitors.

His job prospects now are not good. He works at odd jobs, whatever he can find, shoveling snow, raking leaves, remodeling bathrooms, whatever can earn him money. In the meantime, his wife has been his primary support system through these difficult times, and Ronald does what he can to help pay for food and other household expenses. Friends have also supported the couple, giving Ronald small jobs to try and help.

> Yeah, it's it's what I can scrape together literally cause people hear my story and feel bad and, even though, you know, people here don't even make a lot of money but getting a little $10 or $20 extra if enough of them get together and do it, I could make, maybe make a paycheck by the end of the week, by the time it's done, you know? And there's a lot of people that, that do do that and a lot of people that have gotten to know me.

This has been very important to Ronald, especially after feeling so abandoned by employers after his release from prison.

Ronald must pay child support for his three children in the foster care system. Although the order has been set at $25.00 per month, the state minimum, it has still caused financial strain on the couple. To raise money, Ronald has liquidated all of the possessions he has acquired. This included everything from waterbeds to video games. Ronald hopes to one day find a real job, a good job. However, the felony conviction makes his job search that much more difficult, and limits the kind of jobs for which he can apply.

Notes

CHAPTER 1

1. Hymowitz, K. S. (2006). *Marriage and caste in America: Separate and unequal families in a post-marital age*. Chicago: Ivan R. Dee.

2. Blankenhorn, D. (1996). *Fatherless America: Confronting our most urgent social problem*. New York: HarperCollins.

3. Popenoe, D. (1996). *Life without father: Compelling new evidence that fatherhood and marriage are indispensable for the good of children and society*. New York: The Free Press, a Division of Simon & Schuster, Inc.

4. Murray, C. (2013). *Coming apart: The state of White America, 1960–2010*. New York: Crown Publishing Group, a Division of Random House Inc.

5. Coontz, S. (1992). *The way we never were: American families and the nostalgia trap*. New York: Basic Books, a Member of the Perseus Books Group.

6. Stacey, J. (1997). *In the name of the family: Rethinking family values in the postmodern age*. Boston: Beacon Press.

7. http://www.nytimes.com/2008/06/15/us/politics/15text-obama.html?pagewanted=all

8. http://articles.baltimoresun.com/2006-08-23/news/0608230259_1_cosby-coppin-state-audience.

9. Nock, S. L. (1998). The consequences of premarital fatherhood. *American Sociological Review*, 63(2), 250–263.

10. Cherlin, A. J. (2004). The deinstitutionalization of American marriage. *Journal of Marriage and Family*, 66(4), 848–861.

11. Edin, K., & T. Nelson (2013) *Doing the best that I can: Fatherhood in the inner city*. Berkeley: University of California Press.

12. Thornton, A. (1989). Changing attitudes toward family issues in the United States. *Journal of Marriage and the Family*, 51(4), 873–893.

13. Watkins, E. S. (2011). *On the Pill: A Social history of oral contraceptives, 1950–1970*. Baltimore, MD: Johns Hopkins University Press.

14. Thornton, A., & Young-DeMarco, L. (2001). Four decades of trends in attitudes toward family issues in the United States: The 1960s through the 1990s. *Journal of Marriage and Family*, 63(4), 1009–1037.

15. Wilson, W. J. (1997). When work disappears: The world of the new urban poor. New York: Vintage Books, a Division of Random House, Inc.

16. Anderson, E. (1990). *Streetwise: Race, class, and change in an urban community*. Chicago: University of Chicago Press.

17. Anderson, E. (ed.) (2008). *Against the wall: Poor, young, black, and male*. Philadelphia: University of Pennsylvania Press.

18. Edin, K., & Nelson, T. J. (2001). Working steady: Race, low-wage work, and family involvement among noncustodial fathers in Philadelphia. In E. Anderson & D. Massey (Eds.), *Problem of the century: Racial stratification in the United States* (pp. 375–404). New York: Russell Sage Foundation.

19. Young, A. (2000). On the outside looking in: Low-income Black men's conceptions of work opportunity and the good job. In S. Danziger & A. Lin (Eds), *Coping with poverty: The social contexts of neighborhood, work, and family in the African American community* (pp. 141–171). Ann Arbor, MI: University of Michigan Press.

20. Holzer, H. J., & Offner, P. (2006). Trends in the employment outcomes of young Black men, 1979–2000. In R. B. Mincy (Ed), *Black males left behind* (pp. 11–38). Washington, DC: Urban Institute Press.

21. Sum, A., Khatiwada, I., McLaughlin, J., & Palma, S. (2011). No country for young men: Deteriorating labor market prospects for low-skilled men in the United States. *The Annals of the American Academy of Political and Social Science*, 635(1), 24–55.

22. Murray, C. (2013). *Coming apart: The state of White America, 1960–2010*. New York: Crown Publishing Group, a Division of Random House Inc.

23. Levy, F. (1998). *The new dollars and dreams: American incomes and economic change*. New York: Russell Sage Foundation.

24. Smeeding, T., Garfinkel, I., & Mincy, R. B. (eds.). (2011). Young disadvantaged men: Fathers, families, poverty, and policy. *The Annals of the American Academy of Political and Social Science*, 635(1), 6–21.

25. Sum, A., Khatiwada, I., McLaughlin, J., & Palma, S. (2011). No country for young men: Deteriorating labor market prospects for low-skilled men in the United States. *The Annals of the American Academy of Political and Social Science*, 635(1), 24–55.

26. Wheaton, L., Sorensen, E., Russell, V., & Versteeg, J. (2005). *Benefits and costs of increased child support distribution to current and former welfare recipients*. Washington, DC: The Urban Institute.

27. Mincy, R. B., Klempin, S., Jethwani-Keyser, M., Seith, D., 7 Miller, D. (2012, November). Creating an effective work incentive for low-income non-custodial parents: Lessons from the New York State experience. Paper presented at 2012 APPAM Fall Research Conference, Baltimore, MD.

28. After all, according to the National Survey of Family Growth, men earning up to $40,000 per year represented 60 percent of total male wage earners in the United States.

29. Following our earlier study, which focused on fathers earning up to $10,000, these calculations apply the New York State Child Support guidelines for one and two children, respectively. Federal law requires all states to establish numerical guidelines that, in most cases, judges must use in setting child support orders. In principle these guidelines should result in the child having the same financial resources as they would have had if their parents continued to live together. Some states have achieved this goal using the father's income alone to set the child support guideline, assuming the mother is providing support in kind. Other states use both the mother's and father's income to calculate the amount of the child support order. We use the New York State guidelines in part because they rely only upon the income of the noncustodial parent. Our estimates assume average expenses by expense category for all consumers in a given income category, using estimates from the Consumer Expenditure Survey (CES), US Bureau of Labor Statistics, September 2010. Expenditures for the income categories were calculated as the linear interpolation of the CES reported averages for the income classes just below and above the threshold used.

30. The credit was worth up to $1,095.

31. We compared information from the short survey with the information we obtained from the interviews, and where discrepancies existed, we reported the information from the long interviews because we believed it to be more accurate.

32. Mendenhall, R., Edin, K., Crowley, S., Sykes, J., Tach, L., Kriz, K., & Kling, J. R. (2012). *Social Service Review, 86*(3), 367–400.

33. By contrast, if the mother of his child paid $300 to have her taxes prepared, including the additional information to file for the federal EITC with one dependent, her net gain could be as much as $2,500 if she had two children; earnings gain would have been as much as $4,200.

34. Besides authorizing the credit program, New York legislators also authorized funding for five pilot programs across the state. These programs provided job-placement services to nonresident fathers who were not paying their child support. The staff at these fatherhood programs helped us set up interviews with 30 interested fathers who met all of our study criteria, except full compliance with their child support orders over the tax year. It is likely that the fathers recruited for the study were active and engaged participants in the fathering programs operating at the recruitment site, those that were actively showing up for services, and those that the program staff knew would meet the study criteria.

35. For a complete description of these criteria, please see: Jethwani, M., Mincy, R., & Klempin, S. (2014). I would like them to get where I never got to: Nonresident fathers' presence in the educational lives of their children. *Children and Youth Services Review*. 40, 51–60 (in printing).

36. Jethwani, M., Mincy, R., & Klempin, S. (2014). I would like them to get where I never got to: Nonresident fathers' presence in the educational lives of their children. *Children and Youth Services Review*. 40, 51–60 (in printing).

37. Each participant was given a pseudonym to protect confidentiality. These illustrative quotes are drawn from the interview texts and stay true to the language of the fathers we interviewed.

CHAPTER 2

1. Perry, M. J. (2010). The great mancession of 2008–2009. Statement before the House Ways and Means Committee Subcommittee on Income Security and Family

Support on "Responsible Fatherhood Programs," http://www. aei. org/files/2010/06/17/GreatMancessionTestimony. pdf), accessed December 12, 2012.

2. Sahin, A. (2011). Unemployment gender gap during the current recession. *Current Issues in Economics and Finance,* 16(2), 1–7.

3. Bureau of Labor Statistics, table A-36, Unemployed persons by age, sex, race, Hispanic or Latino and ethnicity, marital status, and duration of unemployment,http://www.bls.gov/web/empsit/cpseea36.htm, accessed August 27, 2013.

4. Bureau of Labor Statistics, table A-36, Unemployed persons by age, sex, race, Hispanic or Latino and ethnicity, marital status, and duration of unemployment, http://www.bls.gov/web/empsit/cpseea36.htm, accessed August 27, 2013.

5. Taylor, P., R. Morin R. Kochhar, et. al. (2010). *A balance sheet at 30 months: How the great recession has changed life in America.* Washington, DC: Pew Research Center, 2010.

6. Bureau of Labor Statistics, table A-36, Unemployed persons by duration of unemployment, http://www.bls.gov/webapps/legacy/cpsatab12.htm, accessed February 17, 2014.

7. Van Horn, C. E. (2013). *Working scared (or not at all): The lost decade, great recession, and restoring the shattered American dream.* Lanham, MD: Rowman & Littlefield.

8. Borie-Holtz, D., Van Horn, C., & Zukin, C. (2011). *No end in sight: The agony of prolonged unemployment.* New Brunswick, NJ: Rutgers University Heldrich Center for Workforce Development.

9. Farber, H. S. (2011). *Job loss in the Great Recession: Historical perspective from the displaced workers survey, 1984–2010* (No. w17040). Cambridge, MA: National Bureau of Economic Research.

10. Sahin, A. (2011). Unemployment gender gap during the current recession. *Current Issues in Economics and Finance,* 16(2), 1–7.

11. Hoynes, H., Miller, D. L., & Schaller, J. (2012). Who suffers during recessions? *Journal of Economic Perspectives,* 26(3), 27.

12. Stykes, J. B., Manning, W. D., & Brown, S. L. (2012). *Estimating nonresident fatherhood: Evidence from the CPS, NSFG, and SIPP.* Bowling Green State University, National Center for Family and Marriage Research.

13. Van Horn, C. E. (2013). *Working scared (or not at all): The lost decade, great recession, and restoring the shattered American dream.* Lanham, MD: Rowman & Littlefield.

14. Borie-Holtz, D., Van Horn, C., & Zukin, C. (2011). *No end in sight: The agony of prolonged unemployment.* New Brunswick, NJ: Rutgers University Heldrich Center for Workforce Development.

15. Van Horn, C. E. (2013). *Working scared (or not at all): The lost decade, great recession, and restoring the shattered American dream* (p. 10). Lanham, MD: Rowman & Littlefield.

16. Edin, K., & Nelson, T. J. (2001). Working steady: Race, low-wage work, and family involvement among noncustodial fathers in Philadelphia. In Elijah Anderson & Douglas S. Massey (eds.), *Problem of the century: Racial stratification in the United States* (pp. 375–404). New York, NY: Russell Sage Foundation.

17. Wilson, W. J. (1996). *When work disappears: The world of the urban poor* (p. iii). New York: Alfred Knopf.

18. Western, B. (2006). *Punishment and inequality in America.* New York: Russell Sage Foundation.

19. The Pew Charitable Trusts (2010). *Collateral costs: Incarceration's effect on economic mobility.* Washington, DC: The Pew Charitable Trusts.

20. Alexander, M. (2012). *The new Jim Crow: Mass incarceration in the age of colorblindness.* New York: The New Press.

21. Holzer, H. J., Raphael, S., & Stoll, M. A. (2003). *Employment barriers facing ex-offenders.* Center for the Study of Urban Poverty Working Paper Series.

22. Holzer, H. J., Raphael, S., & Stoll, M. A. (2003). *Employment barriers facing ex-offenders.* Center for the Study of Urban Poverty Working Paper Series.

23. The Pew Charitable Trusts (2010). *Collateral costs: Incarceration's effect on economic mobility.* Washington, DC: The Pew Charitable Trusts.

24. Anderson, E. (2000). *Code of the street: Decency, violence, and the moral life of the inner city.* New York: W. W. Norton & Company.

25. Venkatesh, S. A. (2006). *Off the books.* Cambridge, MA: Harvard University Press.

26. Edin, K., Lein, L., & Nelson, T. (2002). Taking care of business: The economic survival strategies of low-income, noncustodial fathers. In F. Munger, (ed.) *Laboring below the line: The new ethnography of poverty, low-wage work and survival in the global economy* (pp. 125–147); New York: Russell Sage FoundationRaijman, R. (2001). Mexican immigrants and informal self-employment in Chicago. *Human Organization,* 60(1), 47–55.

27. This would be worth $27,856 in 2009.

28. Waller, M. R., & Plotnick, R. (2001). Effective child support policy for low-income families: Evidence from street level research. *Journal of Policy Analysis and Management,* 20(1), 89–110.

29. Cancian, M., Heinrich, C. J., & Chung, Y. (2009). *Does debt discourage employment and payment of child support?: Evidence from a natural experiment.* University of Wisconsin, Institute for Research on Poverty.

30. Freeman, R. B., & Waldfogel, J. (1998). Does child support enforcement policy affect male labor supply. In I. Garfinkel, S. McLanahan, D. R. Meyer, & J. Seltzer. *Fathers under fire: The revolution in child support enforcement* (pp. 94–127). New York: Russell Sage Foundation.

31. Holzer, H. J., Offner, P., & Sorensen, E. (2005). Declining employment among young black less-educated men: The role of incarceration and child support. *Journal of Policy Analysis and Management,* 24(2), 329–350.

32. Rich, L. M., Garfinkel, I., & Gao, Q. (2007). Child support enforcement policy and unmarried fathers' employment in the underground and regular economies. *Journal of Policy Analysis and Management,* 26(4), 791–810.

33. Miller, D. P., & Mincy, R. B. (2012). Falling further behind? Child support arrears and fathers' labor force participation. *Social Service Review,* 86(4), 604–635.

34. Young, A. (2006) Availability and use of workforce development programs. In R. B. Mincy (ed.), *Black males left behind.* Washington, DC:The Urban Institute.

35. Young, A. & Pam Holcomb (2007). *Voices of young fathers: The partners for fragile families demonstration.* Washington, DC: The Urban Institute.

36. Hamer, J. (2001). *What it Means to be Daddy: Fatherhood for Black Men Living Away from Their Children.* New York: Columbia University Press.

37. Young, A. (2006). *Low-income black men on work opportunity, work resources, and job training programs.* (147–184). In R. B. Mincy, (ed.) *Black males left behind.* Washington, DC: The Urban Institute.

38. Young, A. & P. Holcomb (2007). *Voices of young fathers: The partners for fragile families demonstration.* Washington, DC: The Urban Institute.

39. Anderson, E. (2000). *Code of the street: Decency, violence, and the moral life of the inner city.* New York: W. W. Norton & Company.

CHAPTER 3

1. Legler, P. K. (1996). The coming revolution in child support policy: Implications of the 1996 welfare act. *Family Law Quarterly, 30*(3), 519–563.

2. Huang, C. C., & Pouncy, H. (2005). Why doesn't she have a child support order?: Personal choice or objective constraint. *Family Relations, 54*(4), 547–557.

3. As we pointed out in Chapter 1, most surveys relating to child support undercount nonresident fathers because those who do not pay support are unwilling to admit that they are nonresident fathers. To infer what fathers were paying, Chung and Pouncy relied upon a survey of mothers' receipt of child support payments.

4. Nepomnyaschy, L., & Garfinkel, I. (2010). Child support enforcement and fathers' contributions to their non-marital children. *The Social Service Review, 84*(3), 341.

5. Chambers, D. L. (1979). *Making fathers pay: The enforcement of child support.* Chicago: University of Chicago Press.

6. Sorensen, E., & Zibman, C. (2001). Getting to know poor fathers who do not pay child support. *Social Service Review, 75*(3), 420–434.

7. Cancian, M., Meyer, D. R., & Han, E. (2011). Child support: Responsible fatherhood and the quid pro quo. *The ANNALS of the American Academy of Political and Social Science, 635*(1), 140–162.

8. Bartfeld, J., & Meyer, D. R. (2003). Child support compliance among discretionary and nondiscretionary obligors. *Social Service Review, 77*(3), 347–372; Cancian, M., Meyer, D. R., & Han, E. (2011). Child support: Responsible fatherhood and the quid pro quo. *The ANNALS of the American Academy of Political and Social Science, 635*(1), 140–162.

9. Huang, C. C., Mincy, R. B., & Garfinkel, I. (2005). Child support obligations and low-income fathers. *Journal of Marriage and Family, 67*(5), 1213–1225.

10. Formoso, C. (2003, May). Determining the composition and collectability of child support arrearages. Volume 1: The longitudinal analysis. First part of final report for Section 1115 grant # 90-FD-0027. Submitted to the Office of Child Support Enforcement, Administration for Children and Families. U.S. Department of Health and Human Services. http://www.dshs.wa.gov/dcs/resources/reports.asp; Peters, J. (2003, June). Determining the composition and collectability of child support arrearages. Volume 2: The case assessment. Second part of final report for grant # 90-FD-0027. Submitted to the Office of Child Support Enforcement, Administration for Children and Families. U.S. Department of Health and Human Services. http://www.dshs.wa.gov/dcs/resources/reports.asp, accessed June 2, 2014.

11. Wheaton, L., & Sorensen, E. (2010). Extending the EITC to noncustodial parents: Potential impacts and design considerations. *Journal of Policy Analysis and Management, 29*(4), 749–768.

12. In 2009 dollars, these ranges were between $11,400 and $21,600 and between $1.14 and $11,406.

13. US Department of Health and Human Services. Office of Inspector General. (2002, February). Child Support for Children on TANF. OEI-05-99-00392. http://oig.hhs.gov/, accessed June 2, 2014.

Since most nonresident parents are fathers, we use fathers to describe data on nonresident parents holding child support arrears. However, nonresident has been male or female, and therefore, a more accurate rendering of these findings would be nonresident parents.

14. Sorensen, E., Sousa, L., & Schaner, S. (2007) *Assessing child support arrears in nine states and the nation*. Washington, DC: The Urban Institute.

15. US Office of Child Support Enforcement (2004). *Understanding child support debt: A guide to exploring child support debt in your state*. Washington, DC, http://www.acf.hhs.gov/programs/css/resource/a-guide-to-exploring-child-support-debt-in-your-state, accessed June 2, 2014.

16. Although we included having an active child support case as an eligibility criterion for the study, two fathers were inadvertently included in the study who did not have active cases. One had recently completed his child support obligations after his youngest child turned 21, and one had recently divorced and was expecting a child support order to begin imminently. Thus of the 43 fathers we interviewed only 41 had active child support orders.

17. For this sample, N = 34. Two participants with suspended orders are not included, one due to a lack of information about arrears, and the other due to his exceptional circumstances. His order has been suspended for the duration of substance abuse treatment, but he owes $7,200 in arrears. Five additional participants are not included due to a lack of information. Finally, as previously mentioned, two participants do not have active child support cases.

18. Lin, I. F. (2000). Perceived fairness and compliance with child support obligations. *Journal of Marriage and Family, 62*(2), 388–398.

19. For this part of our study there were only 28 fathers, because the combination of information on length of case and amount of arrears was missing for 13 participants. Two fathers did not have active child support cases.

20. Mincy, R. B., Klempin, S., & Schmidt, H. (2011). Young disadvantaged men: Fathers, families, poverty, and policy; special editors: Timothy M. Smeeding, Irwin Garfinkel, Ronald B. Mincy: Policy papers: Income support policies for low-income men and noncustodial fathers: Tax and transfer programs. *Annals, 635,* 240–240.

21. Sinkewicz, M., & Garfinkel, I. (2009). Unwed fathers' ability to pay child support: New estimates accounting for multiple-partner fertility. *Demography, 46*(2), 247–263.

22. Cancian, M., & Meyer, D. R. (2011). Who owes what to whom? Child support policy given multiple-partner fertility. *Social Service Review, 85*(4), 587–617.

23. US Government Accountability Office. (2011, January). *Child support enforcement: Departures from long-term trends in sources of collections and caseloads reflect recent economic conditions*. GAO-11-196. www.gao.gov/products/GAO-11-196, accessed June 2, 2014.

24. US Government Accountability Office. (2011, January). *Child support enforcement: Departures from long-term trends in sources of collections and caseloads reflect recent economic conditions*. GAO-11-196. www.gao.gov/products/GAO-11-196, accessed June 2, 2014.

25. US Government Accountability Office. (2011, January). *Child support enforcement: Departures from long-term trends in sources of collections and caseloads reflect recent economic conditions*. GAO-11-196. www.gao.gov/products/GAO-11-196, accessed June 2, 2014.

26. US Government Accountability Office. (2011, January). *Child support enforcement: Departures from long-term trends in sources of collections and caseloads reflect recent economic conditions*. GAO-11-196. www.gao.gov/products/GAO-11-196, accessed June 2, 2014.

27. Bartfeld, J. & Meyer, D. R. (2003). Child support compliance among discretionary and nondiscretionary obligors. *Social Service Review* 77(3): 347–372; Meyer, D., Ha, Y., & Hu, M. (2008). Do high child support orders discourage child support payments? *Social Service Review, 82*(1), 93–118; Ha, Y., Meyer, D. R., & Cancian, M. (2006). The stability of child support orders. *Report to the Wisconsin Department of Workforce Development*. Madison,

WI: Institute for Research on Poverty; Ha, Y., Cancian, M., Meyer, D. R., & Han, E. (2008). Factors associated with nonpayment of child support. *Report to Wisconsin Department of Workforce Development*. Madison, WI: Institute for Research on Poverty, University of Wisconsin–Madison; Wu, C. F. (2011). *Child support in an economic downturn: changes in earnings, child support orders, and payments*. Champaign; Urbana: University of Illinois.

28. Beller, A. H., & Graham, J. W. (1986). The determinants of child support income. *Social Science Quarterly, 67*(2), 353–364; Hanson, T. L., Garfinkel, I., McLanahan, S. S., & Miller, C, K. (1996). Trends in child support outcomes. *Demography, 33*(4), 483–496; Sorensen, E., & Hill, A. (2004). Single mothers and their child-support receipt. *Journal of Human Resources, 39*(1), 135–154; Freeman, R. B., & Waldfogel, J. (2001). Dunning delinquent dads: The effects of child support enforcement policy on child support receipt by never married women. *The Journal of Human Resources, 36*(2); 207–225. Case, A. C., Lin, I., & McLanahan, S. S. (2003). Explaining trends in child support: Economic, demographic, and policy effects. *Demography, 40*(1), 171–189.

29. Hatcher, D., & Lieberman, H. (2003). Breaking the cycle of defeat for 'deadbroke' noncustodial parents through advocacy on child support issues. *Clearinghouse Review, May–June; 37*(1 and 2), 5–22. Henry, R. K. (1999). Child support at a crossroads: When the real world intrudes upon academics and advocates. *Family Law Quarterly, 33*, 235.

30. Ha, Y., Cancian, M., & Meyer, D. R. (2010). Unchanging child support orders in the face of unstable earnings. *Journal of Policy Analysis and Management, 29*(4), 799–820. doi:10.1002/pam.20534; Kost, K. A., Meyer, D. R., Corbett, T., & Brown, P. R. (1996). Revising child support orders: The Wisconsin experience. *Family Relations, 45*(1), 19–26.

31. Bartfeld, J., & Meyer, D. R. (2003). Child support compliance among discretionary and nondiscretionary obligors. *Social Service Review, 77*(3), 347–372; Meyer, D., Ha, Y., & Hu, M. (2008). Do high child support orders discourage child support payments? *Social Service Review, 82*(1), 93–118; Sorensen, E., & Hill, A. (2004). Single mothers and their child-support receipt. *Journal of Human Resources, 39*(1), 135–154; Huang, C. (2010). Trends in child support from 1994 to 2004: Does child support enforcement work? *Journal of Policy Practice, 9*(1), 36–53; Nepomnyaschy, L., & Garfinkel, I. (2010). Child support enforcement and fathers' contributions to their non-marital children. *Social Service Review, 84*(3), 341–380.

32. Mincy, R. B., & De la Cruz Toledo, E. (2013) *Unemployment and child support compliance though the Great Recession* (mimeo). Columbia University School of Social Work.

33. Mincy, R. B., Miller, D. P., & De la Cruz Toledo, E. (2013). *Child support compliance during economic downturns* (mimeo). Columbia University School of Social Work.

34. Ha, Y., Cancian, M., & Meyer, D. R. (2011). The regularity of child support and its contribution to the regularity of income. *Social Service Review, 85*(3), 401–419.

35. Bartfeld, J., & Meyer, D. R. 2003. Child support compliance among discretionary and nondiscretionary obligors. *Social Service Review, 77*(3), 347–372.

36. Complete child support information was available for 12 of the 13 chronically unemployed fathers. Of those 12, 8 had no (2 fathers) or low (6 fathers) arrears; 1 had medium arrears, 2 had high arrears, and 1 had very high arrears. Of the 21 laid-off working-poor fathers, child support information was available for 17. Half of these 17 fathers had no to low arrears; half had medium to high arrears. The amount of arrears varied in similar fashion among the 6 out of 9 employed fathers with complete child support information: 2 had no arrears, 1 had low arrears, 1 had high arrears, and 1 had very high arrears.

37. Similarly, a recent study found that while the absolute amount of arrears had no effect on labor force participation or average weeks worked during the year among

low-to-moderate income fathers, those with high arrears in proportion to their income worked fewer weeks during the year and there was some evidence that they were less likely to participate in the labor force. Miller, D. P., & Mincy, R. B. (2012). Falling further behind? Child support arrears and fathers' labor force participation. *Social Service Review*, 86(4), 604–635.

38. Hatcher, D., & Lieberman, H. 2003. Breaking the cycle of defeat for 'deadbroke' non-custodial parents through advocacy on child support issues. *Clearinghouse Review, May–June*, 37(1 and 2), 5–22.; Henry, R. K. (1999). Child support at a crossroads: When the real world intrudes upon academics and advocates. *Family Law Quarterly, 33*, 235.

39. Baron, D. G. (1999). The many faces of child support modification. *Journal of the American Academy Matrimonial Law, 16*, 259.

40. US Department of Health and Human Services. Office of Inspector General. (1999, March). Review and adjustment of support orders. OEI-05-98-00100. oig.hhs.gov/oei/reports/oei-05-98-00100.pdf, accessed June 2, 2014.

41. US Department of Health and Human Services. Office of Inspector General. (2000, July). The establishment of child support orders for low income non-custodial parents. OEI-05-99-00390. oig.hhs.gov/oei/reports/oei-05-99-00390.pdf, accessed June 2, 2014.

42. Hatcher, D., & Lieberman, H. (2003). Breaking the cycle of defeat for deadbroke non-custodial parents through advocacy on child support issues. *Clearinghouse Review, May–June*. 37(1 and 2), 5–22.

43. Roulet, M. (1998). Negotiating their child support system: Report from a discussion of policy and practice. Center for Family Policy and Practice, http://www.cffpp.org/publications/NegotiatingChdSupReco.pdf, accessed June 2, 2014.

44. Chambers, D. L. (1979). *Making fathers pay: The enforcement of child support*. Chicago: University of Chicago Press.

45. Patterson, E. (2008). Civil contempt and the indigent child support obligor: The silent return of debtor's prison. *Cornell Journal of Law and Public Policy, 18*(1). 95–142.

CHAPTER 4

1. Portions of this chapter have been presented in: Jethwani, M., Mincy, R., & Klempin, S. (2014). I would like them to get where I never got to: Nonresident fathers' presence in the educational lives of their children. *Children and Youth Services Review*. 40, 51–60. http://dx.doi.org/10.1016/j.childyouth.2014.02.009

2. Blankenhorn, D. (1996). *Fatherless America: Confronting our most urgent social problem*. New York: HarperCollins; Lessing, E. E., Zagorin, S. W., & Nelson, D. (1970). WISC subtest and IQ score correlates of father absence. *The Journal of Genetic Psychology, 117*(2), 181–195; Popenoe, D. (1996). *Life without father: Compelling new evidence that fatherhood and marriage are indispensable for the good of children and society*. New York: Martin Kessler.

3. Kane, D. C., Gadsden, V. L., & Armorer, K. R. (1997). *The fathers and families core learnings: An update from the field. National Center on Fathers and Families, University of Pennsylvania, Graduate School of Education*. http://eric.ed.gov/?id=ED455906

4. Johnson, W. (2003). Work preparation and labor market experiences among urban, poor, nonresident fathers. In S. Danziger & C. Lin (eds.), *Coping with poverty: The social contexts of neighborhood, work, and family in the African American community* (pp. 224–258). Ann Arbor: University of Michigan Press; Johnson, W. E. (2010). *Social work with African American Males: Health, mental health and social policy*. New York: Oxford University Press.

5. Cabrera, N., Tamis-LeMonda, C. S., Bradley, R. H., Hofferth, S., & Lamb, M. E. (2000). Fatherhood in the twenty-first century. *Child Development*, 71(1), 127–136.

6. Nock, S. L. (1998). The consequences of premarital fatherhood. *American Sociological Review*, 63(2), 250–263.

7. Lerman, R. (2010). Capabilities and contributions of unwed fathers. *The Future of Children* 20(2), 63–85.

8. McLanahan, S., & Sandefur, G. (1994). Growing up with a single parent: What helps, what hurts. Cambridge, MA: Harvard University Press.

9. Sorensen, E., & Zibman, C. (2000). To what extent do children benefit from child support? New information from the National Survey of America's Families, 1997. *Focus*, 21(1), 34–37.

10. Meyer, D. R., & Hu, M. (1999). A note on the antipoverty effectiveness of child support among mother-only families. *Journal of Human Resources*, 34(1), 225–234.

11. Argys, L. M., Peters, H. E., Brooks-Gunn, J., & Smith, J. R. (1998) The impact of child support on cognitive outcomes of young children. *Demography*, 35(2), 159–173; Baydar, N., & Brooks-Gunn, J. (1994). The dynamics of child support and its consequences for children. *Child support and child well-being*, 257–284.

12. Eagly, A.H. (1987). The analysis of sex differences in social behavior: A new theory and a new method. In. A. H. Eagly (ed.), *Sex differences in social behavior: A social role interpretation* (pp. 7–41). Hillsdale, NJ: Lawrence Erlbaum Associates.

13. Chambers, D. L. (1979). *Making fathers pay: The enforcement of child support.* Chicago: University of Chicago Press.

14. Bowman, P. J. (1990). Coping with provider role strain: Adaptive cultural resources among Black husband-fathers. *The Journal of Black Psychology*, 16(2), 1–21; Bowman, P. J., & Forman, T. A. (1997). Instrumental and expressive family roles among African American fathers. In R. J. Taylor, J. S. Jackson, & L. M. Chatters (eds.), *Family life in black America* (pp. 216–247). Thousand Oaks, CA: Sage Publications; McAdoo, J. L. (1993). The roles of African American fathers: An ecological perspective. *Families in Society*, 74, 28–35.

15. Anderson, E. (2008). *Against the wall: Poor, young, black, and male*. Philadelphia: University of Pennsylvania Press.

16. Hamer, J. (2001) *What it means to be daddy*. New York: Columbia University Press; Roy, K. (2004). You can't eat love: Constructing provider role expectations for low-income and working-class fathers. *Fathering*, 2, 253–276.

17. Marsiglio, W., & Roy, K. (2012) *Nurturing dads: Social initiatives for contemporary fatherhood*. New York: Russell Sage; Waller, M. R. (2002). *My baby's father: Unmarried parents and paternal responsibility*. Ithaca, NY: Cornell University Press.

18. Hamer, J. (2001). *What it means to be daddy*. New York: Columbia University Press; Hammond, W. P., Caldwell, C., Brooks, C., & Bell, L. (2011). Being there in sprit, fire, and mind: Expressive roles among nonresidential African American fathers. *Research on Social Work Practice*, 21, 308–318.

19. Gadsden, V. L., & Bowman, P. (1999). African American males and the struggle toward responsible fatherhood. In V. Polite & J. Davis (eds.), *A continuing challenge in times like these: African American males in schools and society*. New York: Teachers College Press.

20. Lamb, M. E. (2000). A history of research on father involvement: An overview. *Marriage and Family Review*, 29, 23–42; Roy, K. M. (2004). You can't eat love: Constructing provider role expectations for low-income and working-class fathers. *Fathering*, 2, 253–276.

21. Anderson, E. (2008). *Against the wall: Poor, young, black, and male*. Philadelphia: University of Pennsylvania Press; Bowman, P. J., & Forman, T. A. (1997) Instrumental and expressive family roles among African American fathers. In R. J. Taylor, J. S. Jackson, & L. M. Chatters (eds.), *Family life in black America* (pp. 216–247). Thousand Oaks, CA: Sage Publications; McAdoo, J.L. (1988). Changing perspectives on the role of the Black father. In P. Bronstein & C. P. Cowan (Eds.) *Fatherhood today: Men's changing role in the family* (pp. 79–92). New York: John Wiley & Sons, Inc.; Wilson, W. J. (2008). The economic plight of inner-city black males. In E. Anderson (Ed.), *Against the wall: Poor, young, black, and male* (pp. 55–70). Philadelphia: University of Pennsylvania Press.

22. Bauman, D. & Wasserman, K. (2010). Empowering fathers of disadvantaged preschoolers to take a more active role in preparing their children for literacy success at school. *Early Childhood Education Journal*, 37(5), 363–370.

23. US Department of Education, National Center for Education Statistics (2005). *Gender differences in participation and completion of undergraduate education and how they have changed over time*, NCES 2005–169, by Katharin Peter, Laura Horn, and C. Dennis Carroll. Washington, DC.

24. US Census Bureau, Current Population Survey (2013). Educational attainment of the population 25 years and over by selected characteristics, http://www.census.gov/hhes/socdemo/education/data/cps/2013/tables.html, accessed February 2014.

25. Skiba, R. J., Michael, R. S., Nardo, A. C., & Peterson, R. L. (2002). The color of discipline: Sources of racial and gender disproportionality in school punishment. *The Urban Review*, 34 (4), 317–342.

26. Skiba, R. J., & Peterson, R. L. (1999). The dark side of zero tolerance: Can punishment lead to safe schools? *Phi Delta Kappan*, 80, 372–376, 381–382.

27. MacLeod, J. (1987). *Ain't no making it: Aspirations and attainment in a low income neighborhood*. Boulder, CO: Westview Press.

28. Sum, A., Khatiwada, I., McLaughlin, J., & Palma, S. (2011). No country for young men: Deteriorating labor market prospects for low-skilled men in the United States. *The ANNALS of the American Academy of Political and Social Science*, 635, 24–55.

29. Goldrick-Rab, S., & Sorensen, K. (2010). Unmarried parents in college. *The Future of Children*, 20(2), 179–203.

30. Waller, M. (2002). *My baby's father: Unmarried parents and paternal responsibility*. Ithaca, NY: Cornell University Press.

31. Rumberger, R., Ghatak, R., Poulos, G., Ritter, P. L., & Dornbusch, S. (1990). Family influences on dropout behavior in one California high school. *Sociology of Education*, 63, 283–299.

32. Nord, C. W., Brimhall, D., West, J. (1997) *Fathers' involvement in their children's schools* (NCES #98-091) Washington, DC: US Department of Education, National Center for Education Statistics; Nord, C. W., & West, J. (2001). *Fathers' and mothers' involvement in their children's schools by family type and resident status*. Washington, DC: US Department of Education, Office of Educational Research and Improvement.

33. Nord, C. W., & West, J. (2001). *Fathers' and mothers' involvement in their children's schools by family type and resident status*. Washington, DC: US Department of Education, Office of Educational Research and Improvement.

34. Amato, P., & Gilbreth, J. (1999). Nonresident fathers and children's well-being: A meta-analysis. *Journal of Marriage and Family*, 61(3), 557–573.

35. Furstenberg, F. F., & Nord, C. W. (1985). Parenting apart: Patterns of childrearing after marital disruption. *Journal of Marriage and the Family, 47*, 893–904.

36. Amato, P., & Gilbreth, J. (1999) Nonresident fathers and children's well-being: A meta-analysis. *Journal of Marriage and Family, 61*(3), 557–573; Hawkins, D., Amato, P., & King, V. (2006). Parent-adolescent involvement: The relative influence of parent gender and residence. *Journal of Marriage and the Family, 68*, 125–136.

37. Roy, K. (2004). You can't eat love: Constructing provider role expectations for low-income and working-class fathers. *Fathering, 2*, 253–276.

38. Baumrind, D. (1972) Socialization and instrumental competence in young children. In W. W. Hartup (ed.), *The young child: Reviews of research* (Vol. 2, pp. 202–224). Washington, DC: National Association for the Education of Young Children; Baumrind, D. (1991). Parenting styles and adolescent development. *The encyclopedia of adolescence* (Vol. 1, pp. 169–208).

39. Baumrind, D. (1972) Socialization and instrumental competence in young children. In W. W. Hartup (ed.), *The young child: Reviews of research* (Vol. 2, pp. 202–224). Washington, DC: National Association for the Education of Young Children; Baumrind, D. (1991). Parenting styles and adolescent development. *The encyclopedia of adolescence* (Vol. 1, pp. 169–208).

40. Amato, P., & Gilbreth, A. (1999). Nonresident fathers and children's well-being: A meta-analysis. *Journal of Marriage and Family, 61*(3), 557–573; Steinberg, L. Lamborn, S. D., Darling, N., Mounts, N. S., & Dornbusch, S. M. (1994). Overtime changes in adjustment and competence among adolescents from authoritative, authoritarian, indulgent and neglectful families. *Child Development, 65*, 754–770.

41. Lamb, M. E., Pleck, J. H., Charnov, E. L., & Levine, J. A. (1985). Paternal behavior in humans. *American Zoologist, 25*, 88–894.

42. Sarkadi, A., Kristiansson, R., Oberklaid, F., & Bremberg, S. (2008). Fathers' involvement and children's developmental outcomes: A systematic review of longitudinal studies. *Acta Paediatrica, 97*(2), 153–158.

43. Amato, P. & Gilbreth, J. (1999). Nonresident fathers and children's well-being: A meta-analysis. *Journal of Marriage and Family, 61*(3), 557–573.

44. Nord, C. W., Brimhall, D., West, J. (1997). *Fathers' involvement in their children's schools* (NCES #98-091) Washington, DC: US Department of Education, National Center for Education Statistics.

45. Fagan, J. & Iglesias, A. (1999). Father involvement program effects on fathers, father figures, and their Head Start children: A quasi-experimental study. *Early Childhood Research Quarterly, 14*(2), 243–269.

46. Nord, C. W., & West, J. (2001). *Fathers' and mothers' involvement in their children's schools by family type and resident status.* Washington, DC: US Department of Education, Office of Educational Research and Improvement.

47. Jones, J., & Mosher, W. (2013). *Fathers' involvement with their children: United States, 2006–2010.* National Health Statistics Reports, no. 71. Hyattsville, MD: National Center for Health Statistics.

48. Mincy, R., & Turpin, J. (2014) *The effect of father engagement on children's academic achievement in fragile families* (mimeo). Columbia University School of Social Work.

49. Nelson, T. J., Clampet-Lundquist, S., & Edin, K. (2002). Sustaining fragile fatherhood: Father involvement among low income noncustodial African-American fathers

in Philadelphia. In C. S. Tamis-LeMonda & N. Cabrera (eds.), *Handbook of father involvement: Multidisciplinary perspectives* (pp. 525–554). Mahway, NJ: Lawrence Erlbaum.

50. Rumberger, R., Ghatak, R., Poulos, G., Ritter, P. L., & Dornbusch, S. (1990). Family influences on dropout behavior in one California high school. *Sociology of Education, 63,* 283–299; Nord, C. W., Brimhall, D., West, J. (1997). *Fathers' involvement in their children's schools* (NCES #98-091) Washington, DC: US Department of Education, National Center for Education Statistics; Nord, C. W., & West, J. (2001). *Fathers' and mothers' involvement in their children's schools by family type and resident status.* Washington, DC: US Department of Education, Office of Educational Research and Improvement; Amato, P., & Gilbreth, J. (1999). Nonresident fathers and children's well-being: A meta-analysis. *Journal of Marriage and Family, 61*(3), 557–573.

51. Mincy, R., & Turpin, J. (2014) *The effect of father engagement on children's academic achievement in fragile families* (mimeo). Columbia University School of Social Work.

52. Blankenhorn, D. (1995). *Fatherless America: Confronting our most urgent social problem.* Scranton, PA: HarperCollins Publishers.

53. McLanahan, S. (2004) Diverging destinies: How children are faring under the second demographic transition. *Demography, 41*(4), 607–627; Reardon, S. (2011) The widening academic achievement gap between the rich and the poor: New evidence and possible explanations. In G. Duncan & R. Murnane (eds.), *Whither opportunity? Rising inequality, schools, and children's life chances* (pp. 91–116). New York: Russell Sage; Phillips, M. (2011). Parenting, time use, and disparities in academic outcomes. In G. Duncan & R. Murnane (eds.), *Whither opportunity? Rising inequality, schools, and children's life chances* (pp. 207–228). New York: Russell Sage.

CHAPTER 5

1. Amato, P. R., Meyers, C. E., & Emery, R. E. (2009). Changes in nonresident father-child contact from 1976 to 2002. *Family Relations, 58*(1), 41–53.

2. Cheadle, J. E., Amato, P. R., & King, V. 2010. Patterns of nonresident father contact. *Demography, 47*(1), 205–225.

3. Furstenberg, F. F. (1991). *Divided families: What happens to children when parents part* (Vol. 1). Cambridge, MA: Harvard University Press.

4. Glick, P. C. (1984). Marriage, divorce, and living arrangements prospective changes. *Journal of Family Issues, 5*(1), 7–26.

5. Furstenberg Jr, F. F., & Nord, C. W. (1985). Parenting apart: Patterns of childrearing after marital disruption. *Journal of Marriage and the Family, 47*(4), 893–904.

6. Manning, W. D., & Smock, P. J. (1999). New families and nonresident father-child visitation. *Social Forces, 78*(1), 87–116.

7. Manning, W. D., & Smock, P. J. (2000). "Swapping" families: Serial parenting and economic support for children. *Journal of Marriage and Family, 62*(1), 111–122.

8. Laughlin, L., Farrie, D., & Fagan, J. (2009). Father involvement with children following marital and non-marital separations. *Fathering: A Journal of Theory, Research, and Practice about Men as Fathers, 7*(3), 226–248.

9. Guzzo, K. B. (2009). Maternal relationships and nonresidential father visitation of children born outside of marriage. *Journal of Marriage and Family, 71*(3), 632–649.

10. Tach, L., Mincy, R., & Edin, K. (2010). Parenting as a "package deal": Relationships, fertility, and nonresident father involvement among unmarried parents. *Demography, 47*(1), 181–204.

11. Seltzer, J. A., & Bianchi, S. M. (1988). Children's contact with absent parents. *Journal of Marriage and the Family*, 50(3), 663–677.

12. Mincy, R. B., Pouncy, H., & Zilanawala, A. (2013, November). Race, romance and nonresident father involvement resilience. Paper presented at *2013 Association for Public Policy Analysis and Management Fall Research*, Washington, DC.

13. Sobolewski, J. M., & King, V. (2005). The importance of the coparental relationship for nonresident fathers' ties to children. *Journal of Marriage and Family*, 67(5), 1196–1212.

14. Carlson, M. J., McLanahan, S. S., & Brooks-Gunn, J. (2008). Coparenting and nonresident fathers' involvement with young children after a non-marital birth. *Demography*, 45(2), 461–488.

15. Fagan, J., Palkovitz, R., Roy, K., & Farrie, D. (2009). Pathways to paternal engagement: Longitudinal effects of risk and resilience on nonresident fathers. *Developmental Psychology*, 45(5), 1389.

16. Fagan, J., & Barnett, M. (2003). The relationship between maternal gatekeeping, paternal competence, mothers' attitudes about the father role, and father involvement. *Journal of Family Issues*, 24(8), 1020–1043.

17. Waller, M. R., & Swisher, R. (2006). Fathers' risk factors in fragile families: Implications for" healthy" relationships and father involvement. *Social Problems*, 53(3), 392–420.

18. Mincy, R. B., Pouncy, H., & Zilanawala, A. (2013, November). Race, romance and nonresident father involvement resilience. Paper presented at *2013 Association for Public Policy Analysis and Management Fall Research*, Washington, DC; Berger, L. M., Cancian, M., & Meyer, D. R. (2012). Maternal re-partnering and new-partner fertility: Associations with nonresident father investments in children. *Children and Youth Services Review*, 34(2), 426–436; Tach, L., Mincy, R., & Edin, K. (2010). Parenting as a "package deal": Relationships, fertility, and nonresident father involvement among unmarried parents. *Demography*, 47(1), 181–204.

19. Tjaden, P., & Thoennes, N. (2000). Prevalence and consequences of male-to-female and female-to-male intimate partner violence as measured by the National Violence Against Women Survey. *Violence Against Women*, 6(2), 142–161.

20. Seltzer, J. A., Schaeffer, N. C., & Charng, H. W. (1989). Family ties after divorce: The relationship between visiting and paying child support. *Journal of Marriage and the Family*, 51(4), 1013–1031.

21. Arditti, J. A., & Keith, T. Z. (1993). Visitation frequency, child support payment, and the father-child relationship postdivorce. *Journal of Marriage and the Family*, 55(3), 699–712.

22. Stephens, L. S. (1996). Will Johnny see daddy this week? An empirical test of three theoretical perspectives of postdivorce contact. *Journal of Family Issues*, 17(4), 466–494.

23. Cooksey, E. C., & Craig, P. H. (1998). Parenting from a distance: The effects of paternal characteristics on contact between nonresidential fathers and their children. *Demography*, 35(2), 187–200.

24. Hamer, J. F. (1998). What African-American noncustodial fathers say inhibits and enhances their involvement with children. *Western Journal of Black Studies*, 22(2), 117–127.

25. Melli, M. S. (2004). American law institute principles of family dissolution, the approximation rule and shared-parenting, *The Northern Illinois University Law Review*, 25, 347.

26. Garfinkel, I., Melli, M. S., & Robertson, J. G. (1993). Child support orders: A perspective on reform. *The Future of Children/Center for the Future of Children, the David and Lucile Packard Foundation*, 4(1), 84–100.

27. Cancian, M., & Meyer, D. R. (1998). Who gets custody?. *Demography*, 35(2), 147–157.

28. Caldwell, C. H., Rafferty, J., Reischl, T. M., De Loney, E. H., & Brooks, C. L. (2010). Enhancing parenting skills among nonresident African American fathers as a strategy for preventing youth risky behaviors. *American Journal of Community Psychology*, 45(1–2), 17–35.

29. Schwartz-Soicher, O., Geller, A., & Garfinkel, I. (2011). The effect of paternal incarceration on material hardship. *Social Service Review*, 85(3), 447–473.

30. We thank Professor Amanda Geller for assistance in updating estimates of the proportion of ever incarcerated fathers in the Fragile Families and Child Well-Being Survey when children were 9 years old and Hyunjoon Um for research assistance in making these estimates. We take responsibility for any errors made in this estimate.

31. Turney, K., & Wildeman, C. (2012). *Redefining relationships: Countervailing consequences of paternal incarceration for parenting.* Yale University working paper.

32. Hairston, C. F. (2002). Fathers in prison: Responsible fatherhood and responsible public policies. *Marriage & Family Review*, 32(3–4), 111–135.

33. Swisher, R. R., & Waller, M. R. (2008). Confining fatherhood incarceration and paternal involvement among nonresident white, African American, and Latino fathers. *Journal of Family Issues*, 29(8), 1067–1088.

34. Mincy, R. B. (2002). *Who should marry whom? Multiple partner fertility among new parents.* (Working paper #2002-03-FF). Center for Research on Child Well-Being, Princeton University; Carlson, M. J., & Furstenberg, F. F. (2006). The prevalence and correlates of multipartnered fertility among urban US parents. *Journal of Marriage and Family*, 68(3), 718–732.

35. Amato, P. R. (2000). The consequences of divorce for adults and children. *Journal of Marriage and Family*, 62(4), 1269–1287.

36. Allen, W. D., & Doherty, W. J. (1996). The responsibilities of fatherhood as perceived by African American teenage fathers. *Families in Society*, 77(3), 142–142; Hamer, J. F. (1997). The fathers of "fatherless"" black children. *Families in Society*, 78(6), 564–578; Hamer, J. (2001). Chapter Six: What fathers say they do as daddies. In *What it means to be daddy.* New York: Columbia University Press. pp. 131–150; Shears, J., Summers, J. A., Boller, K., & Barclay-McLaughlin, G. (2006). Exploring fathering roles in low-income families: The influence of intergenerational transmission. *Families in Society*, 87(2), 259–268, 159.

37. Edin, K., & Nelson, T. J. (2013). *Doing the best I can: Fatherhood in the inner city.* Berkeley: University of California Press.

CHAPTER 6

1. This section focuses on policies that affect fathers and families after children are born. We ignore prevention policies because even if successful, progress in the child support policies we emphasize here would still be desperately needed. Teenage fathers are unable to support their children, and leaving school prematurely to provide for their children is likely to place teenage fathers on a path to low earnings for many years to come. So prevention policies are important. Although many unmarried nonresident fathers are teenagers at the birth of their child, the overwhelming majority of cohabiting fathers are not, and most cohabiting fathers in fragile families eventually become vulnerable nonresident fathers. In addition, any married men with lower earnings also become vulnerable nonresident fathers. See Lerman, R. (2010). Capabilities and contributions of unwed fathers. *The Future of Children*, 20(2), 63–85.

2. Hansen, D. D. (1999). The American invention of child support: Dependency and punishment in early American child support law. *The Yale Law Journal*, 108(5), 1123–1153.

3. Katz, M. B. (1996). *In the shadow of the poorhouse: A social history of welfare in America*. New York: Basic Books.

4. Cancian, M., & Meyer, D. R. (2011). Who owes what to whom? Child support policy given multiple-partner fertility. *Social Service Review, 85*(4), 587–617.

5. Brustin, S. (2012). Child support: Shifting the financial burden in low-income families. *Georgetown Journal of Poverty Law & Policy, 20,* 1–187.

6. In Chapter 2 we identified economically vulnerable fathers by deducting usual expenses and child support payments from non-resident fathers' income. We found that nonresident fathers with two children and incomes up to $40,000 would have disposable incomes just $1,811 above the poverty line. This is why we designated nonresident fathers with incomes up to $40,000 as economically vulnerable. If we deducted only usual expenses, nonresident fathers with incomes of $20,000 would have disposable incomes almost $3,000 below the poverty line. In many states, these fathers would qualify for the self-support reserve.

7. If the parents are unmarried and the father denies paternity, the court may also order a DNA test to establish paternity.

8. Legler, P. (2003). *Low-income fathers and child support: Starting off on the right track. Final Report.* Baltimore, MD: The Annie E. Casey Foundation.

9. Legler, P. (2003).). *Low-income fathers and child support: Starting off on the right track. Final Report.* Baltimore, MD: The Annie E. Casey Foundation. Sorensen, E. (2004). Understanding how child-support arrears reached $18 billion in California. *The American Economic Review, 94*(2), 312–316.

10. US Department of Health and Human Services, Office of Child Support Enforcement. *Entering default orders bench card: Child support and the judiciary* (May 8, 2012), http://www. acf.hhs.gov/programs/css/resource/entering-default-orders-bench-card.

11. US Department of Health and Human Services. Office of Inspector General. (2000, July). *The establishment of child support orders for low income non-custodial parents.* http://oig. hhs.gov/oei/reports/oei-05-99-00390.pdf

12. US Department of Health and Human Services, Administration for Children and Families, Child Support Fact Sheet Series No. 2. *Project to avoid increasing delinquencies* (June 2012), http://www.acf.hhs.gov/programs/css/resource/providing-expedited-review-and-modification-assistance.

13. US Department of Health and Human Services, Administration for Children and Families. *Driver's license reinstatement notification—Ohio, 2007 Best Practices* (March 2007), http://www.acf.hhs.gov/programs/css/resource/drivers-licsense-reinstatement-notification-ohio.

14. US Department of Health and Human Services, Administration for Children and Families. *Turner vs. Rogers guidance* (June 2012), http://www.acf.hhs.gov/programs/css/resource/turner-v-rogers-guidance.

15. Sorensen, E., Liliana Sousa, L., & Schaner, S. (2007) *Assessing child support arrears in nine states and the nation.* Washington, DC: The Urban Institute.

16. US Department of Health and Human Services, Administration for Children and Families, Office of Child Support Enforcement. *Arrears management resource guide* (May 2008), http://www.acf.hhs.gov/programs/css/resource-library/search?keyword=Arrears%20 Abatement&h=1.

17. Miller, D. P., & Mincy, R. B. (2012). Falling further behind? Child support arrears and fathers' labor force participation. *Social Service Review, 86*(4), 604–635.

18. Heinrich, C. J., Burkhardt, B. C., & Shager, H. M. (2011). Reducing child support debt and its consequences: Can forgiveness benefit all? *Journal of Policy Analysis and Management*, 30(4), 755–774.

19. US Department of Health and Human Services, Administration for Children and Families, Office of Child Support Enforcement. State child support agencies with debt compromise policies: Program innovation maps (March 2012), http://www.acf.hhs.gov/programs/css/resource/state-child-support-agencies-with-debt-compromise-policies.

20. US Department of Health and Human Services, Administration for Children and Families, Child Support Fact Sheet Series No. 4. *Promoting child well-being & family self-sufficiency, economic stability* (June 2011), http://www.acf.hhs.gov/sites/default/files/ocse/economic_stability.pdf.

21. Klempin, S. & Mincy, R. B. (2011) Tossed on a sea of change: A status update on the responsible fatherhood field, Center for Fathers Children and Family Well-Being, http://crfcfw.columbia.edu/files/2012/09/OSF-Fatherhood-Survey_Final-Report_9.25.12_SK_RM.pdf.

22. Center of Policy Research, Denver. (November 2008). *Shared parenting: Final report*; US Department of Human Services. Administration for Children and Families. Office of Child Support Enforcement. (2007). *Report on child access and visitation programs: participant outcomes*, http://www.acf.hhs.gov/programs/css/resource/report-on-child-access-and-visitation-programs-participant-outcomes, accessed March 22, 2014.

23. Pearson, J., Davis, L., & Thoennes, N. (2007). *Colorado Parenting Time/Visitation Project.* Denver, CO: Center for Policy Research.

24. Kelly, J. B. (1994). The determination of child custody. *The Future of Children*, 4(1), 121–142.

25. US Department of Health and Human Services, Administration for Children and Families, Office of Child Support Enforcement (2015). *FY 2015 President's budget in brief strengthening health and opportunity for all Americans*, http://www.hhs.gov/budget/fy2015/fy-2015-budget-in-brief.pdf, accessed March 22, 2014.

26. US Senate Committee on Finance. (2013). Description of the chairman's mark the supporting at-risk children act of 2013, http://www.finance.senate.gov/imo/media/doc/120913%20Supporting%20At-risk%20Youth%20Act%20Chairman's%20Mark.pdf, accessed March 22, 2014.

27. Kelly, J. B. (2007). Children's living arrangements following separation and divorce: Insights from empirical and clinical research. *Family process*, 46(1), 35–52.

28. Cancian, M., & Meyer, D. R. (1998). Who gets custody?. *Demography*, 35(2), 147–157.

29. Bauserman, R. (2002). Child adjustment in joint-custody versus sole-custody arrangements: A meta-analytic review. *Journal of Family Psychology*, 16(1), 91.

30. Bjarnason, T., & Arnarsson, A. M. (2011). Joint physical custody and communication with parents: A cross-national study of children in 36 Western Countries. *Journal of Comparative Family Studies*, 42(6), 871–890.

31. Gunnoe, M. L., & Braver, S. L. (2001). The effects of joint legal custody on mothers, fathers, and children controlling for factors that predispose a sole maternal versus joint legal award. *Law and Human Behavior*, 25(1), 25.

32. Amato, P. R. (2000). The consequences of divorce for adults and children. *Journal of Marriage and Family*, 62(4), 1269–1287.

33. Garfinkel, I., Melli, M. S., & Robertson, J. G. (1994). *Child support orders: A perspective on reform.* University of Wisconsin–Madison, Institute for Research on Poverty.

34. Melli, M. S. (2004). The American Law Institute principles of family dissolution, the approximation rule and shared-parenting. *Northern Illinois University Law Review, 25,* 347.

35. Mnookin, R. H., & Kornhauser, L. (1979). "Bargaining in the shadow of the law: The case of divorce." *Yale Law Journal, 88*(5), 950–997.

36. For example, David L. Levy proposes the following three-stage process. First, with the help of a neutral party, a divorcing couple would begin trying to negotiate a parenting plan, including the amount of time the child spends with each parent. If the parents could not agree, they would then seek the assistance of a trained mediator. If the parent could still not agree, they would go to court, and allow a judge to decide. However, all stages of this process would be influenced by the presumption that the child spend no less than 25 percent–30 percent of his or her time with each parent. Though the authors and Levy agree that this is one possible way an administrative process for presumptive joint custody might operate, we do not agree that this process would be desirable. However, the authors greatly appreciate Levy's willingness to discuss the idea of an administrative process for presumptive joint custody, including the likelihood, recognized by all of us, that the presumption of joint custody would increase the likelihood that joint physical custody would be the outcome at all three stages of the process.

37. Mincy, R. B., Pouncy, H., & Zilanawala, A. (2013, November). Race, romance and nonresident father involvement resilience. Paper presented at *2013 Association for Public Policy Analysis and Management Fall Research Conference.* Washington, DC.

38. Amato, P. & Gilbreth, J. (1999). Nonresident fathers and children's well-being: A meta-analysis. *Journal of Marriage and Family, 61*(3), 557–573.

39. Cowan, P. A., Cowan, C. P., & Knox, V. (2010). Marriage and fatherhood programs. *The Future of Children, 20*(2), 205–230.

40. Center on Budget and Policy Priorities. (2009). *Policy basics: The Earned Income Tax Credit.* Washington, DC: Center on Budget and Policy Priorities (CBPP), http://www.cbpp.org/cms/index.cfm?fa=view&id=2505.

41. The example provided is based upon the 2008 credit figures for a single (resident) parent with either one or two children.

42. Mincy, R. B., Klempin, S., & Jethwani-Keyser, M. (2012). *Creating an effective work incentive for low-income non-custodial parents: Lessons from the New York State experience.* Paper presented at APPAM Annual Meeting, Washington, DC.

43. Sherraden, M. (1991). *Assets and the poor: A new American welfare policy.* New York: ME Sharpe.

44. Eyster, L., Anderson, T., & Durham, C. (2013). *Innovations and future directions for workforce development in the post-recession era.* Washington, DC: The Urban Institute.

45. Jacobson, L., LaLonde, R., & Sullivan, D. (2005). Estimating the returns to community college schooling for displaced workers. *Journal of Econometrics, 125*(1), 271–304.

46. US Department of Labor, Employment and Training Administration, Trade Adjustment Assistance Community College and Career Training Grants Program (TAACCCT), *Program summary,* http://www.doleta.gov/taaccct/, accessed April 6, 2014.

47. Jacobson, L., LaLonde, R. J., & Sullivan, D. (2005). The impact of community college retraining on older displaced workers: Should we teach old dogs new tricks? *Industrial and Labor Relations Review, 58*(3), 398–415.

48. Cowan, P. A., Cowan, C. P., & Knox, V. (2010). Marriage and fatherhood programs. *The Future of Children, 20*(2), 205–230.

49. Eyster, L., Anderson, T., & Durham, C. (2013). Innovations and future directions for workforce development in the post-recession era. Washington, DC: The Urban Institute.

50. US Department of Health and Human Services, Administration for Children & Families, Assets for Independence Resource Center (no date). *Ideas for fathers and families*, http://idaresources.acf.hhs.gov/page?pageid=a047000000Df6Ar, accessed March 28, 2014.

51. US Department of Health and Human Services, Administration for Children & Families, Assets for Independence Resource Center (no date). *Child support and asset building providers: Strategies for partnering*, from http://idaresources.acf.hhs.gov/page?pageid=a047000000CNdei, accessed March 28, 2014.

52. US Department of Health and Human Services, Administration for Children & Families, Assets for Independence Resource Center (no date). *Child support and asset building providers: Strategies for partnering*, from http://idaresources.acf.hhs.gov/page?pageid=a047000000CNdei, accessed March 28, 2014.

53. O'Shea, D., Schroeder, D., Khan, A., & Juniper, C. (2013). *Urban fathers asset building project interim implementation report* (mimeo). Ray Marshall Center For the Study of Human Resources, Lyndon B. Johnson School of Public Affairs.

54. Haskins, R, H. Holzer, & Lerman, R. (2009). *Promoting economic mobility by increasing postsecondary education*. Washington, DC: The Pew Charitable Trusts; DeLeire, T. C., & Lopoo, L. M. (2010). *Family structure and the economic mobility of children*. Economic Mobility Project. Washington, DC: Pew Charitable Trusts.

APPENDIX

1. Schwandt, T. (1988). Constructivist, interpretivist approaches to human inquiry. In N. Denzin & Y. Lincoln (Eds.). *The landscape of qualitative research*. Thousand Oaks, CA: Sage Publications. p. 221.

2. Miles, M. B., & Huberman, E. M. (1994). *Qualitative data analysis*. Thousand Oaks, CA: Sage Publications.

3. Strauss, A. & Corbin, J. (1990). Basics of qualitative research: Grounded theory procedures and techniques. Newbury Park: Sage Publications.

4. To stay open to the lived experiences of the fathers, all members of our research team maintained self reflective and process oriented reflections that considered how cultural experiences may have influenced our interpretations. To address validity threats and reinforce the integrity of our conclusions, we also reviewed all coding choices to discuss competing hypotheses or conclusions and conducted coding checks for adequate agreement until inter-coder agreement reached 90% (Miles & Huberman, 1994). We gave participants pseudonyms to protect confidentiality.

Name Index

Subject Index